To Buy
or Not to Buy

Why We Overshop
and How to Stop

April Lane Benson, PhD

TRUMPETER
Boston & London
2008

Trumpeter Books
An imprint of Shambhala Publications, Inc.
Horticultural Hall
300 Massachusetts Avenue
Boston, Massachusetts 02115
www.shambhala.com

9 8 7 6 5 4 3 2 1

First edition
Printed in the United States of America

⊗ This edition is printed on acid-free paper that meets the American National Standards Institute Z39.48 Standard.

♻ This book was printed on 30% postconsumer recycled paper.
For more information, please visit us at www.shambhala.com.

Distributed in the United States by Random House, Inc., and in Canada by Random House of Canada Ltd

Interior design and composition: Greta D. Sibley & Associates

Library of Congress Cataloging-in-Publication Data
Benson, April Lane.
To buy or not to buy: why we overshop and how to stop / April Lane Benson.—1st ed.
p.   cm.
Includes bibliographical references.
ISBN 978-1-59030-599-7 (pbk.: alk. paper)
1. Compulsive shopping. I. Title.
RC569.5.S56B46 2008
616.85'84—dc22
2008024034

To Buy or Not to Buy

To the memory of my mother,
Frances Berman Lane Krebs Mehlman

Contents

Introduction

To Buy or Not to Buy—for overshoppers, *that* is the question. This book is about answering that not-so-simple question. It's also about who you are, what you want, and what you *really* need—and how your deepening understanding of this can help you stop overshopping. The underlying premise of the book is that when we overshop, though we often don't realize it, we are trying to fill emotional needs with material goods. This attempt, like trying to fit a square peg into a round hole, is doomed to failure: you simply can't buy self-esteem or self-acceptance or autonomy. Indeed, the more you focus on acquiring material goods, the less satisfied you're going to be.

What I've learned from a decade and a half of knowing, studying, working with, and writing about overshoppers—and from having been one myself—is that to change your behavior, you've got to change the way you feel about yourself and the way you go about meeting your authentic needs. *To Buy or Not to Buy* is an interactive guidebook for that transformation, in which the concepts, exercises, and activities build on each other, so that what you learn intellectually is regularly tested and reinforced at a gut level.

WHO THIS BOOK IS FOR

This book is for anyone with a shopping problem: anyone whose patterns of shopping and spending damage their relationships, their self-esteem, and their finances. There's no one type of person who tends to be an overshopper. People with this problem differ in age and gender, social and economic status, buying patterns, and underlying motivations. This book is for you if you're a daily overshopper, if you shop only occasionally but go on binges when you do, or if you're a "collector" (which is often the way male overshoppers describe themselves). It's for you if you overshop to project a particular image, if you buy excessively for others, or if you buy multiple versions of the same item. It's also for you if you hunt relentlessly for bargains or if you constantly buy and return.

You've got a shopping problem if you spend so much time, energy, or money on shopping—even if you don't actually *acquire* stuff—that it's impacting your life in a negative way. Perhaps you're one of the many whose attraction to a particular class of things—jewelry or chess sets, clothing or teddy bears, shoes or old maps, electronics or baseball cards—has led to a mountain of debt or other financial problems. Or perhaps overshopping is affecting your work performance, your social life, or your family relationships,[1] or your shopping addiction has put you on the wrong side of the law. This book is also for you if you're insulated from the financial consequences of your overshopping by inheritance or other wealth but you've lost sight of what really matters in life or you feel that your life lacks meaning.

IF YOU HAVE A SHOPPING PROBLEM, YOU'RE NOT ALONE

If any of the overshopping scenarios I've sketched out speaks to you, know that you're not alone. According to a 2006 study conducted by the Stanford University School of Medicine, 5.8 percent of U.S. adults are overshoppers—at least 17 million people.[2] How can we begin to understand or explain this startling statistic?

Two factors, taken together, explain a lot. One is the ever-growing production of goods around the world. In more and more parts of the globe, economic growth is dependent upon selling goods to populations whose basic needs have already been met. To promote that goal—to cultivate in the general public a powerful desire for goods they don't need—a formidable array of resources has been mounted. Advertising and the media shape our material desires, and the credit industry makes these desires seem tantalizingly affordable.

Today, in order to promote the ceaseless stoking of economic engines, every one of us is targeted as a consumer. We are pushed, prodded, *programmed* to purchase. In 2006, 9.2 billion credit card offers went out to America's 300 million people—*more than 30 offers to every man, woman, and child!* Shopping itself has become a leisure and lifestyle activity; malls are the new town centers. We're immersed, cradle to grave, in buy-messages that, with greater and greater psychological sophistication, misleadingly associate *products we don't need* with *feeling-states we deeply desire.*

The second factor in the meteoric rise of overshopping involves the public's radical shift in reference points. Thirty years ago, the Joneses were the people who lived next door, and keeping up with them—attaining a lifestyle at approximately their level—wasn't too much of a problem. By the 1980s, though, the Joneses had become the people we saw on television. They lived farther away—and had a significantly more affluent lifestyle. Soon, everybody, no matter where they were on the economic spectrum or where they lived— but especially in the middle classes—began comparing themselves to the televised Joneses. What people thought they needed, or what seemed an acceptable lifestyle, shifted sharply upward.[3]

The result has been "affluenza," our unprecedented modern plague of materialism and overconsumption. Shopping researcher Paco Underhill puts it concisely: "The economic party that has been the second half of the twentieth century has fostered more shopping than anyone would have predicted, *more shopping than has ever taken place anywhere at any time*"[4] (my italics). In addition to traditional brick-and-mortar fields of commerce, fertile new grounds for the growth of shopping compulsions have been tilled: catalogs, television, and the Internet. So we're now able to shop—and enticed to do so—whether we're dressed or in our underwear, whether we're walking the street, sitting at the computer, or relaxing at the beach with a cell phone.

And shop we do—in spades. Another study more recent than Stanford's showed significantly higher numbers. Ridgway et al. (2008) found that 15.5 percent of college undergrads, 8.9 percent of university staff, and 16 percent of visitors to an Internet retail website exhibited compulsive buying tendencies.[5] Using even the most conservative figure, the one for university staff, this swells the Stanford estimate from 17 to 28 million American overshoppers. And we're not the only ones. The overshopping demographic widens almost daily, with recent research studies and reports of shopping addiction published in Canada, Mexico, Brazil, most of the countries of western Europe, Israel, Australia, South Korea, and now even China. And the *rate* of addiction is growing as well.

Who are these shopping addicts? They can be anyone. Compulsive shopping crosses every social and political boundary. Contrary to popular mythology, the affliction is not limited to women or to certain classes. (The recent Stanford study, for example, demonstrated that men are as likely to have a shopping problem as women.) For every Imelda Marcos—who fled the Philippines leaving behind more than *three thousand* pairs of shoes—there are countless unknown overshoppers: a businessman whose collection of fountain pens has grown obsessive; a language teacher whose closets are stuffed with unworn, still-tagged garments; a waitress who's succumbed to the Jewelry Television network.

A SERIOUS PROBLEM THAT'S GAINING ATTENTION

Long trivialized as the "smiled upon" addiction, overshopping is at last coming out of the closet. Witness the scores of recent newspaper and magazine articles about it, the countless segments on radio and TV, and the mounting number of research studies. There's also growing interest among mental health professionals in specialized training for treating this problem. The conclusion is now inescapable: far from trivial, overshopping is an important source of emotional, social, occupational, financial, and spiritual misery for a great many individuals and families. If you're reading this book, chances are you've experienced some of that misery.

So I congratulate you on having decided, instead of smiling, to do something about your overshopping habit. I know the decision may not have been easy. Strongly reinforced by society, shopping has become the classic mixed-message behavior. On the one hand, it's promoted endlessly (and to the ends of the earth) by those who profit from it. On the other hand, it's regularly the stuff of jokes:

shoppers portrayed as self-involved, materialistic, and empty. As a result, compulsive shopping may be an even greater source of guilt and shame than alcoholism or drug abuse. Those disorders are generally recognized as diseases, or at least widely understood to be serious problems requiring treatment; as a client said to me recently, "It would be much easier to tell people I'm an alcoholic—they'd understand that better." Instead, overshoppers often feel condemned to secrecy, fearing that if others knew about their behavior, they'd be dismissed as superficial, narcissistic, and weak-willed.

Though it may not have been easy, your decision to stop makes a great deal of sense. The results of dozens of studies point clearly to the same conclusion: that beyond the basics of food, shelter, and a little more, a singular focus on material goods, particularly on acquiring them, does not bring happiness. Quite the contrary! In general, *having more things means enjoying life less.* Acquiring and maintaining objects can so fill up our lives and environment that there's little time or space to use what's been acquired. What we consume can end up consuming *us.*

And somewhere inside, every compulsive shopper knows this. Certainly, overshoppers know the frustration and sorrow of the vanishing horizon: how, with each purchase, "the high of the buy" briefly lifts your spirits—but briefly only—and then you're down again, a little lower, already beginning to pin your hopes on the next purchase. Shopaholics know the consequences of their habit—the shame, the guilt, the debt, the discord, the distraction.

But because it takes nearly continuous buying to fuel the economy—it's the engine that pulls the rest of the American train—overshopping is still somewhat trivialized. Just check out the bumper stickers. "When the Going Gets Tough, the Tough Go Shopping," trumpets an SUV in front of me. For those who enjoyed high school Latin, there's "Veni, Vidi, Visa!" A largely female version is "New Shoes Chase the Blues," while men weigh in with "He Who Has the Most Toys When He Dies, Wins."

Behind all the smiles, though, I cringe. I see the fallout in my office, again and again. I know what every overshopper knows: that however clever the bumper stickers may be, overconsumption, like a poisonous vine winding around relationships, work, and financial stability, chokes out joy, self-esteem, and quality of life.

Putting aside the larger cultural and economic factors, what is it that drives some of us to become compulsive shoppers, to chronically overfocus time, attention, energy, money, or any combination of these on material things and their acquisition? Two major factors explain much about compulsive buying. First, nearly all overshoppers suffer from chronically low self-esteem and insecurity and have difficulty tolerating negative moods. As a result, they're prone to fantasizing about what their purchases will do for them, often seeing them as the ticket to feeling better about themselves and being more desirable to other people.

The second factor concerns how overshoppers tend to think about their lives and how they tend to define happiness. Money and material goods are central to their understanding of having a good life. Indeed, most overshoppers make acquiring possessions a central goal in life, imagining that they're the route to identity, success, and happiness. Material goods become the yardstick by which to measure self and others. *Net worth* becomes *self-worth*.

A NATION OF DEBTORS

The most calculable and tangible effect of overshopping is a financial one. Simply put, we've become a nation of debtors. *Three out of every five Americans who carry credit cards carry credit card debt.* Half of them owe more than $6,600, and a full 13 percent owe more than $25,000. The average dollar amount owed on credit cards has risen precipitously, from $2,900 in 1990 to more than $8,000 in 2007.[6]

And over the same period, *savings*—the rock on which any financial house is built, the entire thickness of the door between us and the wolf—has plummeted. In all of U.S. history, there have been only four years with a *negative* personal savings rate, only four years in which the collective American populace spent all its after-tax income and had to dip into savings or borrow to make ends meet: 1932 and 1933, in the belly of the Great Depression, and 2005 and 2006.[7] (We don't yet have 2007 figures, but they're almost certain to show a continuation of the trend.)

It's no surprise, then, that the number of personal bankruptcies has skyrocketed—and continues to increase, despite the fact that Congress toughened bankruptcy laws in 2005. While the precipitating events for filings tend to be job loss, illness, or divorce, over-shopping plays an important role in the financial precariousness that makes these events catastrophic. American personal spending is, quite simply, out of control.

And the news gets worse. Behind the hypnotic glitter of consumerism, a "hidden shadow is now becoming alarmingly visible," as author Stephanie Kaza puts it.[8] We imagine—we are *prevailed upon* to imagine—that the material goods we desire will make us happy, will transform us. But study after study says exactly the opposite! Research confirms what psychologist Paul Wachtel so nicely termed "the poverty of affluence" in his 1983 book of that title: *the more you believe that happiness comes from material wealth, the more likely you are to be depressed, distressed, and anxious—and the less actual well-being you're likely to experience.*

This is quite a pill for an overshopper to swallow. It says that our passion for stuff is badly misplaced; it insists that happiness *isn't* the next purchase away—nor the next, nor the one after that. But, honestly, don't you already know this? In your heart of hearts, hasn't your own experience proved that material goods can't really fill holes in self-esteem, can't really repair self-doubt, can't possibly transform you into that other person you think you want to be?

Yet American culture grows more and more materialistic. Results from the Higher Education Research Institute, which has polled 12 million college freshmen over the last forty years, shows a steady increase in the percentage of students who consider being "very well off" financially to be essential or very important. The figure was approximately 40 percent in the late 1960s, 50 percent in the 1970s, well above 60 percent in the 1980s, and over 70 percent every year since 1990.

This is a prescription for widespread discontent, and there's substantial evidence that it's being filled. In an economy that has grown markedly over recent decades, there's been a documented decline in the culture's overall social and spiritual health. In *How Much Is Enough? The Consumer Society and the Future of the Earth,* A. T. Durning summarizes the widespread unease: "Many of us in the consumer society have a sense that our world of plenty is somehow hollow—that, hoodwinked by a consumerist culture, we have been fruitlessly attempting to satisfy with material things what are essentially social, psychological, and spiritual needs."[9] We're shortchanging ourselves in a fundamental way. We're using up time, energy, and money in the pursuit of things that won't, and *can't,* make us happy. And in doing so, we're missing out on the things that will and can.

Why do we do this? One important reason is the psychological sophistication of the buy-messages that are fired relentlessly at us. "Buy our product and you'll feel like [or *look* like or *act* like or *be* like] the glamorous and successful people who use it in the ads," says the powerful subtext of most marketing messages; "don't buy, and you'll be passed over, an outcast at life's feast." So we get hooked. Simply for profit—and in defiance of overwhelming evidence to the contrary—we're led to believe that happiness can be bought. But less is really more—*much* more—and more is often less. In *The Paradox of Choice,* author Barry Schwartz has written persuasively about how overabundance befuddles and overstimulates us. We're so flooded with choices that simply *choosing* becomes a burden, and in the end, we're led to question whatever decisions we make, whether good or bad. Overabundance just plain worsens our lives: imagine Goldilocks with fifty bowls to choose from, in different styles and colors, some porridge sugared, some buttered, some otherwise doctored, some not.

Overshopping, then, is a culturally induced affliction. But it's grounded in psychological and social needs. In this book, we'll examine how consumerism promotes it. We'll investigate the psychological realities that incline some people more than others toward addictive shopping, and you'll zero in on the relevant aspects of your own particular background and situation. Most important, you'll get an array of practical and proven exercises, concepts, strategies, tactics, tips, tricks, mental rehearsals, and dress rehearsals in actual shopping venues with which you can fight your overshopping habit.

How are we to live in a material world that equates success with possessions, that paints conspicuous consumption as the landscape of happiness? How are we to deal with the pressures of that world, which encourage us to spend more than we make, to work more than we already do, so we can spend more than we're already spending? How are we to regain control and balance, so we can find the time and ease to enjoy what really matters to us—which we may, for the moment, have forgotten? How can we fill the empty spaces inside us, conquering self-doubt with ideas and experiences that nourish the soul? These are the questions this book asks you to ask, and guides you to answer—not for the generic "we" of this paragraph but for you, the very particular and specific person presently reading these pages.

WHAT YOU CAN EXPECT FROM THIS BOOK

If you read it carefully and seriously commit to doing the work, *To Buy or Not to Buy* will lead you on a journey into, through, and beyond your overshopping problem. You'll learn how our culture sucks you into overshopping, enticing you with fabulous promises thinly disguised as products. You'll discover what drives your own particular shopping urges, those underlying personal needs that your shopping presently fills, albeit unhealthily. You'll see clearly what your habit's costing you—in broken or strained relationships (whether with spouse or children or friends), in personal growth, in spirit, and, of course, in financial terms. You'll grasp the sad, central truth of a consumer culture—that *you can never get enough of what you don't really need*—and you'll begin using all this to stop digging yourself in deeper and start digging yourself out. With a clear tally of the costs of your habit, you'll begin to *choose* the path you want to travel instead of being dragged along by unacknowledged needs, heavy baggage in hand. Along the way, and by no means incidentally, you'll discover what you're truly shopping for, what makes your heart sing.

"The journey of a thousand miles," said Lao-tzu, "begins with a single step." In opening this book, you've taken that crucial first step. As with any journey, there'll be difficult places, moments of doubt, occasional setbacks. There's pain underneath your overshopping habit, and kicking the habit involves exploring that pain: acknowledging it, identifying it, and then learning to tolerate it until it eventually subsides. The book's exercises and activities will lead you through this exploration—and ultimately to a better feeling about yourself.

Look at the whole process as an adventure; stay positive, with your eyes and your mind open. Over the journey, you'll identify your personal triggers and the specific aftershocks of these triggers. You'll zero in on what it is you're *really* shopping for, whether those needs are emotional, social, or spiritual. You'll craft strategies and tactics for specific, high-risk situations and then employ and refine them. You'll learn what to expect as you stop overshopping and how to handle any backsliding into old habits.

Money and debt are particular concerns for most overshoppers, and *To Buy or Not to Buy* deals very specifically with these. You'll learn about the centrality of *savings:* that only by *spending less than you make and putting away the difference* can you buttress yourself against life's inevitable emergencies and provide for your future. You'll look directly at the staggering cost (and endless repayment span) of credit card debt, much of it hidden in fine print. You'll map out precisely where your money goes. And you'll identify your values, ask yourself what your goals are, and assess how well your present expenditures reflect those values and goals.

To make the most of this book, work through the twelve parts—this introduction, ten chapters, and a conclusion—*in order* and *completely*. Later chapters build on earlier ones, both conceptually and through the gathering psychological momentum of the activities and exercises. It will also help to work *steadily,* moving a little further along each day. You'll need to allocate forty-five minutes to an hour a day for your *To Buy or Not to Buy* activities—reading, thinking, and writing. It's important, too, at the end of each chapter, to sit down and carefully review your recent work. Fully engaging with this book is a substantial commitment; I know that. But if you go the distance, it will pay off big-time.

Moving through the text, doing all the exercises, responding to the questions, and giving yourself the time to digest new food for thought—expect this process to take a full three months, and expect to refer back to it long after that. Most chapters are designed to be at least a week's work, but there's nothing sacred about the timetable. Don't rush anything. Doing all the work rigorously is far more important than slighting some of it in order to "stay on schedule." Be patient and compassionate with yourself at every step. You've probably struggled with overshopping for a good while. You've re-solved to change your behavior, failed, and tried again; maybe success seems a very long way off—but it doesn't have to be. Put one foot in front of the other, take one step at a time, and you'll get there—first, to relief from debt, shame, and discord, and then to better relationships with others, more security and self-confidence, a stronger sense of self, and a deeper, more meaningful life.

Here are a few other crucial recommendations. First, as you proceed through the book, you'll be answering some questions, creating some lists, and eventually writing down everything you spend and what you spend it on. (You'll do a bit of this writing directly on these pages and most of it in a separate little notebook. More about this Shopping Journal in chapter 1.) The writing process is vital to your progress. Sometimes people feel as though they're writing into a vacuum and begin to lose motivation. Don't let this happen to you. *Writing is often how we discover what we truly think and feel.* Far from going to waste, your written work will lead to uncovering—and recovering—yourself.

Allow friends or comfortable groups (as long as they're not shopping-based) to lend support and encouragement or to share your experience. With a shopping-based friendship, discuss the changes that you're making and then see if the friendship can refocus itself. Many people find it helpful to have a Shopping Support Buddy, a person who's agreed to be an advocate for you as you stop overshopping. (For details about selecting and working with a Shopping Support Buddy, see appendix A.) Some people find Debtors Anonymous or psychotherapy or medication useful. (For a few words about therapy, medication, and the work of this book, see appendix B.) And, increasingly, there are online support groups and message boards specifically focused on compulsive shopping. (For a list of these and other resources, see appendix C.) However you manage it, *feeling connected and understood will substantially boost your chances of success* at the sometimes strenuous, sometimes exhilarating work of stopping overshopping.

Finally, nothing could be more important than to respect and value the self you are now—even as you make room for the kinder, stronger, wiser self who'll emerge as you move toward recovery. To do both of these, adopt this firm, two-legged stance: *see yourself clearly* —face and acknowledge your thoughts, feelings, and behaviors— and *hold what you see with profound compassion,* the way a tuned-in, attentive mother would respond to her small child. If, for example, you get particularly stirred up by a part of the book, notice the way you've been rattled and allow yourself to experience it. But don't dwell on it—and don't do any more reading or exercises until you're feeling more emotionally resilient. Again, you might want to talk your issue through with a supportive friend, family member, therapist, or spiritual adviser.

I've accompanied many overshoppers as they made their journeys from compelled to fulfilled, as they've moved from addictive thinking and behavior to clearheaded self-kindness. You can, too. Work with this book, engaging with its concepts and skills, its tools and strategies; make them your own. Follow *To Buy or Not to Buy* from where you are now to where you want to be—centered, in control, shopping for and getting what you *really* need from now on.

1 | What Are You Shopping For?

So what are you shopping for? Why do you overshop? Where does the urge to overshop come from? What keeps you shopping, even when it doesn't seem to make sense anymore? In this chapter, we take a look at what's underneath the urge to splurge—at the most common reasons we do it and at the kinds of early messages and influences that lie behind those reasons. We're viewing overshopping in the broader context of your life, because the behavior is very much connected to who you are and what you need. Bottom line, overshopping is a coping mechanism, a way you temporarily distract yourself from authentic personal needs that aren't being met. The text and exercises in this chapter will help you begin to tease out the emotional and historical underpinnings of your particular shopping habit. So let's begin: step off the denial merry-go-round and get a solid foothold on the reality of your habit.

WHY DO YOU OVERSHOP?

There are as many reasons to overshop as there are overshoppers. But to keep things manageable, I've distilled most of them into eleven categories. Each one is a way of attempting to deal with thorny individual issues and unmet personal needs; each is based on what real overshoppers have told me over the years. Discovering your own reasons is a necessary and significant step toward stopping overshopping. Ask yourself the questions below, and give yourself permission to be specific, truthful, and nonjudgmental about answering them. *Underline or highlight the parts that hit home,* and feel free to jot down notes in the margins.

Maybe you've already recognized your reasons for overshopping, or at least some of them, and you still continue to do it. Don't let this discourage you. Recognition is not a magic bullet. Rather, it's a kind of radar, allowing you to detect the shape of an incoming urge. The earlier you notice this urge, the easier it is to overcome. But even if you catch it late—when the pressure of the urge makes it almost unstoppable—you gain vital experience for the future. Sometimes the urge is so strong, the hook so sharp, the habitual pattern so sticky, that you can't do anything but succumb to it. Still, seeing the process clearly allows you to lay the groundwork for eventual triumph.

Do you overshop to feel better about yourself or more secure?

Many compulsive buyers have grown up with unrealistically high expectations of themselves. When, inevitably, they fail to meet these expectations, their self-esteem plummets and they become anxious or depressed. To block out the painful self-awareness of failure, they may wholly immerse themselves in buying, focusing intensely[1] on the myriad of sights and sounds and other sensations that go with it. Such immersion brings with it a physiological and psychological high.

Another wrinkle on the same theme is that in general, compulsive shoppers don't accept themselves as they are; they feel insecure and often have a desire to be transformed into some new and idealized version. Amid the dazzle of commercial display—carefully assembled outfits that drape perfectly on sleek mannequins, shiny electronic gadgets that gleam with precision and dynamic capabilities—it's easy to imagine that the next purchase might make you sexier, more powerful, or more commanding. And a massive marketing industry has drummed this message into you almost from birth: "Buy," it tells you, "and you can be like the glamorous and successful people in our ads. Don't buy, and you'll be left out, a loser." The message is clear: dreams are for sale.

Is there a big discrepancy between the way you see yourself and the way you'd like to be? Research has shown that this "self-discrepancy" gap is substantially larger for overshoppers than it is for the normal buyers.[2] If you're reading this, there's a fair chance you're vulnerable to the advertisers' ever-present promises of commercial transformation.

But these promises are false. Buying may distract you from some unpleasant realities in your life, whether they're emotional, financial, relational, or spiritual, but it cannot change them. Instead, you trade destructive long-term consequences for short-term relief, which only winds up making things worse. Self-discrepancy, then, nudges us toward a world of fantasy, a world where what we *wish* to happen takes precedence over what we can reasonably *expect* to happen: the sinkful of dirty dishes evaporates and the unpaid bills dissolve, while the just-bought bracelet sparkles like a new romance. *Who you are* becomes confused with *what you have.* You overfocus on impressing others and shortchange yourself when it comes to taking practical, positive steps to improve your spirit and health (which are your real beauty) or your skills (which are your real power) or your self-acceptance (which is your real strength).

I once had a client named Joanne, a lawyer in her late forties. (All names have been changed to protect privacy.) She recognized that she bought so many clothes and spent so much money and time on haircuts, coloring, makeup, and other cosmetic treatments because she'd never felt pretty. Growing up with a gambler for a father and a disturbed and beautiful mother, Joanne never forgot her father's smirking, oft-repeated lament: "It's such a shame she looks like my side of the family!" Joanne came to the realization that she overshops to feel more attractive and to reward herself for doing the professional work she so often finds tedious.

Do you overshop to avoid dealing with something important?

A particularly strong urge to shop is often a signal of avoidance: you're avoiding some action you know you need to take or ignoring some problem you know you ought to deal with. Is there someone you don't want to see—a friend, a relative, your boss, a doctor? Is there maybe some work you don't want to do? Perhaps you're delaying a next step in your life, like moving or getting pregnant. Maybe you're even afraid of prosperity.

The call to avoidance shopping has to be loud, in order to drown out your own voice telling you to confront your spouse or look for another job. But avoidance shopping cannot silence the very real need for action; it can only briefly muffle that need. Afterward, the situation worsens. The voice of whatever you're avoiding reasserts itself, more forcefully now, and you've also got to deal with the problems that your overshopping has created.

Do you use shopping as a weapon, to express anger or seek revenge?

Rampant overbuying often has negative consequences not only for the buyer but for someone close to her. (For the sake of simplicity, I use the female pronoun *her*, rather than the clumsier *him or her*, in most places in this book. Recent research suggests, however, that men are almost as likely as women to be compulsive buyers.) A partner or spouse (or even a parent) might repeatedly have to bail the buyer out. An overshopper's spouse, partner, or child might feel neglected because of all the time lost to the other's shopping. Because it can hurt others, shopping can be used as a weapon; as a way to retaliate indirectly; as a way to express anger, resentment, or feelings of betrayal. People sometimes do this because they're afraid to express themselves directly, often with good reason. This form of overshopping is usually undertaken as a last resort, after all attempts at productive communication with a spouse, partner, or parent have failed.[3]

If this shoe fits, wear it; look inside for the source of the anger. Anger is usually a sign of buried hurt. Uncover and confront it, and you'll be able to deal with it in a far more constructive way than overshopping.

Suzanne is a client who has been buying compulsively throughout her twenty-year marriage, which has been problematic from the beginning. After an intensely romantic courtship, her husband started dental school and, upon graduation, a lengthy residency. Though he's repeatedly promised to cut back on his hours, each year he seems to work even later. After his training, they moved to a rural community, and Suzanne bore three daughters—and the brunt of rearing them. During these lonely years, she began buying things from catalogs and local stores, which at the time was no financial burden. Over the years, though, her spending grew while her husband's income was reduced because of insurance-reimbursement cutbacks for dentistry. He began to question and resent her purchases, and she came to experience him as withholding. Suzanne acknowledges that some of her overshopping is a form of rebellion against the power disparity in their relationship and her feeling of powerlessness. She's taken to hiding her behavior, believing that the pleasure she gets from buying "special things" for herself is what helps her cope with loneliness, resentment, and frustration.

If you're already aware that you're angry, that you buy things to "get back" at someone, you're ahead of the game. Now you need to find a way to deal constructively with your feelings, so you can enhance, rather than erode, your life, your relationships, and your bank account.

Do you overshop to hold on to love?

Some overshoppers buy incessantly for others. This behavior, though it parades as generosity, is often motivated by a profound underlying fear of abandonment. Out of this fear, the compulsive giver misses the spirit of giving, that gifts be openhanded and without obligation. Instead, he or she imagines each one as an invisible string, tying the receiver—usually a friend, child, or spouse—to her or him. Love, however, can't be bought, coerced, or sustained by compulsive gift giving, and this behavior usually backfires. The following story is typical.

Karen, a twenty-seven-year-old administrative assistant, had terrible fears of abandonment. Her parents' bitter divorce had left her feeling unloved by either one. In adulthood, she developed an intense attachment to a friend, Susan, and it rekindled familiar feelings and fears of loss in her. To avoid experiencing these directly, and to try to keep her friend close and beholden to her, she began buying her lavish gifts. The strategy proved disastrous. Susan felt uncomfortable with the gifts—and in a bind. She didn't want to seem ungrateful, but she couldn't (and didn't want to) respond in kind. Eventually, Karen's worst nightmare came true. Susan backed off and the friendship dissolved.

Do you overshop to soothe yourself or repair your mood?

Everyone who knew Becky knew that she collected teddy bears. It had begun when she was working at a residential facility for developmentally disabled children. She found it thrilling to "rescue" bargain teddy bears at thrift and resale shops and soon realized that she wasn't doing this just "for the children" but for herself. After more than ten years at the facility, burned out and disillusioned by funding cutbacks and staffing changes and a couple of relationships that never really got off the ground, she left her job and moved. Alone in a new city, her collecting intensified. She loved teddy bears because they were cuddly and soft, and she found herself drawn to pillows, terry-cloth bathrobes, and silky things. But the better her purchases felt in the stores, where she'd go whenever she felt bored, irritable, or lonely, the lower she'd sink when she returned home. Her bears grew less comforting than before. She still oohed and aahed over teddy bear gifts, but she was starting to feel like a fake. She felt awkward. After forever having told people how much she loved teddy bears, maybe they weren't what she wanted anymore. She wasn't sure *what* she wanted. She just knew she wanted to feel better.

It's been hypothesized, based on other compulsive or addictive behaviors, that levels of dopamine, a neurotransmitter that mimics opiates, might rise when a compulsive shopper anticipates a purchase or actually makes one. Thus, shopping can be a temporary repair for negative moods. But the fix is short-lived. You're using a Band-Aid on a wound that needs stitches.

Perhaps, like Becky, you're feeling lonely—or sad or scared or angry or bored—and you arrange your schedule so you can be at the mall on nights and weekends, or you spend endless hours surfing

Internet shopping sites. The stores and the websites are familiar, a known quantity, and the excitement of shopping softens the sharp edges of your negative feelings. But this is whistling in the dark. Instead of mustering the courage to meet new people and participate in engaging activities—or learning to ride out your negative feelings—you go through the motions of being with people by imagining that the salespeople or online help associates, or the hosts of the TV shopping networks, are your friends. There is the illusion of close personal connection, but it is only illusion.

A recent study comparing compulsive and ordinary buyers demonstrates a marked difference in mood patterns. Ordinary buyers start out in a better mood than overshoppers, and their mood becomes more positive after the purchase and even more positive when they get home: good, better, best. When a compulsive buyer begins shopping, her mood is typically less positive than that of a normal buyer. Just after the purchase, her mood climbs well beyond that of an ordinary shopper after she's bought. When a compulsive buyer gets home, though, her mood dips far below that of a normal buyer when *she* gets home—and below her own prepurchase mood: somewhat lousy, very good, lousier.[4]

Shopping can, of course, offer a break from inner turmoil. But it can't work for long. What we're looking for when we're lonely can't be found in stores. Depression or boredom can't be reversed by "retail therapy," and no amount of material goods can fill internal emptiness.

Look carefully, then, at your feelings when you experience the urge to shop; ask "What am I *really* shopping for?" Perhaps it's the stimulation of the visual feast, the contact with other shoppers or salespeople, the relaxation of the time away from family obligations, or the need for a reward. Whatever authentic need underlies your urge, there's a healthier and ultimately much more satisfying way to meet it.

Do you overshop to project an image of wealth and power?

In a consumer culture, wealth and power are extremely desirable, since these allow virtually limitless consumption. The subtext is that happiness and self-esteem are directly proportional to the quality (and quantity) of material things an individual can amass. A Lexus, then, is not simply a more reliable and more luxurious automobile than a Ford. It's also a status symbol, an unequivocal indication that its owner is among those lucky few whose houses are on hills overlooking the rest of us. Metaphors for sale.

Of course, for those of us whose houses *aren't* on hills, the Lexus can be bought on credit, even though the purchase may pinch. In other words, some overshoppers buy to project an image, both to the world and to themselves, of the wealth and power they wish they had. This behavior is rooted in the confusion mentioned above, that you *are* what you *have,* and there's a corollary: if you have it, flaunt it. Flaunting what they don't really have, or at least haven't yet paid for, these overshoppers are building houses of straw (though they pretend they're brick). Eventually, the credit wolves will huff and puff and blow their houses down.

If you identify with these overshoppers, it's worth focusing on— and learning to believe—the compelling lesson of repeated research studies: in spite of popular myth, wealth and power *don't* make people happy. Quite the contrary. Happiness comes only from within and has much to do with how you look at the world and its possibilities rather than how the world looks at you. Self-esteem is a function of your internal stock (your values, your role in a family, your contributions to the planet), not your external inventory (your cars or clothing or collections). It's about *who you are,* not *what you own.*

Do you overshop to fit into an appearance-obsessed society?

The American culture's preoccupation with youth, beauty, and style— and its underemphasis on wisdom, growth, and substance—sets us up to overvalue appearance. "Image is everything," said the young Andre Agassi's camera ads, distilling into three words the credo that underlies most advertising. Nowhere is that message more prominent than in the realm of fashion, in which the industry ceaselessly and inventively sells the idea that "clothes make the man"—and even more so, the woman. Buy too heavily into this idea, and you can never keep up with the fashion train, which is carefully scheduled to make costly new stops each season.

Rhonda is single, forty-six, and a senior editor for a top fashion magazine. She spends all her disposable income, and often more, on clothing, shoes, handbags, and jewelry. She's been doing this since she was a young girl getting an allowance. Preoccupied with food, weight, and body shape since her teens, she yo-yo diets and owns wardrobes in three different sizes: thin, thinner, and thinnest. Unmarried, she longs for a committed, long-term relationship with a man and is having difficulty facing the likelihood that she will not bear a child, given her decision not to be a single parent. Rather than experiencing the sadness she feels, she constantly buoys herself with the newest, latest, and greatest that the marketplace has to offer. She calls it a requirement of her job, but, in truth, she buys more than she can possibly wear—and a lot more than she can afford. Her credit card debt is alarming, and she realizes that unless she stops buying and starts to save, she'll never be able to retire. But the need to look as if she walked out of the pages of the magazine that she edits binds her as tight as a corset.

Compulsive clothes shopping is typically an attempt to camouflage a negative body image, both physically and metaphorically—an attempt that can't succeed for long. On the physical level, few of us—however hard we shop, however much we spend—will ever look like the images sold with the goods we buy, those unhealthily willowy women and their square-jawed, six-packed Mr. Cleans. On the metaphorical level, no amount of attention to external appearance can cloak whatever ugliness we see inside.

If you place great importance on the way you look, if you find fashionable clothes essential to looking good, if you doubt your ability to look good without the excessive use of beauty services and/or plastic surgery, you've likely been seduced by the image-mongers. Instead of working endlessly to look like somebody else—or a younger, leaner, buffer, or sexier version of you—it's time to learn to love yourself the way you look and are.

Do you overshop in response to stress, loss, or trauma?

Barbara, a homemaker in her early thirties and a victim in childhood of emotional and physical abuse, began to shop compulsively during college, mostly for clothing, jewelry, shoes, and accessories. A few years before I met her, she had suffered a miscarriage and had a stillborn baby. Devastated and childless, she hardly left the house, closed the curtains, and began losing herself in television. Before long, she found the Home Shopping Network, and in the space of two years, she ran up a staggering amount of credit card debt—nearly $80,000. Virtually all of her spending was for a single category of items: a vast graveyard of porcelain dolls, neatly organized in her basement, every one pristine in its original rectangular box.

Overshopping can function as a relief valve for profound stress or as a balm for the painful wounds of loss or trauma. In the case of chronic stress, you retreat from unbearable tension—the drama of separation or divorce, for example, or the burden of caregiving, whether of children or aging parents, or the yoke of addiction in the family—and enter a frenzy of buying. You focus so hard on your purchases that for a while you insulate yourself from the stress of the real story. Sooner or later, however, this evasion will fail, and you'll be back where you started, needing to deal with the issue directly, and now deeper in debt.

Against the pain of loss or wounds from trauma, *things* seem to offer a compensatory balm. Faced with the loss of a loved one, for example, or serious illness, or scarcity and neglect in childhood, you may find yourself desperately craving a solidness that promises to stay, a permanence you can grasp with your mind and hands. Things can be gathered and controlled, without much fear that they'll disappear. Even the *prospect* of losses can trigger overshopping, like stocking up in the fall to prepare for an anticipated winter, the way a smoker who's about to quit might puff through several final cartons, or an overeater might binge before beginning a diet.

It's a childlike remedy, however, ignoring what adulthood teaches: that reasonable discipline, in shopping as elsewhere, is a centerboard, balancing us as we sail through the turbulent waters of life. And overshopping is a remedy that cannot cure. Physical things can never fill emotional holes. A loss or trauma must be experienced, dealt with, and worked through, so that it can become just another element of the psychic landscape and not its prepossessing central feature.

Do you overshop because it's the lesser evil?

If you, like many overshoppers, have another addiction or compulsive habit—or had one in the past—overshopping may seem less destructive, more acceptable, than this other addiction. If you were first addicted to another behavior or substance—food, drugs, alcohol, gambling, sex, work, or the Internet—you may have merely substituted compulsive buying for the older habit. This could easily happen if you didn't acquire broad-based tools, skills, and strategies to deal healthily with the prior addiction. The strong feelings that surface when you work to kick an addictive behavior sometimes find outlets in a substitute habit, one that provides some of the same highs but is "not as bad." It's a kind of triage. Overshoppers may be deeply in debt or suffering from other negative consequences, but their habit is less likely to damage their physical health than other addictions.

Even if your compulsive buying is the earlier addiction, it's likely to be the last one tackled. This makes sense, as noted above, for reasons of triage. But there's a subtler if equally important reason. Money, for all its public handling, remains the last taboo, far more secret these days than, say, sex or alcohol addiction. So if you're struggling with two compulsions, overshopping, the more private and the less immediately damaging of the two, may be sustained even while you slowly cut the addictive ties of the other behavior.

Do you overshop to feel more in control?

People who see themselves as having few options in central areas of their lives—in relationships, for example, or at work or with family—may seize on shopping as an arena in which they can exercise control through their consumer choices. Such people may experience the heightened state called "flow" during the shopping process, which can also provide a sense of optimism about the future. Research in England with fifty female compulsive buyers suggested that addictive consumption appeared to be the *only* activity during which some of them felt in control, the *only* time they could "self-manage" their lives.[5]

Unlike many areas of life, in which human beings function as part of a team and decisions are the product of collaboration and compromise, shopping offers power and freedom: you buy what you want when you want it, and sellers are always happy to see you.[6] But shopping as a way to experience control soon backfires: it becomes compulsive and, like any addiction, begins to control the addict.

Do you overshop to find meaning in your life or to deny death?

The last question to be asked here is also the most basic. For some people, compulsive buying is an attempt to solve existential or spiritual dilemmas, a way to give meaning to life or to feel part of a bigger whole. A recent ad for a fancy SUV taps lightly into this not-so-light issue: "To be one *with* everything," it says, "you need one *of* everything."[7]

Those of us who use overshopping this way may see it as filling the existential void, as a way to create a contained, predictable world in the midst of chaos. Airplanes crash and burn, trash suffocates our landfills, and teenagers go berserk in their schools: in a maddening and insecure world, some people look for security in what they can control—the things they own. This is not unlike our culture's response to death. We know the end is certain, yet we fear it, we oppose it, we deny it.

Rick, a fifty-four-year-old set designer, has lived with HIV and then AIDS for more than a decade. It was shortly after he first learned of the infection that he began to spend money compulsively on clothes, shoes, and personal services. He'd always been fond of these, but before his diagnosis, he controlled his spending. He's often very sick, but he dresses with an individuality and style that both cheers him and evokes admiration from his friends. "You look great," people tell him, and the momentary reassurance helps him stare down his grim future. Rick's noticed that his overshopping is proportional to the seriousness of his illness. When there's a crisis, he buys wildly. When it passes, the buying slackens. He recognizes how difficult it is to plan anything for the future—including financial soundness—when you're staring death in the eye.

Buying can impart a feeling of immortality and permanence to our ephemeral selves. Social scientist Lauren Lawrence puts it this way: "I buy something that will endure, [so] by extension, I will endure. In this way the object lends the individual a future."[8] Tennessee Williams's Big Daddy says it more rhetorically in *Cat on a Hot Tin Roof*: "The human animal is a beast that dies and if he's got money he buys and buys and buys and I think the reason he buys everything he can buy is that in the back of his mind he has the crazy hope that one of his purchases will be life ever-lasting."[9]

But none of this crazy hope can be realized. Things, no matter how long they endure, can't save us from death. And if we buy things with this hope, we allow getting and spending to rob us of time, energy, money—and the richness of life, right *here*, right *now*.

YOUR SHOPPING JOURNAL

It's time now to look at why *you* overshop—but, first, let's talk about your Shopping Journal, a vital ally in the fight against overshopping. It's simply a notebook, of whatever size you find comfortable, that you keep nearby, whether you're home or out. (Getting a notebook with a pocket will give you the flexibility of keeping receipts or your Reminder Card in it, which we'll talk about later. If you prefer, a premade journal is available for purchase at stoppingovershopping.com/journal.) As you go through *To Buy or Not to Buy*, you'll be making a few different kinds of entries in this journal. Sometimes, you'll create a list of important things to keep in mind in the heat of a shopping encounter. Often, you'll write answers to the kinds of questions posed below. And, eventually, you'll document your expenditures there.

There are two important benefits to keeping a Shopping Journal. First, as I noted in the introduction, in the mental and physical act of writing, we often discover what we really think; and deciding what you *really* think, rather than what you're *supposed* to think, is essential to making the kind of changes you're after. Second, over time, your journal will become a record of your shopping thoughts, feelings, and experiences. Keeping it rigorously will help you to identify and make conscious the often unconscious patterns that bind you to your overshopping behavior. And *that*, more than almost anything else, will enable you to stop overshopping.

Why Do You Overshop?

OK. Looking at what you've underlined or highlighted in this chapter (as well as at any notes you've made in the margins), take some time now to write freely in your journal about how overshopping currently functions in *your* life. Ideally, your narrative will bravely address what lies beneath the surface, will attempt to acknowledge the underground psychological springs from which your overshopping flows. You'll be deepening this understanding in the next subsection, when you start to look at how it all began. Remember, no one else is going to see this. This is the place to be brutally honest with yourself and to listen with interest, curiosity, and kindness to what you're saying.

HOW DID IT ALL BEGIN?

What the child learns, the adult remembers. Whenever you engage in any of hundreds of possible shopping behaviors—clipping a coupon, window-shopping, scrutinizing a product's list of features on the back of the package, trying on a new pair of shoes, checking a price tag, swiping a credit card—you're acting from a set of attitudes and beliefs that you learned when you were young. You may not be *conscious* of the messages you got as a child; you may not *remember* the shopping behavior you observed. But it's all in there, embedded in your psyche. The past lives on in the present, quietly but powerfully shaping it.

Now is the time to take the risk of bringing these messages and behaviors into the light. When you're more aware of your childhood influences, you're less likely to be at their mercy. Instead of shopping or spending automatically or reflexively, like a robot carrying out instructions from a program installed years ago, you can begin to make independent shopping decisions that fit your current life and circumstances. True, calling up your early experiences may reopen old wounds and may therefore require a good deal of courage. But as financial recovery expert Karen McCall observes, "If we are ever to change our financial condition, we have to change our financial conditioning."[10] Stopping overshopping, then, involves more than simply mastering the practical skills you'll learn throughout this book; it also depends on acknowledging the emotional underpinnings of your attitudes and behavior—and then moving beyond them.

Money is far more than mere currency; like the Maltese falcon in the Bogart movie, it's the stuff that dreams are made of. And "stuff," the material things we buy with money, can have profound emotional significance, becoming inextricably linked with happiness, love, power, freedom, security, independence, control, and self-worth. Each of these connections, heavily reinforced by advertising, is a myth that exacts a high price from believers.

One way or another, the shopping myths imprison rather than free us, affixing us to the iron wheel of commerce, tethering us to the future rather than the present. Instead of empowering, they weaken us. What we need to do is to pry these embedded fictions loose— and shop, not for more stuff, but for ideas and experiences that will fill our lives with passion and commitment. It's these that constitute genuine wealth, these that provide enduring self-esteem.

To warm you up for the exercises below, check off the shopping myths you grew up with. With which of the following was shopping or "stuff" equated?

❑ happiness   ❑ security
❑ love   ❑ independence
❑ power   ❑ control
❑ freedom   ❑ social connection
❑ fun   ❑ self-worth
_____ (other)

Messages about Shopping, Spending, and Stuff

We all heard a variety of messages—views, attitudes, beliefs, lore, morals, advice—when we were growing up. Some came from our parents and relatives, some from other people. Some came from books, magazines, movies, or plays. Some came from the music we listened to, and some from the advertising that surrounded us. The following is a list of common messages about shopping, spending, and stuff. *Underline the ones you heard as a child and put a star next to the ones you bought into.* This will help prepare you for the autobiographical thinking and writing that you'll be doing at the end of this section.

Pro-shopping Messages

"Diamonds are a girl's best friend."

"Clothes make the man."

"Always look your best."

"You get what you pay for."

"Whoever said money can't buy happiness didn't know where to shop."

"A little retail therapy goes a long way."

"You can never be too rich or too thin."

"Shop 'til you drop."

"Never settle for less than the best."

"New shoes chase the blues."

"You'll never have to worry about money."

"You can't take it with you."

"It's cheap at twice the price."

"The right dress means more than the right religion."

"We have to keep up with the Joneses."

"In the land of the Golden Rule, he with the gold rules."

"He who has the most toys when he dies, wins."

Anti-shopping Messages

"Money doesn't grow on trees."

"Do you think I'm made of money?"

"Money is the root of all evil."

"Don't dress in a way that calls attention to yourself."

"Waste not, want not."

"Half a loaf is better than none."

"You should only buy things on sale."

"Don't spend it all in one place."

"Make do with what you have."

"Don't talk about money."

"Money talks. Sometimes all it says is 'good-bye.'"

"Don't trust anyone with your money."

"When we were kids, we didn't spend money like that."

"Save your best things for company."

"Never ask for things. Wait until they're offered."

"That's for rich people."

"Be grateful for what you have."

Family Patterns

What about family dynamics? How does your family history relate to your present feelings and behavior about shopping, spending, and stuff? The following are a number of common familial scenarios that can foster the development of compulsive buying in a child. Each one has an infinite number of variants. Can you recognize yourself and your family in one or more of these?

- Some parents of compulsive buyers were abused and/or neglected during their own childhoods—and given gifts to compensate. Maybe there was a bitter divorce or serious mental or physical illness in the family. Maybe there was an addiction or some other dysfunction. When these children become adults, they tend to follow the familiar pattern with their own children; it's what they know. They shower the children with presents to offset their own real or perceived parental deficiencies. In such families, the children often feel inadequate, as though something vital were missing in themselves and their lives; when they grow up, they buy compulsively to fill this internal emptiness—to feel, at least temporarily, more complete and less alone.

- Parents who demand that children earn their love through "good" (probably compliant) behavior, achievement, and performance often have children who feel emotionally undernourished. If you felt valued only when you achieved, then you were deprived of being loved unconditionally, loved no matter what. Deprivation keeps people hungry for love and acceptance, keeps them fixated on the idea that to be loved, they have to conform to a certain ideal. Some of these compliant people try to buy love with gifts or overshop to maintain the warmth and recognition that they get from salespeople. These safe, limited, one-way relationships are often a substitute for reciprocal, lasting relationships, which are more difficult to cultivate and maintain.

- When "good" behavior, performance, and achievement are rewarded with money and gifts rather than affection and affirmation, this behavior often passes to the next generation, where it may result in compulsive buying, compulsive gift giving, and/or compulsively picking up the tab. This deprivation of nurturance leads to dependence on the gratitude expressed by the recipients of gifts or dinners, because it seems an important confirmation of the buyer's inherent worth.

- In some families, parents don't give children the time or energy that would allow them to feel secure, loved, valued, and important. They grow up believing they're not worth being paid attention to, feeling lonely and empty—and they look for something to fill up on. Perhaps the parents work nonstop, typically to acquire and maintain possessions they don't really need and may not even use. Because possessions have been given so much value at a formative stage of the child's development, the natural longings for personal acknowledgment and familial love become redirected into wishes for material objects. The resultant compulsive shopping can be seen both as an act of aggression—it will require rescue from significant others, forcing parents or spouses to make up for what the compulsive buyer has missed growing up—and as an attempt to confirm self-worth.

- Another common scenario involves the family that has suffered financial reversals. They may fixate on lost luxury and deeply envy the more financially fortunate, and their reduction in status may lead to lowered self-esteem. If the family members' view of themselves continues to be associated with the quality and quantity of possessions they can acquire, compulsive buying may become the unconscious solution to their problem. Recent economic conditions in the United States, including the bursting of the Internet bubble in the 1990s and now the subprime mortgage crisis, have led to significant financial reversals for many households. Whether or not we'll see a compulsive-buying upsurge in the next generation is uncertain, but it's a distinct possibility.
- In families where a *feeling* of both emotional and financial impoverishment has dominated—even if the financial circumstances were comfortable—compulsive buying can be fostered. By itself, being poor doesn't necessarily lead to feelings of deprivation; but when emotional impoverishment is also present, the combination is lethal. Then, children's needs for things *and* attention go unmet, and they feel alone, unworthy, angry, mistrustful, or rebellious. Powerlessness, shame, or pain dominate their lives, and if these feelings aren't faced and dealt with, the grown children may try to ward them off with overshopping. Typical is this plaintive cry: "I've been so deprived for so long, it's time for me to have things." Another version is, "I felt so deprived as a child, I'll do anything to avoid ever having to feel that way again."
- Some families give no real financial guidance or education to their children. The children may not be given any responsibility for money while growing up and may be overprotected in other ways as well: no chores, no allowance, no babysitting jobs, for example. Alternatively, the parents may provide some guidance but be extremely critical of any mistakes or misjudgments the children make. As these children become young adults, they lack confidence in money matters. Often, they haven't learned to manage a checking account and can't handle the responsibility of a credit card. Such young adults are at great risk for overshopping.

Your Personal History with Shopping, Spending, and Stuff

Now it's time to get personal. In order to understand your relationship with shopping and the meanings you attach to getting or having material things, you need to examine the early messages you received and the circumstances in which you received them. This process may bring up painful memories—of physical, emotional, or spiritual deprivation; of neglect or abuse; of low self-esteem or persistent feelings of inadequacy. Painful feelings—sadness, anger, fear, and shame, for example—are also likely to surface as you take the honest, introspective look that writing this shopping autobiography entails.

Here's the place to open a protective umbrella of care. Imagine yourself ministering to a child with a scraped knee or cut finger—though, of course, you are both the child and the mother. First of all, you'd be calm, to help soothe the child. You'd acknowledge both the physical pain and the emotional upset. Then, you'd reassure the child that everything was going to be OK. And then you'd engage: first, you'd clean and bandage the wound, and then, a little later, perhaps, you'd think through with the child what had happened and how to prevent it next time. Treat yourself this same compassionate way—calm, acknowledge, reassure, and engage. It's how to care for yourself when the going gets tough.

Hang on to that open umbrella, see what you're discovering or rediscovering calmly, and acknowledge whatever feelings the process brings up. Be proud of yourself for having the determination and courage to do this memoir, and reassure yourself that something good will come of it. If the feelings get too painful, take some time to nurture yourself before you go back to the work. Get support from other people as well; talk to a trusted friend, mentor, or therapist about what you're experiencing so that you're not alone with it. Ultimately, this reflection on your personal history will promote healing. It will help you begin to envision a you who cares for yourself in healthy ways, free from the burden that overshopping creates in your life.

YOUR EARLIEST MEMORIES ABOUT
SHOPPING, SPENDING, AND STUFF

Now let yourself wander back in time to the days when you were growing up. How did your family influence you about shopping and stuff? What attitudes, habits, or skills did you learn from your own first shopping experiences? Who were your role models? What did you learn about shopping from peers, community, and the media? How did you learn to use money? Thinking about and answering these questions will help you see how early influences helped shape your current beliefs and behaviors. Even if you discover only a few significant connections between the past and your present overshopping, you'll have taken a meaningful step forward. Remember, there are no right or wrong answers here—just your memories and impressions. Your story is your own, unique and personal.

JOURNAL TIME

Writing Your Shopping Autobiography

Use the questions that follow to structure your story. I've organized them into three sections: "Early Family Influences"; "Peers, Community, and Media Influences"; and "Learning to Use Money." Relax and give yourself plenty of time for this trip down memory lane. Don't even think about doing it all in one sitting. You might want to ask family and/or friends for their recollections.

Early Family Influences

1. What's your first memory of shopping? What was the situation, who was there, how did you feel, and what happened?
2. What do you remember about shopping trips when you were a child? Who went shopping? Where did they go? What was the emotional climate like? What was your role?
3. What did your family do for fun? How did shopping figure into your family's recreation and vacations?
4. When you were a child, how were birthdays and holidays celebrated? What part did shopping and buying play in the celebration?
5. Did you get extra presents when you were sick? What about for an achievement? If so, what was the impact?
6. Do you remember really wanting something badly and not getting it? If so, what was it?
7. Do you feel you were deprived of your share of material possessions? Do you feel you got more than your share of material

goods? If you answered "yes" to either question, what was the situation and how did you feel about it?

8. Was your family poor? comfortable? wealthy? Did this fluctuate?

9. How did your family's economic situation affect your views, attitudes, and messages about buying and owning?

10. Did you ever feel envious, guilty, ashamed, or competitive about how much or how little money and possessions your family had, as compared with your friends or others around you? What do you remember about that?

11. Were there any addictions, mental or physical illnesses, or life circumstances (either positive or negative) that affected your family's views, attitudes, and messages about buying and having? If so, what were they and how did they affect you?

12. Do you remember frequent discussions or arguments in your family about shopping? About amassing stuff? About getting rid of stuff? If so, how were they resolved?

13. Whose attitudes or beliefs dominated the family view? What effect did this have on you?

14. Were there shopping or buying secrets in your family? What were they? For example, did anyone hide their purchases, have bills sent to other addresses, forge checks, or open credit cards in someone else's name? If so, how did the secrecy affect you? Is it still going on?

Peer, Community, and Media Influences

1. How old were you when you first went shopping with your friends without parental supervision? Describe the scene: who was there, how did you feel, where did you go, and what happened?

2. As a child and then as a teen, how often did you go shopping with friends? Never or rarely? Sometimes? Often? What was the experience like? How often did you buy something? How did you feel after the purchase?

3. How did you and your peers determine what was "cool" or "in" in terms of clothes, music, and so forth? How important were brands?

4. How did your peers' tastes or attitudes affect your shopping or buying as a child? As a teen?

5. Were you allowed to use your parents' credit card to go shopping? If so, did you have a spending limit? Were there any problems surrounding the use of their credit card?
6. Can you remember a specific incident involving your peers and shopping that is still with you today? If so, what were the circumstances? How did you feel at the time, and how might this still affect you?
7. What messages about shopping, buying, or having material things did you get from your religious community? From your town or neighborhood?
8. Was there any conflict between the messages you got from your family, your peers, and your community? If so, what was the conflict and how did you react to it?
9. Looking back, were there celebrities, specific television shows, or television commercials that influenced your shopping as a child? as a teen? Who or what were they, and what influence did they have?

Learning to Use Money

1. As a child, did you get an allowance? If so, at what age did it begin and how long did it continue? Did you have to earn it in some way and, if so, how? Was it ever taken away as a punishment?
2. If you got an allowance, were you (a) told what you could buy or (b) asked to account for how you spent it or (c) free to do with it as you wished? How did you feel about how the allowance issue was handled?
3. How and when did you first get your own (nonallowance) money—for example, as gifts from relatives or from odd jobs such as selling lemonade, lawn mowing, or babysitting? Were you free to do with it as you wished? What kind of advice or guidance did your parents or others give you about whether, when, or how to spend it? What do you remember using it for?
4. At what age did you start to give gifts to friends and family for birthdays and/or holidays? How did you decide what to give and how much to spend (if you bought the gifts)? How did you pay for the gifts?
5. When did you get your first savings account? Your first checking account? Did someone teach you how to use the accounts?

Did you make regular deposits in your savings account? Did you keep a running balance and reconcile your checkbook with your monthly bank statement? Did you often bounce checks?

6. When did you get your first paycheck from a regular part-time job? From your first full-time job? How did having regular paychecks affect how you shopped and what you bought?

7. When did you get your first credit card? Did anyone teach you about using it and about compound interest? Did you pay your bill in full, or did you run up a balance? Was this a source of friction with anyone?

8. Did you know the interest rate on your card(s)? Did you know what you owed? Were you ever out of control with your credit card as an adolescent or a young adult? If so, what were the circumstances and what happened?

9. If you went to college or other training after high school, who paid for it, and what were your thoughts and feelings about how your tuition was being paid?

10. What messages did you receive from your parents about supporting yourself? Did you think that you'd be supporting anyone else as an adult and, if so, who?

11. Looking back on your childhood, what *positive* shopping role models did you have? What *negative* shopping role models did you have?

12. What unfulfilled expectations or unsatisfied dreams are currently feeding into your shopping or buying?

HOW IT ALL BEGAN, WHERE IT LED YOU, AND HOW YOU SEE IT NOW

One final set of reflections. Now it's time to connect the past and present, putting together the early influences on your attitudes and beliefs with your subsequent overshopping behaviors. You'll use sentence completion to connect what you saw, thought, and believed during three distinct periods in your development with what you know now.

To give you an idea of how useful this can be, read how Jennifer, a twenty-five-year-old yoga instructor I worked with, completed these sentences.

In my childhood, I saw *my friends wearing cool shoes,* so
I picked up the message that *if I had shoes like theirs, I would be
    cool, too.*
Later, I overshopped when I *begged my mom to buy them for me,*
still thinking or believing that *the shoes made me cool.*
Now I realize *that I make myself cool, not the shoes,*
which will help me stop overshopping because *I know I'm not defined
    by what I own.*

In my teens, I saw *that you needed to look a certain way to fit in,* so
I picked up the message that *I need to keep up with trends.*
Later, I overshopped when I *bought trendy clothes that I didn't need,*
still thinking or believing that *being "in style" is vital.*
Now I realize *that I should buy things that don't go out of style,*
which will help me stop overshopping because *I'll resist the urge to
    buy clothes or other items that are trendy.*

As a young adult, I saw *that my boyfriend seemed to love me more
    when I bought him something he really wanted,* so
I picked up the message that *gifts equal love.*
Later, I overshopped when I *bought him things I couldn't afford,*
still thinking or believing that *he'd love me more if I did.*
Now I realize *that gifts and material possessions don't equal love or
    happiness,*
which will help me stop overshopping because *I'm not going to buy
    things to make someone love me. If someone doesn't love me for
    who I am, he's not the right guy for me.*

Now it's your turn. Review the three sets of autobiographical questions
you've just answered, and then complete the sentences below in your
journal.

In my childhood, I saw . . . , so I picked up the message that . . .
Later, I overshopped when I . . . , still thinking or believing that . . .
Now I realize . . . , which will help me stop overshopping because . . .

In my teens, I saw . . . , so I picked up the message that . . .
Later, I overshopped when I . . . , still thinking or believing that . . .
Now I realize . . . , which will help me stop overshopping because . . .

As a young adult, I saw . . . , so I picked up the message that . . .
Later, I overshopped when I . . . , still thinking or believing that . . .
Now I realize . . . , which will help me stop overshopping because . . .

Congratulations! I know that dredging up old memories wasn't easy or necessarily pleasant—but it's important to be able to see that your over-shopping behavior is the end product of a long chain of causes and effects. In the next chapter, you'll first explore what triggers you to overshop today—and what the consequences of that overshopping are. Then, you'll get a chance to explore and examine your ambivalence about stopping, to see both sides of the coin. Finally, you'll begin to learn how to use this informa-tion to interrupt the overshopping cycle—and practice doing just that.

2 | What Hooks You and What Unhooks You

Triggers and Aftershocks, Values and Vision

In the previous chapter, we looked from a broad psychological perspective at what lies behind overshopping. Now our focus narrows to the immediate precipitants, which we call "triggers," and to the negative consequences of overshopping, which we call "aftershocks." In this chapter, you investigate and document your personal triggers and aftershocks—and then you begin to connect the dots between them. You look at the overshopping *sequence*—triggers → actions → aftershocks—whose three elements unfold like a little Rube Goldberg machine: a squirrel drops a nut on a lever, the tripped lever releases a trapdoor, and a ballerina drops down onto a miniature hay bale. Triggers lead to overshopping, and overshopping leads to aftershocks.

Once you've worked with your triggers and aftershocks, you look at them within the context of your values and vision. Then, so you can make an informed decision about stopping, you identify and balance the benefits and costs, learn what to do when your heart and head disagree, and discover ways to maintain and boost your motivation. Finally, having learned about getting hooked and unhooked, you arm yourself against the inner grinches that may kick and scream (and try to steal from you) as you stop overshopping.

THE URGE STRIKES: WHAT'S TRIGGERING YOU?

A trigger is a starter, some stimulus that elicits a response, something that stirs you up, an itch that makes you want to scratch. It's anything that inclines *you in particular* toward shopping: something you see or hear or think or feel or experience or remember that stimulates you. It can be as pointed and specific as a Sale sign or as all-encompassing as the loss of a loved one. A trigger can lead directly and immediately to the action of buying—you pass a store window with an eye-catching display of the exact shoes you've coveted—or it may initiate a chain of intermediate steps that culminate in buying. (It's worth noting that being in an emotionally or physically vulnerable state predisposes you to being triggered. *H*ungry, *a*ngry, *l*onely, *t*ired—these and many more physical and emotional states are times to pause, to *halt* rather than do something impulsive. On a day when you're feeling physically strong and in high self-esteem, it's much less likely that your usual triggers will set you off.)

To organize our consideration of triggers, I've divided them into five types—*situational, cognitive, interpersonal, emotional,* and *physical*—and offered common examples of each in the self-recognition exercises below. As you read through the questions, statements, and phrases below, check off any that apply to you (even if not exactly). Then, dedicate a page in your Shopping Journal for a list of your triggers, copying any important ones from this exercise. Write only a word or a few words on each line, just enough to jog your memory, but make the list as clear and complete as you can. Put your most potent and/or typical triggers toward the top, and put down as many as you can think of. You might even want to paste in a visual reminder, something you've cut out from a magazine, perhaps, or a price tag, a receipt, a sketch, a business card, a piece of fabric—anything that will remind you of what you need to steer clear of. Throughout your work with this book, add additional triggers to the list as you discover them.

Common Situational Triggers

❑ If you see a Sale sign in a store window or get an announcement of a sale in the mail, do you have trouble passing it up?

- ❏ Do you almost always buy something new when you have an important party or event to attend?
- ❏ Do birthdays and other holidays lead you to overshop, either for yourself or for other people?
- ❏ Do you feel compelled to buy things you see in magazines or on television?
- ❏ Do you spend a lot of time looking through catalogs?
- ❏ Do you see someone wearing something and decide you have to have it?
- ❏ Does rainy, cloudy, or snowy weather bring out the shopper in you?
- ❏ Does being homebound (for whatever reason) cause you to shop?
- ❏ Does merely *being* at the computer tempt you to shop online?
- ❏ Does being off from work with no plans set you up for overshopping?
- ❏ Do you overshop when you go on vacation?
- ❏ Is your living space so cluttered and disorganized that you buy things you think you need but in fact already have?

Common Cognitive Triggers

- ❏ "If I don't buy this DVD now, I'll never be able to get it."
- ❏ "I've done a terrific job on this paper; I deserve something special."
- ❏ "I feel so guilty for yelling at my daughter that I've got to buy her that jacket she wants."
- ❏ "I've kept my cool with my teenage son this week; I need a reward."
- ❏ "Those sneakers [or earrings or gloves or boots] are so cool! I want a pair, too."

- "I look terrible! Some Botox and some new makeup would help. This is an emergency. I'll put it on my credit card."
- "My Volvo has no sex appeal. I really want a Mercedes."
- "When I find pants that make me look thin, I'd be a fool not to buy them."
- "This high-end attaché case spells success to everyone who sees it. It'll get me new accounts."
- "I'm not going to retire for at least twenty-five years. Why start preparing now?"
- "I'll never save up enough money for a trip to Japan. I might as well liquidate my vacation account and buy that fabulous designer suit."

Common Interpersonal Triggers

- Do you shop when you've had a fight with a friend or a family member?
- Does someone's commenting negatively—or positively—about your appearance send you shopping?
- Does wanting to fit in or impress your peers drive your shopping?
- Does being with a particular friend predispose you to go to the mall?
- Does seeing someone else get something you want lead you to overspend?
- A favorite salesperson calls to tell you that there's something new in the store, "with your name on it." Are you off and running?
- Is retail therapy your favorite response to a demanding or sick parent or child?

Common Emotional Triggers

- Life is looking pretty dull and gray to you. Does shopping always connect you with a brighter emotional shade?

❑ Something or someone is really annoying you. Do you shop to forget about it?

❑ It's hard to shake the sadness that you're feeling in your gut. Does this send you in search of mood-enhancing bargains?

❑ You're feeling underconnected and lonely. Do you go shopping to be around other people and then find yourself buying?

❑ Do you habitually use people you pay—personal trainers, for example, or beauty experts, yoga instructors, dance teachers—to fill some kind of emotional void?

❑ You're excited, maybe even euphoric. Does a mood like that send you shopping?

❑ You remember a happy experience—maybe even a good shopping trip. Do you shop to try to re-create those feelings?

❑ You feel stressed and overloaded. Do you find that one way to decompress is browsing (which in your case all too often leads to buying)?

❑ You often judge yourself: whatever goes wrong seems to be your fault. To drown out some of the self-blame, do you submerge yourself in stuff?

❑ You're constantly hounded by thoughts about what you should or shouldn't be doing and what you should or shouldn't have done. Have you found that one of the only ways to keep such thoughts at bay is to get in touch with your inner shopper?

❑ You feel embarrassed or ashamed about some aspect of your behavior, character, or lifestyle. Do you use shopping as a way to try to cover it up?

❑ Whether vaguely or distinctly, you're anxious and restless. Does shopping seem to calm you down?

❑ Do you think you have to keep buying gifts for friends, family, or coworkers, either in order to be liked or because you believe you owe it to them?

❑ You're constantly comparing yourself with other people.

Is shopping a way you try to silence your feelings of envy, jealousy, or inadequacy?

Common Physical Triggers

❑ You're trying to watch your weight, and you're feeling hungry. You shop in order to avoid eating.

❑ You've got a stress headache, and, rather than take care of yourself by lying down or taking aspirin, you figure you'll distract yourself by browsing in a store with soft music.

❑ Your lower back is acting up again; one way to forget it temporarily is to spend an afternoon at the mall with some friends.

❑ It's 3:00 A.M., and you've been tossing and turning for hours. Why not put on the TV and see what's happening at QVC or HSN?

❑ You're out with friends after work, and you've had a few drinks. On your walk to the train station, you see a pair of shoes you have no business buying, but the alcohol has affected your judgment.

AND *THEN* WHAT HAPPENS? AFTERSHOCKS

Aftershocks are the undesirable consequences of overshopping—the costs, whether financial or otherwise. Until now, the consequences of your overshopping, even if they haven't been positive, have been positive enough for you to continue with this behavior. The fact that you're working with this book, however, suggests that you're beginning to recognize and face the aftershocks.

Shopping aftershocks span at least as wide a territory as triggers; I've organized them into seven categories. The *financial* impact of your overshopping behavior is the most concrete and most countable aftershock, but it's merely the visible tip of the iceberg. Lurking beneath are other, sometimes even more important costs—costs to your *relationships*, your *emotional life*, your *work life*, your *physical body* or your *living space*, your *personal development*, and your *spirit*.

To head off any possible confusion here, it's worth noting that one shopper's trigger can be another's aftershock. Feelings such as guilt, anxiety, or shame, for example, might *propel* one person to shop; those same feelings might be the undesirable *consequences* of someone else's shopping. It's even possible that the same thing could function as trigger *and* aftershock for the same overshopper: remorse about something he or she did or said, for example, could trigger overshopping, which could easily lead to more remorse.

As above, check off each question or phrase that applies to you, even if roughly, in each of the categories. Then dedicate another page in your Shopping Journal and enter any important aftershocks you identify in the exercise. Here, too, you might want to paste in a visual reminder: maybe the balance from your credit card bill, or the description of a course you want to take but can't afford because of overshopping, or a photo of some clutter in your house or apartment—again, anything that will remind you of why you want to stop overshopping. As before, put the most important ones near the top and add additional aftershocks whenever you discover them.

Common Financial Aftershocks

- ❑ Your overshopping has led to a situation in which you can't pay off your credit card bills and don't know when you'll be able to.
- ❑ You have very little, if any, money for retirement.
- ❑ Your home is sorely in need of repairs, but the money you're paying to the credit card companies makes any thought of having the work done a pipe dream.
- ❑ You're besieged by calls from creditors. A lawyer has told you that bankruptcy is your best option.
- ❑ You're trying to get a mortgage, and you've discovered that your credit rating is poor.
- ❑ You're often hit with late fees and penalties; you're chronically disorganized and in denial about your finances.
- ❑ You've borrowed money from family or friends, and you don't know when or if you're going to pay it back.

❑ You don't have enough money to cover your living expenses should an emergency arise and you couldn't work for several months.

Common Relationship Aftershocks

❑ Are you lying to yourself about your behavior?

❑ Are you lying to someone else about it?

❑ Are people acting as if they don't trust you?

❑ Are you neglecting or withdrawing from your family?

❑ Are you fighting with a spouse or partner?

❑ Are people expressing concern about your overshopping?

❑ Are you impatient with your children?

❑ Are you having conflicts with or hiding from friends or loved ones?

❑ Are you canceling social engagements?

❑ Are you keeping your problem a secret?

❑ Do you live amid enormous clutter that's affecting other people negatively?

❑ Are you or your spouse considering separation or divorce because of the fallout from your overshopping problem?

Common Emotional Aftershocks

As a result of overshopping, do you feel

❑ depressed?   ❑ secretive?

❑ anxious?   ❑ greedy or selfish?

❑ irritable?   ❑ angry?

❑ ashamed or guilty?   ❑ like hurting yourself?

❑ unworthy?   ❑ defeated and ready to give up?

❑ out of control?   ❑ helpless?

❑ narcissistic or vain?   ❑ hopeless?

❑ shallow?

Common Work Aftershocks

❑ Are you in danger of being fired for excessive shopping during work time, whether on the Internet or out of the office in stores?

❑ Are you stealing from your company in some other way—falsifying expense reports, perhaps?

❑ Are you working overly long hours, in one job or more, to maintain a lifestyle that you can't really afford?

❑ Are you missing work because of your shopping problem?

❑ Is your performance at work suffering because of your shopping problem?

❑ Are you being passed over for promotions because your shopping problem is keeping you from doing the best job you can?

Physical Body or Living Space Aftershocks

❑ Are you neglecting your need for regular checkups or specific medical care because you've spent your money supporting your overshopping habit?

❑ Are you so anxious about your debt that you're having stomach problems or developing high blood pressure?

❑ Are you having trouble sleeping because you're so upset about your debt?

❑ Is your overshopping giving you stress or migraine headaches?

❑ Are you forgoing regular exercise because you don't have the time for it or the money to go to the gym?

❑ Are you skimping on high-quality food because so much of your money goes to feed your shopping addiction?

❑ Are you having trouble thinking clearly or concentrating?

❑ Are you in a constant state of overstimulation because of this problem?

- ❏ Are you neglecting everyday tasks such as cleaning the house and taking out the garbage?
- ❏ Do you resist inviting people to your home because you're embarrassed about how cluttered and disorganized it is?
- ❏ Does the state of utter disarray in your home make you feel stressed, overwhelmed, and emotionally exhausted?

Personal Development Aftershocks

- ❏ Have you wanted to go back to school or take classes but been unable to afford it because of shopping?
- ❏ Have you wasted time shopping that you could have used to nurture your creativity?
- ❏ Has your shopping distracted you from even thinking about personal development?
- ❏ As a result of your overshopping, have you let go of a hobby you enjoyed?
- ❏ Have you been unable to travel and broaden your horizons because you've used your money for shopping?
- ❏ Have you stopped challenging yourself intellectually because of your preoccupation with shopping?

Common Spiritual Aftershocks

- ❏ Do you feel as if your life lacks meaning or is going nowhere?
- ❏ Would your life be richer if you weren't shopping so much?
- ❏ Have you made the almighty dollar your God?
- ❏ Have you lost your connection with nature and the outdoors?
- ❏ Are you unable to be alone with yourself?
- ❏ Have you lost a sense of community?
- ❏ Do you feel as if your values and your lifestyle are mismatched?
- ❏ Have you lost your capacity to use humor to deal with contradiction and adversity?

- ❑ Do you feel hollow?
- ❑ Have you lost your capacity to deeply appreciate beauty and elegance?
- ❑ Have you lost your generosity of spirit?
- ❑ Have you lost your awareness that growth is about *being* more, not having more?

SHOPPING STORIES

Soon, it'll be time to synthesize these trigger and aftershock exercises, to weave them together into your personal shopping story. First, though, we'll look at the detailed first-person narrative of an overshopper we'll call Gwen, with its real-life choreography of triggers and actions and aftershocks. Then we'll see how several other overshoppers wrote out their personal overshopping sequences. I think you'll see how doing this exercise can expand and solidify awareness.

Gwen's Shopping Story

I left the house feeling stressed and anxious this morning. I was thinking about all I needed to get done before the end of the day, some of which I'd much rather *not* do. I got to the office and almost immediately had an irate phone call from Harold, who'd just opened our joint credit card statement and seen a balance quite a bit higher than he was expecting. I kicked myself for letting the bill get so high and felt anxious and self-critical all through the workday. When I left work, I drove to the nursing home where my elderly father is being somewhat disruptive with the staff. I tried to mend fences with the administrator in charge, tried to calm Dad down, and left thinking, "I'm totally wiped out. I've simply got to get into some kind of protected space and lose myself a little. I'll stop by the mall."

As I made my way there, I started feeling excited. I remembered that my nephew's college graduation is coming up, and I hadn't yet bought him a present. I told myself I'd just buy the gift and go home. I walked into the mall, found the present, bought it, and turned back toward the car. On the way out, though, a pair of pants snagged me.

I couldn't take my eyes off of them. I had to try them on, and they were *wonderful*. But I reminded myself of my pledge—*only* buy the gift—and put them back.

Then, as I neared the exit, I ran into Hope. She was carrying an unbelievable belt she'd just bought for 50 percent off! I completely forgot my resolve. She took me back to where she'd bought her belt so I could get one, too—50 percent off! I barely noticed the sign indicating that all sales were final. I felt satisfied for the first time all day. But the moment I got back into my car, it hit me. "What's wrong with me?" I wondered. "What was I thinking? If I return it right now, the charge won't even show up on my credit card bill." I walked back into the store and went up to the cashier, who showed me the Final Sale, No Returns sign. I drove home anxious, guilty, and a little ashamed. When I got there, the kids were playing outside and Harold was trimming the hedge. He seemed glad to see me. I slunk into the house, trying to hide the little package in my purse. But my cell phone rang, and as I rummaged around for it, the purse opened wide enough to reveal the brightly labeled store bag. Harold saw it and wanted to know what it was. When I showed him, he got furious: "There's only so far you can push me," he said darkly. Why, I wonder, do I have to bite the hand that feeds me?

In this scenario, Gwen's emotional vulnerability has opened her to any number of possible triggers: the long list of the day's tasks, her husband's irate phone call, her own self-denigration, her subsequent anxiety, her eldercare responsibilities, the sensual excitement of the mall, and finally, irresistibly, a friend with a bargain. Her day is a little dance of triggers, actions, and aftershocks, an intertwining of thoughts, feelings, and behaviors; but she, in the middle of it all, has little control over the dance steps. In the end, there are two profound aftershocks (neither of which, we might note, is financial): her husband's not-so-veiled threat and her own further self-flagellation.

Trigger-to-Aftershock Sequences

In the shorter examples below, Sarita, Wes, and Raquel each begin with the emotional state that made them vulnerable to overshopping, then list any thoughts or feelings or actions that led to their behavior.

Next, they describe their immediate emotional experiences *after* over-shopping and say how those feelings developed and changed: whether, for example, excitement turned to regret. Finally, they articulate the thoughts that followed those feelings.

Sarita

Situational trigger: a colorful catalog

Action: shopping

Financial aftershock: debt

Emotional aftershock: shame

When the J. Jill catalog comes in the mail, I'm so overexcited I actually start to sweat. I want something on every page, and I often end up ordering three or four items I really don't need, especially if I'm having a hard time with the children. I call rather than order online. I like the personal attention of the sales associate, who sometimes knows things about the garments that aren't in the catalog descriptions. I place my order, get off the phone, and I'm elated. What I've ordered seems like it's going to be really beautiful. It's almost as if I have amnesia at the moment I order. I have more than $12,000 of credit card debt that my partner doesn't know about. What am I doing buying anything? I manage to get busy with e-mail and forget all about what I've done until my order comes. Then I look at the boxes, remember my debt, and all the bad feelings I've pushed under seem to come popping up everywhere. I tell myself that I'm a sorry excuse for a human being and have about as much discipline as a two-year-old. Why am I allowing myself to go down this slippery slope that could end in bankruptcy?

Wes

Interpersonal trigger: tension between me and my new boss

Action: shopping

Physical aftershock: a sinking feeling in the pit of my stomach

I don't know if I'm ever going to get comfortable with my new boss. He's a micromanager, and he hovers—it makes me crazy! I don't feel very competent when I'm around him, and I wonder when the other shoe is going to drop—that is, whether I'll be fired. I've been taking long lunch hours just to get away from the office—and after wolfing down a hero, I've been finding wonderful rare books in a shop near the office. I've gotten some really gorgeous volumes, but I can't afford them, and that's making me even more stressed. I get a sinking feeling in the pit of my stomach the moment I leave the store. I've had a lot of gastric distress at other times, too, lately; maybe I'm giving myself an ulcer. I'm worried that I'll never be able to attract the kind of woman I'd like to be with and I'll turn into an aging curmudgeon.

Raquel

Emotional trigger: loneliness

Action: shopping

Spiritual aftershocks: feeling hollow, making the almighty dollar your God

I finish with work at 3:30 P.M., and my husband, Rob, doesn't get home until three hours later. It's been this way for years, and I feel lonely and out of sorts during those hours, despite the fact that I've known forever that his job, which provides the vast majority of our income, requires him to work until 6:00, at the earliest. I just don't like sitting around an empty apartment, so I often find myself stopping at my favorite stores on the way home, despite the fact that we're trying to put money away for retirement. I tell myself that I'll just go and look, more as a social activity than to shop. The salespeople know me and seem as happy to see me as I am to see them. Then they start bringing me handbags that are just being unpacked. If I don't buy one of them now, the store will be out of them; there are already so many advance orders. I decide to buy one, and, initially, I feel very relieved to have one. But then I get scared, and I start to berate myself about what my life has become and lament that I don't seem to have any purpose higher than chasing the almighty dollar, so that I can buy what I think is going to make me feel full. By now, I should know that I can't fill the emptiness inside me with a handbag. When I think about how out of control my buying has gotten,

I imagine myself as a different kind of "bag" lady. I think about running away, but where to? And what will I do when I get there?

JOURNAL TIME

Write Your *Shopping Story*

Your own overshopping story is an original creation. It follows a particular trigger-to-aftershock sequence, one generated by a lifetime of experience that has colored the way you deal with unmet needs. As you've read and probably know firsthand, overshoppers respond to very different triggers—what's irresistible to you may leave someone else completely unaffected—and the aftershocks of overshopping are a very personal chapter as well. Not only is each *story* unique, but so is each overshopper's *awareness* of the overshopping sequence as it plays out in his or her life. Some overshoppers can describe their triggers, actions, and aftershocks with considerable accuracy and in great, often painful, detail; however, all of this is information gathered from careful observations of their patterns *in retrospect*. As soon as the next urge to shop strikes, their self-knowledge flies out the window. Swept up in the thrill of the hunt, they ignore what they "know." They "forget" about stopping (or make other excuses) and opt for the short-term payoff of continued overshopping. If this sounds at all like you, what you need is more *on-the-spot* awareness—and then the capacity to take skillful action based on that awareness. You need a way to hold on to and *use,* even in the heat of the overshopping moment, what your wise mind knows.

Other overshoppers avoid thinking about their habit. They may feel out of control and know there's something wrong, but they may not have much of a clue about their overshopping cycles. They don't know what's triggering them or even that they're being triggered. Maybe they're starting to feel some aftershocks—deepening debt, perhaps, or money discord with a spouse—but not putting the pieces together, not seeing the pattern behind the difficulties. If this sounds like you, work toward a thorough recognition of each step in your overshopping sequence. Once you scrutinize the links in your overshopping chain, you'll be in a position to find the weakest ones and break them.

Owning and articulating *in writing* your personal overshopping sequence is a powerful tool for stopping. This work encourages you to connect the dots, to see the *pattern* of your triggers, actions, and aftershocks. Such knowledge helps you maintain on-the-spot awareness, and a proven premise of this book is that understanding your particular overshopping sequence *in the heat of the overshopping moment* (not merely in retrospect) helps you learn to stop.

OK, then. Take some time, open your Shopping Journal, and, following the pattern of the three examples above, write your own overshopping story. First, choose your most potent or most typical trigger(s) and connect the dots to the action of overshopping and then to one or more of your most troublesome aftershocks. Write a detailed narrative that describes how, when, where, and why this particular trigger led to the action of shopping. Then describe the aftershock: how, when, where, and why it occurred and what aftereffects it had on your life. Also write something about where you fall along the continuum of awareness. Are you conscious, most of the time, of your triggers, actions, and aftershocks? Or are you only vaguely or rarely aware? Without the prompts in the previous exercises, would you have recalled most of the triggers and aftershocks that resonated with you?

Write at least a paragraph, preferably two, including all the links in the chain that you recall. (Using a recent example may help with the level of detail.)

ON-THE-GO EXERCISE

Record Your Shopping Urges

An important technique for gaining control of your shopping urges is to be fully conscious of them, and the best way to do this is to log them in your Shopping Journal. If you have a great many shopping urges each week, logging at least three of them will give you the best chance of slowing yourself down.

While you're feeling the urge, *before* you allow yourself to act on it, open to a blank page. (You might want to title it "The Urge Strikes" and attach a small Post-it as a tab, so it's easy to find again.) Then note the day, date, time, and place. Now take a few slow, full breaths, and answer, in writing, these questions:

1. How does your body know you want to shop? (Is it trembly, hot, tense, jumpy, achy, something else?)

2. Are there any negative or positive thoughts, feelings, images, or memories that go along with the urge? If so, what are they?
3. What do you think is triggering you?

Even when you don't log an urge in writing, ask yourself these questions. For this work to pay off, you need to *pay genuine attention to yourself*. When your triggers shout "Shop!" to you, step back a little and watch. Slow yourself down. Make it a point of honor to take several full, deep breaths and then ask yourself the questions. Almost always, there's a strong emotion or internal experience that's prompting you to want to shop. Increasing your awareness will help you to locate it and create some space around it, giving you a little distance from the impulse.

VALUES AND VISION

The focus and persistence you're showing in getting to this point suggest how seriously you're engaging with your overshopping problem. You've already done a lot of hard work, and you've stepped far enough back from your habit to take a nonjudgmental and even curious look at the elements of its sequence. You're beginning to gather some positive momentum. Soon, you'll need to make a decision about whether or not to stop your overshopping. But before you make that decisive choice, you've got to consider the pros and cons of both alternatives, and part of doing *that* is to do a slow-forward from the present into the future.

What direction do you want your life to take? What do you value the most? How does overshopping fit in with your direction, your values? Values are the intentional choices we make that empower us and propel us in a particular direction. Our values define both the small and the large about us, what we want to pursue from day to day and what we want our overall lives to be about. When you've discovered and identified your values—or allowed them to reveal themselves—you're in possession of a sturdy and reliable compass, one that will guide you in the direction of your long-term vision and reorient you if and when you deviate from it. Living true to your values is an act of faith in yourself and your long-term vision.[1] Because it's so critical to discover and zero in on your values, we'll be taking two different paths. In this chapter, you complete a eulogy exercise; in the next, you take an online survey of your values in action.

JOURNAL TIME

How Do You Want to Be Remembered?

One common way to tap into your values and long-term vision is to think about how you'd like to be remembered after you die. What do you want to leave behind? What do you want to have stood for? Allow yourself to imagine—to picture—living your life, *from this moment forward,* according to your most cherished values. What would be clear about the kind of life you led? Give concrete shape to this vision by pretending that you're attending your own funeral and listening to yourself being eulogized. Write your responses in your Shopping Journal. (This exercise can evoke strong feelings, so go slowly with it and let these questions percolate before you start to write.)

1. What's being said about your relationship with yourself, your health, and your physical well-being?
2. What about your relationship with an intimate partner, either a relationship you were still in when you died or a relationship you had earlier in your life?
3. How are your relationships with family members being described?
4. What about your relationships with friends?
5. Has anyone mentioned your relationship with your work? If so, what's been said?
6. Someone is describing your interest in community. Let's listen in.
7. Someone is talking about the way you developed yourself over time, about your pursuit of truth, your inner wisdom. What's that person saying?
8. Someone else is talking about the way you most enjoyed spending your time. What are you hearing?
9. What's being said about your values, about what you stood for, about the model you left behind for others to follow?

10. What has this exercise evoked in you? What thoughts, feelings, and body sensations were stirred up as you thought and wrote? Does the way you're living your life *today* reflect accurately what was said about you? How does the way you're living your life today *contradict* what was said about you?

The way you want to be *remembered* will give you a pretty good idea of what you value and how you want to *be*, right here, right now. You're getting in touch with your vision and preparing to follow it. Committing to that vision will give you a bigger stake in your life, keeping you focused not on short-term payoffs but on the bigger picture.

TO STOP OR NOT TO STOP?

You're working with this book because your shopping behavior is causing you grief. But you didn't wake up one morning last week and suddenly, out of the blue, realize this. Chances are, you've struggled with overshopping for some time: vowed to stop, wanted to stop, started to stop—but *haven't* stopped. Why? Simply because even though your overshopping behavior is clearly *costing* you, you're *benefiting* from it as well. If you weren't, you wouldn't still be doing it.

What this says is you're ambivalent about stopping—your heart and head disagree. You're finding that "My sweet tooth says I wanna, but my wisdom tooth says no," as the Fletcher Henderson 1930s classic colorfully puts it. A more academic formulation is a little more direct: "Ambivalence is a common human experience and a stage in the normal process of change."[2] In a few pages, you'll look into that ambivalence and work at comprehensively laying out both sides of it. First, however, a few words about preparing for change.

Nothing is more central to stopping overshopping than being highly motivated to do so. What do you notice about your motivation level? What have other people in your life said to you about your shopping behavior? How much do you agree or disagree with what they have to say? This is an excellent issue to discuss with your Shopping Support Buddy; check out the possibility that even now, working with this book, you may still be denying the full extent of your habit. Strong motivation depends on a wholehearted recognition of the need for change.

It depends as well on having the tools to make change happen. When you have them, change isn't pie in the sky, something devoutly wished for but likely out of reach; instead, it's a birdhouse you build. When you have tools, you have confidence; you know the path from milling the wood to drilling the bird-sized opening to nailing the pieces together. Coming to understand how, why, and what your shopping costs you, and learning the strategies and tactics for stopping—this, too, is building a safe structure, and inside of it you'll shelter the readiness, will, and ability to change. The following exercise is designed to foster this. It lets you gauge how much you want to change and puts you in touch with what you need to do to make it happen. It's a confidence builder, worth repeating anytime your motivation flags.[3]

JOURNAL TIME

Conduct a Motivational Interview with Yourself

Carefully choose one particular overshopping behavior you'd like to change in the coming week—for example, "I don't want to look at a single catalog for the next seven days." Now, in your journal, answer the following questions about this change:

1. On a 0–10 scale (0 = totally unimportant, 10 = essential), how important is it to you to make the change—for example, to actually *not* look at catalogs this week?
2. Why are you at this number and not at 0?
3. What would it take for you to go from this number to a higher number?
4. How might you go about making this change?
5. What would be a good first step?
6. What obstacles do you see, and how might you deal with them?

7. Now how confident (0–10) are you that you can make this change this week?
8. What gives you that level of confidence?

What are you waiting for? Go for it!

COSTS VERSUS BENEFITS

Motivation and confidence are the rails that change runs on. To keep moving, though, the train needs to chug through a field of perfectly understandable ambivalence; it needs to see what's on the track that's keeping it stuck. We'll do that here by considering what overshopping does *for* you as well as *to* you, by identifying and organizing both the benefits and the costs. Complement this kind of analysis with at least the beginnings of a long-term vision, and you're ready to make a responsible, informed, and *sustainable* decision about stopping.

Central to the balance between the benefits and costs of stopping overshopping—or of continuing—is the distinction between short- and long-term effects, because what feels good right now may feel anything but good later on. Eventually, those calming cigarettes may irreparably damage your lungs; over time, that glittering new jewelry could wind up costing you your marriage. In the midst of a culture that insistently pushes instant gratification, we also need to look *beyond* the moment, to balance now against later, to weigh the short-term payoff against the long-term cost.

When you do that, you'll likely find that *continuing* to overshop offers you plenty of short-term benefits but few long-term ones. *Stopping*, however, offers both short-term benefits *and* substantial long-term ones. When we focus on costs instead of benefits, the situation is reversed. *Continuing* to overshop has significant short- *and* long-term costs, but the costs associated with *stopping* are mostly short-term. Once the overshopping habit has been broken for a while, almost all the effects are positive.

This is something you can't take at face value. You've got to see for yourself. The following exercise asks you to sit on both sides of the seesaw and feel how it tips. There's a matrix of eight cells to fill in, four cells for the short- and long-term costs and benefits of *stopping* overshopping and four cells for the short- and long-term costs and benefits of *continuing*. As you complete the matrix, keep in mind what really matters in your life, what you value most—whether it's family, relationships, work, health, self-respect, spirituality, or a solid financial footing—and let this animate your perception of costs and benefits. (Since costs are synonymous with aftershocks, add any new ones you discover to the page in your Shopping Journal where you've listed aftershocks.)

To give you a feel for the process, take a look at the matrix of a recovering overshopper whom we'll call Danielle. Sitting on both sides of the seesaw, as we want her to, she finds plenty of entries for each cell. When you've read through them all, however, it's not much of a challenge to decide which side weighs more.

Danielle's Matrix

	If I Stop	If I Continue
Short-Term Benefits	• I'll have money in the bank. • I'll feel proud of myself. • I won't have to keep hiding things. • I'll have more time, so I won't always be rushed and behind schedule. • I'll have more control of myself and feel less anxious.	• I'll get more new clothes. • I can hold on to the comfort of the familiar. • There'll be continuing excitement in my life. • Salespeople will like me. • I'll look fashionable. • I'll feel important.
Long-Term Benefits	• My house will be uncluttered. • There's a strong chance that I'll develop more genuine relationships. • I'll have money for retirement. • My life will be considerably simplified. • I may very well be a more joyful person.	• I'll always be well dressed. I'll feel more like I belong when I'm with my friends who have lots of money. • I won't have to focus on how unfulfilled I am in my marriage. • I'll keep attracting a lot of attention.

	If I Stop	If I Continue
Short-Term Costs	• I may overeat. • I won't see my "friends" at the shops. • I'll feel deprived. • I won't feel special.	• I'll quickly run out of room for my stuff. • I'll be constantly short of money. • I'll stay frightened about the future and have to hide this fear. • My husband will be angry with me.
Long-Term Costs	• Some people may not like me if I don't keep buying them gifts. • I won't know what to do with myself, which will make me anxious. • I'll have to set boundaries and deal with my feelings of unworthiness. • People will pay less attention to me if I don't keep buying so much new stuff.	• My children will grow up with the same skewed sense of values. • My husband will find out, and things at home could fall apart. • I won't have money for retirement. • I'll have to keep living with shame, guilt, and worthlessness. • I won't develop the muscles to have better relationships. • I'll never feel free.

Your Matrix

Take your time and write what comes to mind now. Whenever you think of additional costs or benefits, add them to this living document.

	If I Stop	If I Continue
Short-Term Benefits		

	If I Stop	If I Continue
Long-Term Benefits		
Short-Term Costs		
Long-Term Costs		

JOURNAL TIME

Observations from Your Matrix

Now that you've filled out your own matrix, answer the following questions in your journal.

1. What have you noticed?
2. What contradictions do you see, if any?
3. Which list was easiest to write? Why?

4. Which list was the hardest to write? Why?
5. When you look at the whole form, what do you see in terms of the balance of costs versus benefits?
6. If you work on stopping overshopping, what's likely to happen?
7. If you don't work on stopping overshopping, what's likely to happen?
8. What, if anything, would have to change in your life for the overshopping costs to outweigh the benefits?

WHEN YOUR HEART AND HEAD DISAGREE: STAYING MOTIVATED

Even if you've come to a firm decision to stop overshopping, and your heart and head agree on this, it's fairly likely that they'll soon lock horns about a particular shopping excursion. Facing a specific purchase, you may lose sight of the reasons for stopping. In the heat of the moment, when the urge to overshop has struck, your heart will argue passionately that even though, yes, in principle, you're going to stop overshopping, it's OK to go shopping again "just this once" or "just to look." It may even be so brazen as to insist that you *simply must have this one last thing right now!* This is a great moment to take out your Shopping Journal, a moment to slow down and articulate what's happening. Answer two questions: What is my heart saying? What would be good about shopping?

But also listen to your head. Whenever overshoppers overshop, they're strengthening their pattern and working against recovery. To break a pattern, you've got to stop enacting it. Even innocent-seeming shopping indulgences tend toward harm. And indulgent indulgences, of course, can wreak a *lot* of havoc. So answer these two questions: What is my head saying? What would be not-so-good about shopping?

To shop or not to shop—for the shopaholic, this is a critical decision, made and remade, day in, day out. What we're after in this process is tyranny of neither heart nor head but a self-respecting, well-considered balance between costs and benefits, between momentary pleasure and enduring contentment, between doing what *feels* good to you and doing what *is* good for you. When your heart and head disagree, I urge you to listen respectfully to both. Maybe it's a spectacular spring day and a nice stroll past some favorite stores on the way back from lunch will be lovely—and won't put you at serious risk of overshopping. Or maybe the item is inexpensive and something you could genuinely use. You might choose to grant your heart's wish. On the other hand, maybe you're feeling crushed by the weight of the credit card bills and by your anxieties about paying them and the electric bill next month, to say nothing of the rent. No matter what you see, no matter how much your heart goes pitter-patter, your head must win out. It's not worth putting another ounce of pressure on yourself or making yourself sick. If you decide to resist your impulse, congratulate yourself, and celebrate your success in some way that doesn't involve money, knowing that you're strengthening a very important muscle.

If, after listening to both heart and head, you decide to shop, ask and answer the following questions *before you proceed*. It's best to do this in writing, in your journal.

Reminder Questions

1. Why am I here?
2. How do I feel?
3. Do I need this?
4. What if I wait?
5. How will I pay for it?
6. Where will I put it?

Make it a regular practice to stop and ask yourself these six questions before making any purchase that might conceivably constitute overshopping. These questions are printed on a detachable card on the last page of this book. Keep it in your purse or wallet or otherwise strategically located—next to your computer, perhaps, if you're an internet shopper.

GETTING HOOKED AND GETTING UNHOOKED

Now let's step back for a moment and try to gain some perspective on the problem. At its simplest level, overshopping is the exaggerated outcome of desire, of wanting things. If we did not grow up *conditioned* to want, *expecting* to want, so *programmed* to want that *want* and *need* become equated, the problem would vanish. We assume our desire is "natural," but, in fact, the ravenous craving we experience is a hallmark of modern consumer-driven cultures (and those heading in that direction). In these cultures, "inundated by material goods, we consume until we're drowning in . . . things we don't really need or want. [In these cultures,] the fevered mind of entitlement reigns large. . . . If we want it, we feel we deserve it, and therefore we should have it—now!"[4]

How can we rein in this toxic sense of entitlement? The first step is to recognize it for what it is. But recognition is only the beginning. After that, we need to choose, consciously, to engage our better judgment, to act in our own best interests. We can counter the prevailing winds of entitlement by embracing a generous spirit, by "a willingness to give, to share, to let go. The cultivation of generosity offers a very strong antidote to the wanting mind and would be a powerful corrective [to materialism] if taken up in a widespread way across our culture."[5] Overstuffed as many of us are in this life, we're at the same time starved for connection, vitality, and engagement. Generosity feeds these needs and is far more satisfying than getting and spending.

The popular Buddhist teacher Pema Chödrön offers specific correctives to detach us from desiring things, from feeling entitled to them, in her essay "How We Get Hooked, How We Get Unhooked." She likens addictive consumerism to a perpetual itch, flaring up and moderating, but always there. To overcome it, she suggests a process of four *R*s: *R*ecognizing the itch, *R*efraining from scratching, *R*elaxing into the underlying urge to scratch (letting yourself experience it), and *R*esolving to continue interrupting your habitual patterns by learning and consistently practicing the four *R*s.[6] This process begins, in other words, with self-awareness, with articulating and acknowledging what you feel. It continues with self-restraint, with exercising your power to decide *not to act* on your urge. The next step is self-acceptance: you hold your urge gently and comfortingly and allow yourself to feel it even as you refuse to act upon it. Finally, you reinforce your refusal to scratch by committing yourself to continuing it, now and in the future. Eventually, the itch will either disappear or fade into the background.

As we've observed earlier, the cultural itch to acquire stuff activates in overshoppers some kind of underlying pain, which the compulsive buying is an attempt to anesthetize. This pain and its connection with overshopping is largely unconscious—until you devote the time and energy to begin making it conscious, as you're doing right now. What is this pain? Only you can say. Perhaps it's the as yet unfulfilled desire for a life partner, or the need for more harmony in a current relationship. Perhaps it's wanting a better job, better health for you or someone you love, or better friendships. Maybe it's the fear that you'll never have what you really want. Maybe it's the pain of knowing that there's very little in your life *other than shopping* that you derive much pleasure from. Maybe it's the profound loneliness of feeling that your life lacks meaning.

Whatever the underlying pain is about, habitual shopping is an attempt to deflect it, to ignore it, to reject it. Of course, it's human nature to resist dealing with pain. "I'm too tired to think about this right now," we say, or "Everybody does it; I'm no different." "It's not so bad." "I can stop whenever I want to," we may tell ourselves, or "I have other, more important issues to deal with." But doing this regularly only worsens things. It amplifies our discomfort and entangles us more deeply in it. In addition, the psychological gymnastics we do to avoid negative feelings dull *all* of our experiences—the pleasure as well as the pain—and keep us at a distance from those experiences. This compromise makes the vital data that our feelings provide us with much less accessible. We're now vulnerable to making costly mistakes, literally and figuratively.

Accepting your pain, on the other hand, can paradoxically help to end your suffering. Experience your experience and it disappears; what you resist persists. Again, think about an itch. If you *don't* scratch it—and you allow yourself to experience what it feels like— the itch eventually goes away or recedes into the background. If you *do* scratch it, it reddens. And if you *keep* scratching, it inflames and may even become infected.

Once you're ready to face the possibility that avoiding the pain hasn't worked, doesn't work, will *never* work, you've got to build the strength to tolerate your pain and make space for it. One important ingredient in the recipe for creating this space is a generous dollop of compassion for yourself. What does that mean? It means, *Cut yourself some slack!* Don't think of yourself as a loser, a weakling, or some other pejorative epithet; don't call yourself names. Instead, look clearly and kindly at yourself. Notice and allow what you see. Food for thought: *allow*, not swallow; *allow*, not wallow.

Just look at how much you've done to try to manage this pain. You didn't know what else to do; it's not your fault. What you tried could never have worked—but you didn't know that, certainly not the way you're beginning to know it now. You've got to accept your urges to overshop; accept the feelings of loss that may result from giving up the behavior; and accept the emotional pain that will come, at least initially, when you stop relying on overshopping to manage your feelings. Once you seriously entertain the idea that you're going to have to accept, tolerate, and come to terms with this pain, you've taken a solid step toward transformative change.[7] When you can allow yourself to feel all of your feelings without acting on them in negative ways, your will builds muscles. You become unstoppable.

I know. All this is a little abstract. But these abstractions form a sturdy armature, a frame on which you hang the more concrete work to come. Giving up overshopping, like overcoming any addiction, is a serious, strenuous, and gradual process—but it *can* be done. There *is* a real alternative. And it helps, particularly in the middle of the toughest parts, to remember that what you're letting go of has genuinely eroded your life and that what you're patiently allowing to emerge will greatly enhance it.

AS YOU STOP OVERSHOPPING

OK. You're on board. You're overcoming your ambivalence about stopping. You're ready to take the plunge, to do the work of this book, and to change your behavior. Before you do, know this and be prepared for it: the out-of-control spender who starts setting limits on spending behavior may experience what Olivia Mellan calls "a genuine inner temper tantrum."[8] After all, overshopping is a technique by which you cope with difficult feelings. As you abandon this technique, those feelings will probably surface, threatening your progress. Be ready. Whether the upsurge of feelings is mild or sharp, *recognition of what's happening* is your first line of defense.

- Understand that the difficult feelings *preceded* your overshopping habit, that your buying behavior is an excitement designed to mask those feelings, to distract you from them. Naturally enough, when the distraction ceases, the feelings reemerge, unmasked now and raw as ever.

- Brace yourself. When you first begin to resist the impulse to shop, your feelings are likely to be strongest. Having solid strategies for riding out those intense initial feelings is crucial. In this book, you'll learn a variety of such strategies.

- Take comfort in the power of process. As you continue to resist the shopping impulse and begin to practice healthier ways of dealing with your feelings, the intensity of the difficult feelings will lessen, and your power to resist overshopping will grow.

- Don't judge yourself. "Overshopper" has been a part of your identity, and as you cast that part away, you may feel disoriented, scared, hurt, angry, or lost. *This is typical and normal.*

- Certain relationships, particularly those that have revolved around shared shopping, may grow strained. Find a healthier footing for them, steering toward different areas of mutual interest. If that fails, allow the relationships to wither, accept this as a cost of change, and trust that new and better relationships will follow.

- If you've struggled with other addictive behaviors in the past, you may find them creeping back when you stop overshopping. If this happens, reach out for help right away. Ultimately, the tools, skills, and strategies that you acquire in *To Buy or Not to Buy* will apply to *any* addictive behavior.

Hang on to what you learn here. *It works.* The change you're making is a significant one—if it weren't, you wouldn't be struggling so hard with it. *Major change is always accompanied by anxiety.* Defuse that anxiety by focusing on your new tools and strategies and by visualizing what you'll gain: self-control, self-esteem, and better relationships; relief from debt, shame, and secrecy; and a general feeling of being grounded and competent. Keep your eyes on the prize!

3 | Your Shopping Self-Portrait

I hope by now you've made some exciting discoveries about why you overshop, how it all began, what triggers you, and what the consequences or aftershocks are. Maybe in the process of the eulogy exercise you've discovered or rediscovered something about what you value in life. It's now time to extend your self-learning by painting your unique shopping self-portrait.

The Shopping Patterns Checklist is the initial, pencil-sketch stage of your self-portrait. Here you assemble information, asking questions as a journalist would—when, where, with whom, and for whom you shop, as well as what you buy and what you tell yourself about why you're buying it. You also begin to sort out some of the assembled information. Then you go on to the next stage, a visualization, in which you revisit a specific purchase you made and later regretted and then follow up with some written observations. Because it's sensory rather than analytic, the visualization brings color and immediacy to your portrait. These two different perspectives on overshopping are then connected in the final section of the chapter, a series of questions about the relationship between buyer and purchase, the You and Your Stuff Questionnaire.[1]

THE SHOPPING PATTERNS CHECKLIST

It's important to begin sketching the unique profile of your shopping/overshopping behaviors. If you were sketching a still life, you'd spend a good deal of time looking at each of the elements. You'd examine their interrelatedness, their relative sizes, colors, shapes, and so on. It's the same with sketching your shopping portrait. You'll look at when you shop, where you shop, with whom you shop, and for whom you shop. You'll look at the way you shop; the kinds of goods, services, and experiences you buy or acquire; your shopping signature; and the "justifiers" you use to give yourself permission to overshop. As you read over each list below, check all items that apply. Then look over the lists and star the items in each category that create the most trouble for you.

When *Do You Shop?*

❑ Before work

❑ On my lunch hour

❑ After work

❑ Weekend days

❑ Weekend evenings

❑ While others are sleeping

❑ Before holidays or special events

❑ After holidays

❑ Before the start of a new season

Where *Do You Shop?*

❑ Stores or malls

❑ Department stores

❑ Specialty stores or boutiques

❑ Discount stores

❑ Consignment shops

❑ Flea markets, garage sales, or auctions

❑ Trunk shows, sample sales, or using a personal shopper

❑ Internet shopping

❑ TV shopping

With Whom *Do You Shop?*

❑ Alone

❑ Alone, with help from one or more salespersons in stores

❑ Alone, with help from a telephone salesperson

❑ Alone, with help from an online salesperson

❑ With a spouse or significant other who actively participates

❑ With a spouse or significant other who just tags along (waits while I shop)

❑ With another family member who actively participates

❑ With a family member who mostly just tags along (waits while I shop)

❑ With a friend who actively participates

❑ With a friend who mostly just tags along (waits while I shop)

❑ With a friend who knows about my overshopping problem and helps me resist

❑ With two or more friends

❑ With a friend who may also have an overshopping problem

For Whom *Do You Shop?*

❑ For myself, primarily for my own pleasure or satisfaction

❑ For myself, but primarily to impact (please, impress, appease, anger, and so forth) someone else

❑ For my spouse or significant other

❑ For my child/children

❑ For my parent(s) or grandparent(s)

❑ For my sibling(s)

❑ For members of my extended family

❑ For my friend(s)

❑ For my acquaintance(s), such as club member(s)

❑ For my coworker(s)

- For use by a group (for example, art supplies for my son's classroom) without me
- For use by a group (such as at a party) that includes me
- For someone specific, but I often don't actually give away the gifts
- For no one specific, and I often don't actually give away the gifts

How *Do You* Acquire *Something You Want?*

- Cash
- Debit card
- Credit card that I pay off completely
- Credit card that I don't pay off in full
- Get it for free (off the curb or from someone giving it away)
- Money I've borrowed from a domestic partner, family member, or friend
- Money I've borrowed from a financial institution (payday or bank loan)
- Direct request that someone buy it for me as a gift (right now or very soon)
- Indirect request or hint for someone to buy it for me as a gift (right now or soon)
- Direct request that someone buy it for me for a birthday, holiday, or special occasion
- Indirect request or hint for someone to buy it for me for a birthday, holiday, or special occasion
- Barter my services in exchange
- Promise to barter my services but don't follow through (so actually get it for free)
- Scrape together cash lying around the house
- Return/exchange something I've bought

- ❏ Sell/trade something to get the money
- ❏ Help myself to products that belong to my company, church, or other organization
- ❏ Deceive someone intentionally
- ❏ Shoplift

What Kinds *of Goods, Services, or Experiences Do You Buy/Acquire?*

CLOTHING

- ❏ Business clothes
- ❏ Leisure clothes
- ❏ Outerwear
- ❏ Special-occasion clothes
- ❏ Lingerie, underwear, hosiery
- ❏ Shoes
- ❏ Handbags
- ❏ Fashion or other accessories
- ❏ Jewelry or watches

SELF-CARE

- ❏ Toiletries
- ❏ Haircuts, coloring, perms, and the like
- ❏ Waxing, manicures, pedicures, and so forth
- ❏ Cosmetics
- ❏ Massage, other body treatments
- ❏ Plastic surgery; laser, Botox, fillers, or other treatments
- ❏ Gym, personal trainer, classes

HOME FURNISHINGS AND DECOR

- ❏ Furniture, occasional pieces (indoor)
- ❏ Art, prints, and pictures
- ❏ Indoor plants (flowers)
- ❏ Candles, vases, scents, and so on

- ❑ Kitchenware
- ❑ Tabletop china, tabletop linens, baskets, boxes, and so forth
- ❑ Bed and bath items
- ❑ Holiday and seasonal decor
- ❑ Antiques and collectibles
- ❑ Furniture (outdoor), garden equipment
- ❑ Materials for home improvement
- ❑ Outdoor plant materials

ENTERTAINMENT, RECREATION, HOBBIES, GIFTS, AND HOME OFFICE

- ❑ Books, magazines, newspapers, other print materials
- ❑ Prerecorded videos, CDs, DVDs, and so on
- ❑ Software, computer and video games
- ❑ Movies, video rentals
- ❑ Telephones, including cellular
- ❑ Concerts, ballet, theater, museums
- ❑ Computers, TVs, DVD players, and the like
- ❑ Musical equipment (for listening or playing)
- ❑ Gizmos or gadgets (such as an iPod)
- ❑ Greeting cards and stationery
- ❑ Writing implements
- ❑ Toys, books, classes for children
- ❑ Craft, sewing, and knitting supplies
- ❑ Other hobby supplies
- ❑ Photography equipment and supplies
- ❑ Sports/exercise equipment
- ❑ Tickets to sports events
- ❑ Outdoor adventures
- ❑ Pet food/supplies
- ❑ Entertaining others

- ❏ Alcohol, cigarettes, recreational drugs
- ❏ Casino or other gambling
- ❏ Gifts: birthdays, holidays, and other special occasions
- ❏ Vacations

What's Your Shopping Signature?

- ❏ Free items, giveaways, or great bargains
- ❏ Inexpensive items for comfort or delight (flowers, candles, soap, lipstick, and so forth)
- ❏ Practical or necessary items, but I buy more quality or features than I need or can afford, designer styles, status brands
- ❏ Luxuries or extravagances that express my lifestyle, values, interests, or passions (fine art, cars, collectibles, fine jewelry)
- ❏ Going shopping with a particular item or goal in mind but then buying something else
- ❏ Impulsive purchasing, enjoying the "find"
- ❏ Extensive planning or researching, enjoying the anticipation as much as the purchase
- ❏ Shopping "just to look," as entertainment
- ❏ Unplanned shopping trips to brick-and-mortar venues
- ❏ Unplanned browsing on internet or TV shopping venues
- ❏ Spending more money than I intended

What Do You Tell Yourself?
How do you give yourself "permission" to overshop? "It's OK to buy this because . . ."

- ❏ it will improve my quality of life.
- ❏ it just makes me feel good.
- ❏ it makes me feel special.
- ❏ I've had a hard day.
- ❏ it'll help me relax, and I *need* to relax!

- [ ] I deserve it.
- [ ] I'm bored.
- [ ] it makes me laugh.
- [ ] I need this to distract myself.
- [ ] it's so pretty! (or "interesting!" or "perfect!")
- [ ] it's such a good value.
- [ ] it makes me feel more like my ideal image.
- [ ] it gives me a feeling of having made it.
- [ ] I'm worth it.
- [ ] it'll impress someone.
- [ ] it'll really please someone.
- [ ] it'll really annoy someone.
- [ ] it'll help me to get closer to someone.
- [ ] it'll beautify my home.
- [ ] it's for education (or some other good cause).
- [ ] it's to replace an item that's worn or outdated.
- [ ] I don't remember if I already have one, so I'll get it just in case.
- [ ] it might come in handy someday.
- [ ] it's for my hobby or special interest.
- [ ] it expresses something unique about me.
- [ ] I need to get a gift for an occasion.
- [ ] it's not for me; it's for someone else.
- [ ] I've *got* the money!
- [ ] I can afford it.
- [ ] I can do whatever I want.

In each section of the Shopping Patterns Checklist, you've checked the items that reflect your shopping profile and starred those items that pose an overshopping threat to you. Now it's time to reflect on those stars. Look closely at them. What do you see that might help you to stop overshopping? You might notice, for example, that you often overshop with one particular friend, whereas with another friend, you're not in the least tempted. What might you do with that kind of information?

You might see that your worst shopping binges are on the Internet, in the middle of the night, when others are sleeping—but that you almost never overshop on weekend evenings, even though you sometimes spend them at the mall browsing. What might you do with *that* kind of information?

You might realize that when you tell yourself, "I can do whatever I want," you often overshop. But when you tell yourself, "It's OK to shop, because I can afford it," you mean what you say, and you don't overshop. What would *that* suggest to you?

Take a good look at what you've indicated on the checklist. Were there any surprises? Were there any inconsistencies? Make some notes in your Shopping Journal about what you've learned, recognized, seen, or figured out about the following:

Where you shop

When you shop

With whom you shop

For whom you shop

How you *acquire* what you want

What you *buy*

Your *shopping signature*

What you *tell yourself*

They'll serve as a valuable reference.

And, finally, having now taken a close analytic look at your shopping/overshopping behavior, write on a page of your journal the single most important thing you learned from doing the Shopping Patterns Checklist.

EXERCISE

Shopping Visualization

Let's put the checklist to work for you. You've got a pencil sketch of your shopping self-portrait firmly in hand. Now add color and immediacy to it by reexperiencing a particular shopping event from the inside out, using your recollection to choose the different shades and textures you want to apply.

For this work, we turn to a visualization. You can read the text aloud and then answer the questions or, better, have someone else read it to you or download the audio file at www.stoppingovershopping.com/audiofiles of my voice guiding you. Bringing the human voice into this process has its own way of evoking feelings and memories; tuning in to this different channel, even briefly, is likely to shake loose a few more connections. However you ultimately do this visualization, give yourself a quiet, uninterrupted twenty to thirty minutes to read or hear the text and then respond.

This visualization is designed to help you get in touch with the personal meaning of what goes into your overshopping behavior and what comes out of it.

Maybe what you'll get out of this exercise will be something that you can use the next time you're in a store, or in front of the computer, the TV, or with a catalog, and have that impulse to buy something you don't need.

You might find it more comfortable to do this exercise with your body relaxed and your eyes closed.

Begin by taking a few full, deep breaths, in . . . out . . . in . . . out . . . Allow yourself to feel your breath as it enters your nose, and as it fills your diaphragm and then again as you breathe in . . . and out . . . in . . . and out . . . in . . . and out . . .

Now, when you're ready, allow yourself to remember a time when you bought something that you were sorry you bought, either then, when you first bought it . . . or that you now regret.

You might imagine something you have in your closet or in your home that you haven't used in a long time, or possibly never used. Maybe it's a service you purchased, that you were sorry about.

Maybe you wonder why you ever bought it in the first place.

Allow yourself to be curious, without judgment, about why you bought this thing, whatever it was . . .

Allow yourself to go back to the time when you were getting ready to buy it and remember . . .

What was going on?

What made it seem so attractive, or so important, or so necessary?

Maybe something had happened that day or that week that made you want to buy something . . .

Maybe it was something about the way you were feeling . . .

Maybe you were hoping that special thing would give you something, or change something . . .

Maybe you were hoping that buying this thing or this service would help you leave someone or something behind . . .

Or maybe it was something about the act of shopping itself . . .

Maybe you were bored. Maybe you were angry, or lonely. Maybe you needed excitement, activity, companionship, to feel affirmed, to feel welcomed . . .

Maybe it was about someone who was part of the shopping experience, or someone you were shopping for . . .

Or maybe some other reason . . .

Stay with this experience for a few more breaths and see if anything else arises . . .

Now, allow yourself to explore your disappointment . . .

Why are you sorry that you bought this thing?

Maybe you didn't really want it in the first place and it was something else that you wanted . . . maybe not even a thing . . . but maybe what you wanted was to be able to express something . . .

Perhaps you lost interest and found that you weren't using it or wearing it . . . or soon after you bought it, you were attracted to something else . . .

Or perhaps you began to feel that it wouldn't change your life the way you'd hoped . . . That it wouldn't make you look good or feel good . . .

Maybe there was something else you wished you had done with your time . . .

Or maybe you were really upset about spending your money that way . . .

Maybe you began to feel ashamed about buying it . . .

Or maybe about having to hide it or having to tell someone about having done it. Or some other reason . . .

Whatever it was, notice how it feels to look at this purchase so closely . . . how it feels to get in touch with what the shopping and the purchase were all about for you . . . when you first bought it . . . and then later on . . .

Let yourself be with the whole experience now . . .

Take a few full, deep breaths . . .

And whenever you're ready, open your eyes and come back to the room.

JOURNAL TIME

Shopping Visualization Follow-up

What came up for you during the visualization? Take a look at what revealed itself—first, as you recalled the purchase and then as you recalled the regret. Let what you learned from doing the visualization percolate before you proceed to answer these follow-up questions.

THE PURCHASE

1. As you listened to the visualization, what was the time you remembered?
2. Where were you?
3. Were you alone or with someone else?
4. If you were with someone else, who was it?
5. What else do you remember about the scene?
6. What do you remember about the way you *felt* at the time?
7. What was it you purchased?
8. What do you recall about why you bought it? What was going on?
9. What made it seem so attractive or important or necessary?
10. Did you actually *need* it? Would you say it was essential, very necessary, somewhat necessary, or entirely unnecessary?
11. If you didn't need it, what do you think you were *really* shopping for?
12. What did you tell yourself? How did you justify your purchase?
13. How did you pay for this purchase?
14. What did you do with it? Where did you put it?
15. Did you use it?

THE REGRET

1. Why are you sorry you bought it?
2. Were you sorry right away?

3. If not, how soon after you bought it were you sorry?
4. Are you just regretting it now, for the first time?
5. What were the aftershocks of this purchase?
6. Did it lead to debt, shame, fear, guilt?
7. Did this purchase have an effect on anyone besides you? If so, who was it, and what effect did it have?
8. How does it feel to look at this purchase so closely?
9. What do you see now that you couldn't see before?
10. What could you do differently next time?

JOURNAL TIME

You and Your Stuff Questionnaire

Now it's time to take a look at your relationship with actual *items* you've acquired. What's the relationship been like? A hot romance followed by a quick breakup? A lovely honeymoon but then a gradual loss of interest? Was there a lifelong happy marriage? Have you grown to hate some of the items or already thrown them out? Let's play twenty questions to find out! Answer them in your Shopping Journal, quickly first, "off the top of your head"; then go back and reflect to see if you have any further observations.

1. What are some of your most prized possessions?
2. For each of these prized possessions, when and how did you acquire it?
3. What sorts of items that you typically acquire bring you the greatest joy or satisfaction, both immediately and over the long term? (Refer to the categories on the Shopping Patterns Checklist.)
4. What sorts of items that you typically acquire bring you the greatest disappointment or dissatisfaction, either immediately or over the long term? (Again, refer to the categories on the Shopping Patterns Checklist.)
5. After an item arrives in your home (you bring in the bag, UPS delivers an order, or whatever), how soon do you tend to unpack it?
6. What do you do with it after you've unpacked it?

7. Do you try to hide it in some way? If so, how and where do you hide it?

8. If you hide it, who, including yourself, are you hiding it from, and why are you hiding it from them?

9. If you don't hide a new purchase, how long does it normally take you to install it in your life—to start enjoying it or consuming it fully?

10. Do you usually remember what you bought, or is it a surprise when you see it again?

11. For what percentage of the items you acquire do you have in mind a specific planned use? (That is, you picture to whom you'll give the gift and when, or you envision the specific event to which you'll wear the shoes or take the camera.)

12. How often do you actually use the item for that planned purpose? If you don't use it for that specific purpose, what do you normally do with it?

13. What percentage of the time do you purchase an item with the idea that you might return it?

14. How often do you actually return it?

15. How many items are in your possession right now that you intend to return?

16. How often, after purchasing or acquiring an item, do your initial positive feelings become neutral or negative? Over time, does excitement turn to guilt? disgust? embarrassment? sadness?

17. What do you do with possessions you no longer want?

18. What kind of clutter do you have in your home?

19. What's the impact of your overshopping—and any clutter you may have—on the significant relationships (spouse, significant other, parents, children) in your life?

20. Given all the work you've done in this section, and all that you've noticed, what's the most direct, honest, accepting thing you can say to yourself at this point?

In these first chapters you've charted many of the features of your shopping self-portrait: why you overshop and how it all began, your specific triggers and aftershocks, the conflict between your head and heart, and your reasons both for stopping and for continuing. You've begun to stockpile motivation by looking at your values and vision, and you've examined the psychological mechanism that hooks you and then read about a four-step process for getting unhooked. Finally, you used all the observations you've made to this point, first generating a pencil sketch of your unique shopping self-portrait and then filling it in with color and texture. You'll take this portrait, now a living, breathing work of art, into the next chapters. I'll meet you there, where you'll acquire and begin to process information to help you become financially fit.

4 | Becoming Financially Fit

Just as you need a comprehensive approach to *physical* health—solid nutritional information and advice, an exercise regimen, and preventative and reparative medical care as needed—*financial* health, too, requires a broad base of knowledge. You need self-control, of course—but you need much more. You need a clear picture of your financial position. You must recognize the central importance of savings and the lurking subtleties of the credit system. Finally, you also need to recognize the ways in which our culture works to undermine monetary well-being and learn what strategies are available to turn financial dis-ease into financial health. In this chapter, we concentrate on the nitty-gritty of money. You begin by learning to record and collect important data about all of your expenditures. It's the essential first step in getting your financial house in order.

LIVING BY SKILLFUL MEANS

Let's begin to reshape your thinking about money by recognizing the need *to live by skillful means*. Though you often hear or talk about living "within" or "beyond" or "below" your means, what you really need to do is live by *skillful* means: to live your financial life mindfully and with utmost consciousness, examining your expenditures, your goals, and your values, and making sure they all line up. The work of this chapter—recognizing the centrality of savings, grasping the appalling cost of credit card debt, and recording and categorizing every expenditure—will point the way.

Before we move to more general remarks about how to achieve this, I want to say this right up front: one of the most important things to jump-start your recovery is to *stop using credit cards right now*. Not tomorrow, not next week, but *today*! Not cut back, but *cease and desist*—cold turkey. Use only cash and checks and a debit card. There are risks associated with using debit cards that you need to be aware of. If someone misuses your credit card number, you can dispute any erroneous charges that show up on your bill and just pay the amount that's not in dispute. In contrast, if someone misuses your debit card number, the funds are immediately removed from your bank account. By the time you discover the misuse, the damage may already be done—facing you with bounced checks (together with any associated fees) and the task of attempting to recover your money. So exercise particular caution about giving out your debit card number. If in doubt, use cash or don't buy! Studies confirm what you probably already realize: if you use cash for your purchases, you'll spend far less. The immediacy of cash is vastly more "real" than the very muffled impact of plastic.

Financial health and living by skillful means can only be achieved if you know what you earn, what you spend, and where it goes. Astonishingly, many people know none of this and are in a state of continual financial fog. So we start with the essential step of organizing your financial documents. David Bach, Jean Chatzky, Karen McCall, Suze Orman, Dave Ramsey, and many others have written extensively about methods for doing this. It doesn't much matter which of these financial recovery gurus you read; what matters is that you *get your financial documents organized and then keep them organized!* It's not very different from organizing your closet: you find out what you have and where it is, and then you periodically update and reorganize it, often seasonally. When it comes to your financial documents, this means holding on to all the important ones and keeping similar documents together: a separate folder for each credit card, each bank or investment account, medical receipts, and the like.

Weighing In, a process that you begin in this chapter, will go on throughout—and beyond—the rest of the book. Once you've completed the book and have been doing it for a number of months, it's often useful to create a nurturing and realistic spending plan. Some people go to accountants or financial planners for help with this process, but you don't necessarily need to. Many of the books written by the financial gurus mentioned above contain clear and detailed information about creating a spending plan. Karen McCall's MoneyMinder system is one of the most comprehensive.

And you certainly don't have to wait until you finish the book to gather new and better ideas about money. You can begin to understand now, for example, that *making* more money is not necessarily the way to *have* more; savings and better money management is. And *having more*, as you've now read several times, *is certainly not the way to be happier.* Study after study has shown that when people seek money or material goods to wield power, gain status, control others, show off, or massage self-doubt, they tend to grow *less* happy. It's important, then, to remember—and to remind ourselves repeatedly—that the American reverence for the so-called good life, with its emphasis on competitive material acquisition and its unrealistic sense of material entitlement, is the worship of a false idol.

In order to live by skillful means, you must avoid the common confusion of *physical wants* with *psychological needs*, a confusion that underlies a great deal of overshopping. A *physical want* is a wish, a desire for a material thing: a new dress for the upcoming party, a candy bar, an electronic gadget, a mocha cappuccino, a vacation to Thailand, a pair of ruby earrings. *Psychological needs*—the need to belong, for example, or for self-esteem or autonomy—go deeper and in general cannot be satisfied by material things. That new dress for the upcoming party can't really meet your need to belong; the three-gigahertz notebook can't satisfy your need to feel control or self-esteem; that Montblanc pen can't buy you meaningful autonomy.

One last observation before we move to the centrality of savings: living by skillful means includes providing adequately for self-care, something overshoppers often neglect. Compulsive spenders frequently defer such fundamentals as "regular medical and dental care [and] keeping a car safely maintained and properly insured. . . . If needs are neglected, however, over time they become *deprivations,* and usually lead not only to a serious deterioration in . . . physical well-being, but [also]—by supporting . . . low self-esteem and feelings of 'not being worth it'—a downward emotional spiral that makes any meaningful recovery impossible."[1] *You* have to come first, in other words, but that means satisfying your *real* needs, not your "Emperor's New Clothes" needs.

THE CENTRALITY OF SAVINGS

It's vital to understand the centrality of savings. Savings is the base of sound financial management, the foundation of your financial house. It's the protective cushion between you and the wolf at your door; it's what makes a solid future possible. Yet our American culture is astonishingly deficient in this area, with *the lowest rate of savings in the entire Western world*. In fact—this is startling enough to mention again—for the years 2005 and 2006 (and, in all probability, for 2007 as well), our savings rate was *negative*, the only time in American history, except two years in the Great Depression, that this has been the case. This has happened for a variety of reasons, but the root cause is simple: as a nation, we've been hoodwinked into somehow believing we're entitled to getting whatever we want and getting it *now*. This sense, deeply enabled by the credit industry, has made borrowing the essential lubricant of the American consumer machine.

Even reasonably careful Americans, prudent in other areas, often consider it sound finance to "spend no more than you make." In fact, however, sound finance, living by skillful means, necessitates spending *less* than you make—and *saving* the difference. But few of us have been taught this; saving is neither a habit nor a skill we've developed. The bill of goods we sell ourselves about why we can't save is that we "don't have enough money" to start saving, or "there's plenty of time to save later," and we've "got more important things to spend our money on now." You may very well see, when you write your savings script later in this chapter, that you didn't have role models of saving when you grew up. Also, you may have adopted the belief that there's only one kind of savings, a fund that should never be touched. If so, this austere concept could make you very reluctant to put any money away. Last, you might imagine that unless you save a considerable sum, and do it regularly, the fund will never amount to much.

None of this is true. Saving even a very small amount adds up, through the magic of compound interest, to a meaningful sum—as long as you do it regularly. And the sooner you begin, the more dramatically your savings will grow. Further, there are different types of savings. One kind is for unanticipated, costly needs: a major plumbing expense, a significant illness, the loss of a job. For this, financial advisors suggest that you establish a liquid—or "prudent," as it's sometimes called—reserve of a certain number of months of expenses; three to six months is a pretty common figure. Another kind of savings provides for expected, nonmonthly but regularly occurring expenses, such as taxes, insurance premiums, vacations, and the kids' educations; for this, you establish a periodic expenses account, with money in it to pay the periodic expenses as they come due. A third kind of savings is for a comfortable retirement. For this, a regular investment program is essential—and surprisingly productive. Consult the financial experts mentioned earlier in this chapter for further details about saving. Note that although a full-scale savings program, with prudent reserve, periodic, and retirement accounts, is ideal, *any savings program is better than none*. And once you make saving a habit, you'll likely find it possible to expand your initial program.

One trend in the working world bears particular emphasis here. The burden of funding retirement is shifting more and more to the individual, further and further away from corporations and government. This makes retirement planning all the more critical. In *Deal with Your Debt*, Liz Pulliam Weston suggests that retirement savings should now take precedence over practically every other financial goal. Though some experts weigh in differently on this issue, there's universal agreement on a related point: if your employer *matches* retirement contributions, you'd be foolish not to accept this free money. In that situation, it's almost always better to contribute to your retirement plan as much as your employer will match. Again, for specific details on retirement planning, refer to the work of the financial experts mentioned earlier.

But specific details aren't necessary to give you an introductory idea of the way that modest savings can grow into a meaningful retirement fund. Just look at the following chart.

Savings Chart

Daily Investment ($)	Initial Investing Age	Total Return at Age 65		
		4%	6%	8%
1	25	$35,959	$60,772	$106,991
1	35	$21,105	$30,617	$45,570
1	45	$11,148	$14,067	$17,972
1	55	$4,474	$4,985	$5,572
5	25	$179,794	$303,861	$534,953
5	35	$105,525	$153,084	$227,852
5	45	$55,741	$70,336	$89,862
5	55	$22,369	$24,923	$27,860
10	25	$359,588	$607,722	$1,069,907
10	35	$211,049	$306,169	$455,704
10	45	$111,481	$140,673	$179,725
10	55	$44,739	$49,846	$55,719
20	25	$719,175	$1,214,444	$2,139,813
20	35	$422,099	$612,337	$911,408
20	45	$222,963	$281,345	$359,449
20	55	$89,478	$99,693	$111,438

Of course, the first thing most overshoppers, who are usually in debt, ask is, Where will I find the money for savings? David Bach has a refreshing answer. He's coined a term to suggest how unnecessary expenses can add up over time and deny us the rewards of financial freedom. Bach's "Latte Factor" is the amount you throw away on pricey coffee, junk food, candy bars, and other very avoidable costs: late-payment fees, for example, parking tickets, and taxis when you could have used public transportation or walked. Identifying and avoiding these unnecessary expenses allows you to redirect that money to savings, where it will appreciate and grow into a surprisingly generous amount by retirement; "no matter how small your paycheck happens to be, if you save consistently, you can finish rich."[2] The savings chart certainly supports his contention.

My prescription for rescuing that Latte Factor money comes a little later in this chapter, with the Daily Weigh-in. In this process, you learn to honestly assess how necessary each of your expenses is, and you calculate a *Necessity Cost* for each item. Doing so enables you to see how much you could be saving on a weekly and an annual basis if you were buying only things that were more necessary rather than less. Here's the place to hold any sense of entitlement you're aware of under the microscope and begin to tease out any wants masquerading as needs.

A second savings question that arises for indebted overshoppers is whether to first pay off credit card balances, which are very expensive to carry, and postpone saving, with its much more modest return, until all debt is erased. This is a thoughtful question, and, again, different financial experts weigh in differently. Liz Pulliam Weston urges people to pay off credit card debts before anything else—and, of course, to stop using the cards while doing so (barring a genuine emergency). Karen McCall, on the other hand, suggests balancing debt repayment and savings. She notes that failure to save is a major pathway to debt in the first place and recommends making savings an unswerving habit, even while you're paying off debt. What both of them agree on—along with virtually every other writer on finance—is that you need to stop incurring additional debt immediately and begin digging yourself out of the hole.

One caveat here: just as you're developing mindfulness in shopping and spending, you must begin to *save mindfully*, too. Begin your savings program immediately, and sensibly. Don't go from being a compulsive shopper to being a compulsive saver; saving is a means to an end, not an end in itself. Start with a fund for your periodic expenses, followed by a gradual buildup of your prudent reserve fund. Only when those two are adequate should you create an investment account for retirement.

(Again, though, if your employer matches retirement contributions, *immediately* do what you have to in order to claim your share of free money; it dramatically increases your return.)

It's sensible, even as you save, to allocate some money every month to experiences that make your heart sing—I call them *heart-songs*. Otherwise, you'll be prone to serious relapses, wild spending swings that sap your sense of purpose along with your account balance. It's also sensible, as you repay all the debt you prudently can, to provide for your basic needs: decent shelter and medical care, adequate nutrition, safe transportation. What you're after is balance, a comfortable equilibrium.

JOURNAL TIME

Your Savings Scripts

As your answers to How Did It All Begin have already shown, self-defeating adult behavior such as compulsive shopping is often shaped by childhood messages. These messages, first heard at a time when you were vulnerable and relatively powerless, can stay with you and exert a continuing influence on your life—even if the messages don't make sense anymore, even, in fact, if they *never* really made sense. Such shaping messages are often called *scripts,* in recognition of their power to direct us, like actors in a play. Answer the questions below in your Shopping Journal. Their aim is to help you see whether childhood messages about money have shaped your attitudes toward saving and whether any of the scripts in your head may need some adult rewriting.

1. What were you told about saving as you were growing up? Common savings messages are: *"Always save your money." "A penny saved is a penny earned." "A penny saved is a penny." "Save your best things for company." "Always save for a rainy day."*
2. How might these early messages be affecting your present ability to save?
3. What were your parents' thoughts, feelings, and behaviors related to savings?
4. What's your first memory about saving your own money?
5. What were you saving for?
6. Where did the money come from?

7. Did you use it for that purpose?

8. How do you think this memory affected you?

CREDIT CARDS AND FACING THE FACTS ABOUT YOUR DEBT

Here's the lowdown on credit card debt—and it's pretty low down. We touched on it earlier, noting the extraordinary ease with which credit cards are made available to us, beginning toward the end of high school (and in some cases much earlier) and following us to the grave. Earlier, we emphasized how important it is for overspenders to stop using credit cards immediately, thereby stabilizing their debt. Now we'll examine the specific financial consequences of credit card debt—and several strategies for paying it off. If you want more detail, more practical help—and more inspiration—read Jerrold Mundis's *How to Get Out of Debt, Stay Out of Debt, and Live Prosperously*. It's a classic.

OK, here it is again: except in the case of dire emergencies, *no sane person should carry credit card debt*. Credit cards are the ultimate legal drug in a materialist culture, the crowning strategic coup in the battle for instant gratification, impossibly convenient and psychologically well insulated from the feel of spending. How very different it is to run your card through a machine (or merely hand it to someone else) than to count actual greenbacks out of your wallet! Credit cards are *designed* for impulsiveness.

Worse, what comes with the impulsiveness is a set of extraordinarily harsh repayment terms. Worse yet, the terms are cloaked in the complexities of compound interest and in an assortment of quasi-deceptive and outright deceptive practices that can even include retroactive penalties.[3] Worst of all, everything's spelled out in print so small that most of us would need a magnifier to read it. Almost nobody does. That's why it comes as such a shock to the "minimum-payment set," that sizable group of Americans who make only the required minimum payment each month, to learn that a $20,000 credit card debt *will likely outlive the debtor*, requiring—with a 2 percent monthly minimum payment and an interest rate of 18 percent—precisely sixty-nine years and two months to repay! The following chart offers further shocks. Read it and weep, then dry your tears and start planning!

Sad Truth for the "Minimum-Payment Set"

Credit Card Balance ($)	2% Minimum Payment ($)	Annual Interest Rate (%)	Total Interest Paid ($)	Payoff Period
10,000	200	18	28,930	57 years 6 months
20,000	400	18	58,932	69 years 2 months
30,000	600	18	88,931	75 years 8 months
40,000	800	18	118,930	80 years 1 month

This is so outrageous a prospect that in 2006, the federal government issued new guidelines to increase the required minimum payment and thereby shorten the payoff period. It's a very modest step in the right direction, and the guidelines are not being widely followed, but however you slice it—old guidelines or new—credit card debt makes no sense. For every purchase, you wind up paying through the nose, often as much as two or three times the original sales price, or even more. (Differences in either minimum-payment percentages or interest rate—or both—will affect total interest paid and payoff period; see the payment calculator at Bankrate.com, referenced below.)

Still, if you've incurred that debt, all is not lost. A small change such as paying the *initial* minimum payment *each month* (rather than paying the declining minimum as the balance declines) can make an almost unbelievably dramatic difference:

Happier Truth for Initial Minimum Fixed Payers

Credit Card Balance ($)	2% Fixed Payment ($)	Annual Interest Rate (%)	Total Interest Paid ($)	Payoff Period
10,000	200	18	8,622	7 years 10 months

Credit Card Balance ($)	2% Fixed Payment ($)	Annual Interest Rate (%)	Total Interest Paid ($)	Payoff Period
20,000	400	18	17,243	7 years 10 months
30,000	600	18	25,867	7 years 10 months
40,000	800	18	34,489	7 years 10 months

Compare this with the previous chart. Pretty impressive stuff for so slight a change! For the $20,000 example, becoming an initial minimum fixed payer saves you $41,689 in interest—more than twice the amount you originally charged!—and reduces your repayment time by a cool sixty-one years. Sixty-one *debt-free* years!

One more version of the chart, and then I leave you to further tinkering of your own with an online credit card payoff calculator. Suppose you rescue enough "Latte Factor" money to pay a little more than the fixed initial minimum: 2.5 percent instead of 2 percent. Now there are very nice additional savings: you reduce your interest payment a further 38 percent, your payoff time a further 36 percent. Debt repayment starts to look almost tolerable.

Still Happier Truth for Fixed Payments a Little above the Initial Minimum

Credit Card Balance ($)	2.5% Fixed Payment ($)	Annual Interest Rate (%)	Total Interest Paid ($)	Payoff Period
10,000	250	18	5,386	5 years 2 months
20,000	500	18	10,772	5 years 2 months
30,000	750	18	16,135	5 years 2 months
40,000	1,000	18	21,545	5 years 2 months

Enough charts. The lesson is obvious: paying off your credit card debt—and incurring not a penny more—is a fundamental step toward financial responsibility. How can you do this? By recognizing the importance of it, by providing for it when you construct a spending plan, by helping yourself, and, if you need it, by getting help from others. For starters, try negotiating a better interest rate from your current credit card company, something you can do for yourself. Let them know you've been offered a substantially better rate by another company (your mailbox should confirm this) but would *prefer* remaining with them—*if* they'll match the better rate. Even if you can't afford the minimum payment, be in touch with your creditors. They're much more likely to work with you if you proactively inform them that you're aware of your debt and committed to paying it off. Graciously but forcefully challenge any genuine credit card mistakes—they do happen—and learn to use your consumer's leverage. Credit is a competitive business, and most card companies will bend over backward to keep you.

If you're overwhelmed and need external guidance, consider credit counseling. However, make sure to use a not-for-profit service. Often free to you, these services are paid a portion of what you repay to your creditors. Such services negotiate lower interest rates for you, can sometimes even get the interest totally eliminated, and will help you organize and consolidate your debt. For really substantial credit card indebtedness, financial institutions can provide consolidation loans, wiping out one or several high-interest debts and replacing them with a single, lower-interest loan. *But do this only if you're totally committed to living without credit cards!* Otherwise, your good intentions are very likely to backfire, and you may well end up with more debt rather than less.

One more thing: avoid temptation (and the possibility of fraud should your mail go astray) by putting a stop to the endless flow of credit card offers; simply call the National Opt-Out Center, toll-free, at (888) 567-8688 or contact the center at www.optoutprescreen.com.

None of this, of course, is magic. Until you make changes, until you stop being driven by the forces that got you into debt, no mere strategy will solve your problems. Once you're there, though, credit card debt, however horrendous, *can* be overcome. Here's an exercise to make you fully conscious of your situation, and a tool for seeing what it's actually costing you.

Credit Card Exercise

On the chart below, list creditor, balance, monthly minimum payment percentage, interest rate, payoff period if you pay only the minimum payment, and payoff period if you pay the initial minimum as a fixed payment each month. These payoff period figures are available at www.bankrate.com/brm/calc/MinPayment.asp. Just plug in your data.

Name of Creditor	Outstanding Balance	Minimum Payment (%)	Interest Rate (%)	Payoff Period	
				Minimum	Fixed

Notice again how dramatically a fixed payment will improve the situation if you continue paying it even though your required minimum drops with each payment. It bears repeating that in the $40,000 credit card debt example above, doing this will reduce the length of the repayment period from more than eighty years to less than eight—and save you more than $84,000 in interest! Experiment with this calculator—and with the lower interest rate you may negotiate with your creditors—to gain further insight into the nature of compound interest.

Weighing In

Now it's time to start tracking *everything* you spend, each and every day. You've absolutely got to do this to gain control over your buying behavior. Weighing In is a process that helps you in two ways: you begin to keep close track of your expenses—how much and for what—and you start to see what you could be saving on a weekly and a yearly basis *if you only made purchases that were more necessary rather than less.*

You can write this data on blank pages in your journal or, better yet, make photocopies of the three different forms you'll be using—the Daily Weigh-in, the Weekly Weigh-in, and the Weekly Spending by Categories—and keep those copied pages in your journal's pocket.

THE DAILY WEIGH-IN

Here's what the Daily Weigh-in form looks like:

Daily Weigh-In			Date	
Item Purchased	Category	Actual Cost (AC)	Necessity Score (NS) 0, ⅓, ⅔, 1	Necessity Cost (NC) AC x NS = NC
		$		$
		$		$
		$		$
		$		$
		$		$
		$		$
		$		$
		$		$
		$		$
		$		$
	Daily Totals: AC	$	NC	$

Daily Weigh-in Instructions

- Write the date at the top of each Daily Weigh-in page in advance.
- Record every purchase you make, use only cash, check, or debit card; *no credit cards*.
- Record the *Actual Cost* (AC) of *every* purchase. Write down amount and item *as soon as you make the purchase,* whether you pay with cash, check, or debit card. Write down the amount to the penny. This minimizes the possibility that financial fog will roll back in. (Don't save up receipts and enter them later; it's too easy to forget that way.)
- As you log each purchase, assign it a *category,* selecting from the list of categories, described below, which you'll see on the Weekly Spending by Categories form.
- Next, *evaluate each purchase* and assign it a *Necessity Score* (NS): 0 if the item was *entirely unnecessary,* ⅓ if it *wasn't very necessary,* ⅔ if it was *pretty necessary,* and 1 if it was *essential*.
- Assign a Necessity Score right away—even though, upon later reflection, you may decide to change the score.
- Finally, calculate a *Necessity Cost* (NC) for each item. This is AC x NS, the Actual Cost multiplied by the Necessity Score.
- At the end of each day, total the Actual Cost of your purchases and separately total their Necessity Costs.

Assigning a Necessity Score is a somewhat subjective decision, dependent to a certain extent on your psychological awareness, existing debt level, and present and future expenses. Here are some rough guidelines. If you fell and broke your leg during the week, the check to the orthopedist would be entirely necessary and you'd give that a Necessity Score of 1. If a pair of $500 Jimmy Choo sandals caught your eye, and, despite the fact that you have other sandals in a similar color and heel height and are $8,000 in debt, you bought them anyway, you'd have to stare truth in the face and rate your purchase a 0, totally unnecessary. The occasional computer gamer who shells out $300 for surround-sound computer speakers when a carefully chosen $75 set would be entirely adequate has a subtler decision. If his old speakers were working, probably the Necessity Score is 0; if the old ones had failed, maybe a ⅓ is justified.

As you're assigning each Necessity Score, keep in mind that you can't meet psychological needs through overshopping. However bad a day you've had, however angry or lonely you may be, buying something won't really address your authentic needs. If you're angry, you need to know it, feel it, and handle it constructively; the same for loneliness. Whether it's a Baby Ruth or a little black dress, a cutting-edge video camera or an amber necklace, if you buy it to repair your mood, it probably gets a Necessity Score closer to 0 than to 1.

As far as categorizing your expenditures, it's straightforward but essential. Categorization enables you to begin recognizing the *patterns* of your spending, to see that the particular pie of your income gets sliced in a very specific way: so much for food, so much for clothing, so much for health care. There are fifteen expense categories—Savings/Investment, Heartsongs, Home, Food and Drink, Clothing and Accessories, Self-Care, Health Care, Personal and Spiritual Growth, Transportation, Entertainment, Dependent Care, Vacation, Gifts, Dues / Fees / Personal Business, and Debt Repayment—and each of your expenditures falls into one of them. Virtually all of them are self-explanatory; only Heartsongs—activities *other than shopping* that make you glad to be alive—need a little clarification.

Heartsongs are special investments in your particular joy of living: concert tickets, supplies for a hobby you love, taking your grandchild to the movies, a day at the beach perhaps; heartsongs make your heart sing. (*Nothing* you buy compulsively can be a heartsong because it doesn't only make your heart sing, it also makes your heart ache.) Allocate a certain amount of money each month to this category; just how much will depend on your income, your expenses, and your debt. For now, just think about what constitutes a heartsong for you; and when you spend on one, use that category name to record it. Providing yourself with heartsongs makes it all worthwhile—including the hard work of this book—and makes it a lot less likely you'll feel so deprived that you binge-spend.

By the time you've kept a couple of months of Weigh-in data, you'll know exactly how much you're spending and pretty much what you're spending it on. There are several important distinctions that will help you think more clearly about the structure of your spending. The first of these is the distinction between nondiscretionary (essential) and discretionary (optional) expenses. While it may seem obvious, it's extremely important to cover nondiscretionary expenses first. The mortgage or rent has to be paid (and the car payment, the grocer, the electric company, and so on) or the consequences will be direct and dire. These are nondiscretionary expenses. New clothing and vacations and kitchen cabinet upgrades come afterward. They're discretionary.

Even here there are shades. If you need a car for basic transportation, then yes, the car payment is nondiscretionary. But if the vehicle in question is a Mercedes when your circumstances would justify a Hyundai, it makes sense to consider trading down. In general, the distinction between discretionary and nondiscretionary expenses is the one you're already making with Necessity Scores when you weigh in. Nondiscretionary purchases get a 1; the closer to 0 the Necessity Score, the more discretionary the purchase.

A few further distinctions will help you organize your spending. It's vital to notice that some expenses are *fixed* (such as mortgage or car loan payments) while some are *flexible* (such as food, utilities, and telephone). It's even more critical to notice that some expenses are *monthly* (health insurance premiums, for example, or garbage fees); others are *occasional* (such as stereo gear or a new puppy); and the rest, which are regular but less frequent than monthly—and often quite significant—are *periodic*, including, among others, school taxes, property taxes, most homeowner's or automobile insurance, medical and dental checkups, and gifts. Effective planning requires that you recognize these distinctions. You must, in particular, prepare for periodic expenses. That's the second kind of savings you read about earlier in this chapter.

To give you a feel for the Weighing-in process, we now follow a week in the life of Eileen, a civil service worker in her midfifties. Eileen's shopping addiction has left her with a staggering $75,000 in credit card debt, and the consequences are profound. Although eligible for retirement and attractive pension benefits, she has to continue working to pay off this debt. Eileen and her husband cannot afford to move out of their cramped, one-bedroom rental apartment, and they've had to rent additional storage space for her purchases, which continue to cost them many times over in exorbitant interest charges and storage fees. Eileen despairs about not having been able to control her spending and about how little she has to show for all her years of hard work. Her data is recorded on Daily Weigh-in forms. All the bulleted comments are hers, except for those in italics, which are mine.

Daily Weigh-In	Oct 15, 2007			
Item Purchased	Category	Actual Cost (AC)	Necessity Score (NS) 0, ⅓, ⅔, 1	Necessity Cost (AC x NS)
subway	Transportation	$2.00	1	$2.00
lunch	Food	$8.55	⅔	$5.70
subway	Transportation	$2.00	1	$2.00
Dr.'s app't	Health Care	$200.00	1	$200.00
Daily Totals		AC: $212.55		NC: $209.70

- I spent $8.55 for lunch, but I could have spent less. In my neighborhood, the same soup's cheaper, and I could have brought it to work and heated it in the microwave.
- *Although Eileen rates the $200.00 doctor's appointment as entirely necessary, the cost could have been less. Overwhelmed by a backlog of paperwork, she's let some of the deadlines for filing insurance claims pass. As a result, she hasn't yet met her yearly deductible, and so won't be reimbursed for charges her insurance company would have covered.*

Daily Weigh-In	Oct 16, 2007			
Item Purchased	Category	Actual Cost (AC)	Necessity Score (NS) 0, ⅓, ⅔, 1	Necessity Cost (AC x NS)
bus	Transportation	$4.00	1	$4.00
breakfast	Food	$3.63	⅔	$2.42
lunch	Food	$11.46	⅔	$7.64
snacks for the office	Food	$16.98	⅓	$5.66
subway	Transportation	$2.00	1	$2.00
Daily Totals		AC: $38.07		NC: $21.72

- I could've spent less for lunch by walking a little farther; the places closest to my office are the most expensive. And I'd be killing two birds with one stone; I could use the exercise.
- I gave the snacks a ⅓ because I bought six to eight bags of rice cakes and I could have bought less. Also, I bought fancy sodas for the office, and I'm the only one who does that. I can't believe there's still that part of me that thinks people will like me if I buy them things. I'm selling myself short when I do this. Time to stop!

Daily Weigh-In Oct 17, 2007				
Item Purchased	Category	Actual Cost (AC)	Necessity Score (NS) 0, ⅓, ⅔, 1	Necessity Cost (AC x NS)
breakfast	Food	$8.53	1	$8.53
lunch	Food	$18.94	1	$18.94
subway	Transportation	$2.00	1	$2.00
subway	Transportation	$2.00	1	$2.00
Robert S	Health Care	$125.00	1	$125.00
Macy's: work-out clothes	Clothing	$94.79	⅔	$63.19
dinner	Food	$19.09	1	$19.09
Daily Totals		AC: $270.35		NC: $238.75

- *Eileen treated coworkers to both breakfast and lunch, another instance of buying to please. A Necessity Score of 1 for these seems unjustified. This is probably an example of attempting to fulfill psychological needs by overspending.*
- When I went to Macy's, I bought only workout clothes, which I really needed. But I could've bought less, as I don't work out all that often. I tend to buy three things when one would be enough. *A Necessity Score of ⅔ is overgenerous, given Eileen's debt level. Restraint here is as important a workout as the one at the gym.*

Daily Weigh-In Oct 18, 2007				
Item Purchased	Category	Actual Cost (AC)	Necessity Score (NS) 0, ⅓, ⅔, 1	Necessity Cost (AC x NS)
subway	Transportation	$2.00	1	$2.00
coffee	Food	$3.06	1	$3.06
lunch	Food	$13.27	⅔	$8.85
lunch for secretary	Gift	$5.79	0	$0
Barnes & Noble	Entertainment	$65.66	⅓	$21.89
Daily Totals		AC: $89.78		NC: $36.34

- I need to eat, but I could have had a less expensive lunch. I chose what was closest at hand, and it was somewhat more than I had to spend.
- I brought something back for my secretary to eat, which she'd asked me to do. I paid for her lunch, which she didn't ask me to do; but I tend to overdo it because I want to be liked and thought of as generous. I didn't have to do this.
- I went to Barnes & Noble for something specific, and I bought other books that were not on my list. I looked at the books and said, "I want these," but I didn't have to buy them. I don't even really know if I'll read them.

Daily Weigh-In Oct 19, 2007				
Item Purchased	Category	Actual Cost (AC)	Necessity Score (NS) 0, ⅓, ⅔, 1	Necessity Cost (AC x NS)
bus	Transportation	$4.00	1	$4.00
lunch	Food	$8.57	1	$8.57
subway	Transportation	$2.00	1	$2.00
subway	Transportation	$2.00	1	$2.00
candy contribution	Gift	$50.00	0	$0
dinner	Food	$95.27	⅔	$63.51
Daily Totals		AC: $161.84		NC: $80.08

- This was lunch out with associates at work, and it was really the least I could spend at this restaurant. It didn't feel like a splurge because I was out, not eating at my desk—and I needed to get out of the office.
- I bought $50.00 of candy from a coworker, who was selling it for her daughter who was raising money for a good cause. I did it to be nice, but I could have bought one box and then used the extra money to pay off more of my debt. Again, this is me: one thing I seem to do with money—something I need to stop doing—is trying to buy love.
- Dinner was pretty expensive. I could have eaten for less. But the restaurant was convenient, the food was exceptionally good, and a little splurge now and then makes life worthwhile. *Hmm . . . This sounds*

pretty cavalier and surely not very realistic. Eileen could have eaten for a great deal less. Given her debt, $95.27 for dinner is an extravagance she can't afford. Even a Necessity Score of ⅓, rather than the ⅔ she gave it, would be stretching things.

Daily Weigh-In Oct 20, 2007				
Item Purchased	Category	Actual Cost (AC)	Necessity Score (NS) 0, ⅓, ⅔, 1	Necessity Cost (AC x NS)
lunch	Food	$49.93	⅔	$33.28
jacket	Clothing	$125.47	1	$125.47
bagels	Food	$8.55	1	$8.55
alterations	Clothing	$100.00	1	$100.00
shoes	Clothing	$9.99	0	$0
earrings	Clothing	$69.75	0	$0
bracelet	Clothing	$79.06	0	$0
sweater	Clothing	$89.51	⅔	$59.67
Walgreens: cosmetics	Self-care	$27.45	1	$27.45
jacket	Clothing	$325.83	0	$0
Daily Totals		AC: $885.54		NC: $354.42

- I took two friends to lunch. I wanted to reciprocate to one, who'd taken me to lunch the last time; I didn't have to take the other. But it would just have been awkward to treat only one, and I didn't want to look cheap. *What if Eileen had thought this through in advance? Taking the time to troubleshoot is a great investment.*
- *Eileen has a number of jackets. Having recently lost sixty pounds, she didn't have outerwear that was suitable to be altered. She bought two jackets that day. The $125.47 jacket was something she knew she'd get a lot of use from. The more expensive one she gave a 0 to, because she knew it was unnecessary. Did she think about returning it? She didn't feel she could, because the store had special-ordered it*

for her. (It's not a good idea to accept a store's offer to special-order for you, for just this reason.)

- I gave the shoes, earrings, and bracelet all 0s. The earrings and bracelet were costume jewelry, and I don't even wear costume jewelry! They just looked good to me at the time, and I didn't think them through. I don't even remember what the shoes were, so they couldn't have been very important. I sometimes buy things and just put them away in a closet, where I may not find them until the next season; occasionally, they don't even get worn.
- The sweater was something I needed, but I could definitely have found a similar one for less money.

Daily Weigh-In Oct 21, 2007				
Item Purchased	Category	Actual Cost (AC)	Necessity Score (NS) 0, ⅓, ⅔, 1	Necessity Cost (AC x NS)
Soda/snack	Food	$6.50	1	$6.50
Daily Totals		AC: $6.50		NC: $6.50

THE WEEKLY WEIGH-IN

Eileen took these seven days of data and summarized them on the second of the three forms you'll be using, the Weekly Weigh-in. Her expenditures, transferred to the Weekly Weigh-in form, tell a compelling story. To be sure, it's only a single week's story, but it's certainly an eye-opener. Have a look.

Weekly Weigh-In Oct 15–21, 2007		
	Day's Actual Cost	Day's Necessity Cost
Monday	$212.55	$209.70
Tuesday	$38.07	$21.72
Wednesday	$270.35	$238.75
Thursday	$89.78	$36.34
Friday	$161.84	$80.08
Saturday	$885.54	$354.42
Sunday	$6.50	$6.50
Weekly Totals	AC: $1,664.63	NC: $947.51
Week's Possible Savings (AC – NC) $717.12		

Project this week's arithmetic forward a full year, and Eileen might save an astonishing amount: $37,290.24. Remember, not every dollar of possible savings can be realized; but if Eileen could save just half this amount, she could pay off her debt in less than five years—instead of amassing even more and reinforcing this vicious cycle.

Here's a blank version of the Weekly Weigh-in form and instructions for how to use it. Again, you can simply enter your own weekly data on a journal page or make copies of the form.

Weekly Weigh-In	Dates _____	
	Day's Actual Cost	Day's Necessity Cost
Monday	$	$
Tuesday	$	$
Wednesday	$	$
Thursday	$	$
Friday	$	$
Saturday	$	$
Sunday	$	$
Weekly Totals	AC: $	NC: $
Week's Possible Savings (AC – NC) $ _____		

Weekly Weigh-in Instructions

- At the end of each week, transfer your Daily Weigh-in totals to the Weekly Weigh-in form.

- Then total the seven days' Actual Cost to get a Total Week's Actual Cost. Total the seven days' Necessity Cost to get a Total Week's Necessity Cost.

- Finally, subtract the Total Week's Necessity Cost from the Total Week's Actual Cost. This will give you the Week's Possible Savings. If you multiply that number by 52, you'll have a ballpark idea of what you could save over the course of a year if you bought only things that were more necessary rather than less.

WEEKLY SPENDING BY CATEGORIES

The Daily and Weekly Weigh-in forms tell you a great deal about your spending, but one more form is necessary to complete the picture. The Weekly Spending by Categories form allows you to begin seeing the *patterns* to your spending. It creates a virtual X-ray of your week's spending habits. Here's a blank version of the form and instructions for how to use it. You can make copies for the eight to twelve weeks you'll keep this data, or simply rewrite the form into your journal.

| Weekly Spending by Categories Dates _____ – _____ | | | | | | | | |
Category	Mon	Tues	Wed	Thu	Fri	Sat	Sun	Total
Savings/Invest								
Heartsongs								
Home								
Food								
Clothing								
Self-care								
Health Care								
Education								
Transportation								
Entertainment								
Dependent Care								
Vacation/Travel								
Gifts								
Personal Business								
Tax & Insurance								
Debt Repayment								
Other								

Weekly Spending by Categories Instructions

- At the end of each week, X-ray your spending habits by transferring your Daily Weigh-in data to the Weekly Spending by Categories form.
- Then total the seven days' expenditures for each category in which you've spent.
- Don't agonize about categories; just use your common sense. I've largely followed the excellent work of Karen McCall in naming and organizing these categories, and you aren't likely to have much trouble deciding where to put any expense. If you're in doubt—does an expensive premovie dinner count as Entertainment, or is it Food?—make a reasonable decision. What's most important is that you enter all your expenses; where you place them is secondary.

A few final points about what and how you spend. You'll notice Savings/Investment at the top of the Weekly Spending by Categories form. That's to emphasize the centrality of this much-neglected category; remember, *pay yourself first*.[4] By the same token, though Debt Repayment is listed last, it is by no means least important; *paying down your debt is a cornerstone of financial health*. And don't forget Heartsongs. As you move from excessive spending to realistic spending, play yourself some joyful tunes. Balance, here and in all things, is the watchword. Finally, as you keep your numbers, allow me to remind you one more time: use only cash, check, or debit card. *A credit card for an overshopper is like lighter fluid for a pyromaniac.*

It's genuinely exhilarating to climb out from under the burden of debt, to take control of your financial life, to envision and plan for a fulfilling future. Though personal and cultural issues may have kept you until now from achieving this, you can—you genuinely *can*—do it. Approach the task with a positive attitude—see your purse or wallet as half full rather than half empty—and consciously practice self-kindness. However you got here, this is where you are; see it clearly and compassionately, notice and allow. Now start moving toward where you want to be. Identify what really matters, map a path in that direction—and stay on it!

5 | What Are You *Really* Shopping For?

And How to Get It

Although an overshopper's urges are responses to cues, to triggers that ignite her impulses and propel her into overshopping, these cues are only catalysts, not causes. Behind them lie real needs—some emotional, some social, some spiritual. In this chapter, you work toward two important goals: you begin to pinpoint the needs your shopping is an attempt to satisfy (or to distract you from), the underlying issues that drive your behavior; and you start designing healthier and more satisfying ways to meet those needs. In the process, you find ways to bring pleasure and delight into your life, along with comfort, health, and safety. You improve your capacity both to connect with others and to act independently. And you identify your most pressing needs and dominant character strengths, then see how you can build a better life with them. Go through this chapter particularly slowly and thoughtfully—and by the end you'll have a much better idea of what you're *really* shopping for and how to get it.

SELF-KINDNESS, SELF-CARE, AND SELF-RESPECT

Mother: Now, Jenny, I know there are lots of things you like to do for fun, but from now on, I'm not going to let you do them. The only thing you'll get to do is go shopping.

Jenny: Ride my bike?

Mother: Nope.

Jenny: Go exploring in the woods with Wylie?

Mother: No. Just shopping.

Jenny: Play my ukulele? Make finger puppets? Color by numbers? Talk on the phone? Do puzzles? Hike with you guys?

Mother: Nope.

Jenny: Visit Grandma and Grandpa? Swim at the lake? Have a picnic in the park? Go to the circus with Sarah and her family? Play cards with Danny and Jason? Go to gymnastics class? Learn to steer the sailboat? Play in the mud?

Mother: No. Just shopping.

Jenny: Just shopping!? Why are you being so *mean*??

Self-Kindness

Shopping can bring us pleasure. So can (or used to, or might) any of a thousand other activities. If shopping's become the first thing you think of for fun—maybe the *only* thing you think of—then you're being as mean to yourself as Jenny's mother is to Jenny.

Self-kindness is essential for stopping overshopping. If Jenny's mother weren't so mean, she'd not only *allow* her daughter to play in the ways she wants to, she'd *propose new ideas and opportunities* for Jenny. She'd actively look for new and better ways to provide an interesting, nurturing, safe environment for her daughter—and she'd relish doing it. In the spirit of being your own good mother, in this chapter you'll explore a myriad of ways to treat yourself with the kindness, care, and respect you inherently deserve as a human being.

Let's first explore ways of giving pleasure or delight to yourself, of letting yourself *play*. Kids know how to play. As adults, we often dramatically narrow our range of play options, at serious risk to our well-being. We set ourselves up for emotional deprivation, which makes us sitting ducks for self-destructive habits. If you've gotten into the overshopping rut, it might be time to kindly allow yourself—and proactively provide opportunities for yourself—to play.

Listed below are some ideas, loosely categorized according to the particular sort of pleasure they offer. This is hardly a full inventory, for the possibilities are endless; rather, it's a tickler, a way to get you started. Any or all of these acts of self-kindness might be used as alternative behaviors, healthier and more fulfilling than shopping. Many of them are also less expensive, but that's not the primary point here. You want to expand your options, so you'll always have a wide array of activities from which to choose. For each of the categories, reflect, imagine, *feel*. Check off the suggestions that speak to you, consider *exactly* what it is about shopping that you enjoy, and then brainstorm. What alternative activities might provide the same pleasure in a healthier, more satisfying way than shopping?

JOURNAL TIME

Acts of Self-Kindness

Start a page in your journal for Acts of Self-Kindness. On it, you'll list some of the activities you check below and others you think of that are both appealing and doable. You'll then have a handy reminder of at least a dozen acts of self-kindness that are alternatives to shopping.

Action. For some people, the need for activity is what drives the shopping urge. The hustle and bustle of being out in a busy store is a big part of the fun. What else might you do that could meet that need? Is there something you've always wanted to try?

- ❑ Go dancing, running, roller skating, hiking, or biking.
- ❑ Play tennis or Ping-Pong.
- ❑ Take a movement class, such as dance, power yoga, or aerobics.
- ❑ Walk your dog or your neighbor's dog.
- ❑ Join a softball team or bowling league.
- ❑ Go swimming, rowing, kayaking, or canoeing.

Spontaneity. For many overshoppers, the delight is that you can do it on the spur of the moment. The Internet, catalogs, and television shopping channels are right there at your fingertips, 24-7. Even many brick-and-mortar stores are open whenever you get the urge. If you especially love being spontaneous, what else might you do?

- ❑ Head out to the all-night diner at 3:00 A.M.
- ❑ Stop in at the public library in the afternoon.
- ❑ Go for a walk on the beach.
- ❑ Do a crossword puzzle on your lunch hour.
- ❑ Turn on the radio and dance in your living room.
- ❑ Drop in on a friend.
- ❑ Take a walk in the park—and climb a tree while you're there.

Relaxation, lounging, taking it easy. Rather than hustle and bustle, is gentle relaxation what you need? Is this why you find yourself zoning out in front of a shopping channel or wandering onto eBay? What else might do it for you?

- ❑ Watch a video in bed (a nice, easy bit of fluff).
- ❑ Listen at home to an audiobook.
- ❑ Lie on the couch and listen to some soft music.
- ❑ Get a chair massage.
- ❑ Hang out on your porch.
- ❑ Make yourself a cup of tea and sip mindfully.
- ❑ Do nothing; simply *be.*

Sensual joy. Our five senses offer us unlimited opportunities for pleasure. Sensuous self-kindness can soothe or celebrate the body, the heart, the mind, and the soul. Touch, smell, taste, sight, and hearing each bring something unique and wonderful to life's table.

Touch. Do you love silky fabrics? Nubby tweeds? The feel of velvet? The texture of metal or wood? When you're out shopping, are you reaching for tactile delights? What else could offer you the comfort or joy of touch—and not break the bank?

- ❑ Play in the mud or the garden.
- ❑ Take a bath with fragrant oils or get a massage.

❏ Pet a kitten, hold an infant, or stroke someone's hair.

❏ Sew or knit.

❏ Do some woodworking.

❏ Throw a pot.

❏ Bake some bread or make a pie crust.

Taste and smell. Chocolates? Scented candles? Yellow roses? Perfume? Even if you don't actually seek out the sensuous pleasures of taste and smell while you're shopping, fantasies about *future* mouth and nose pleasure may drive overshopping—for kitchen equipment, backyard barbecues, even clothing to wear at expensive restaurants. What healthier ways can you think of to feed your craving for these experiences?

❏ Prepare food for yourself, and slow down and *taste* it.

❏ Enjoy coffee at home, and grind the beans yourself.

❏ Smell the roses whenever and wherever you see them.

❏ Go for a walk after a rain; *notice* the freshness.

❏ Inhale the scent of newly cut grass.

❏ Breathe in the perfume of freshly baked chocolate chip cookies.

Sight: color, pattern, beauty. Do you love color? Do you buy too many beautiful things or spend more than you can afford on things so exquisite they take your breath away? If you deeply appreciate well-made, high-quality objects, stopping overshopping doesn't have to mean depriving yourself. Congratulate yourself on your capacity for aesthetic appreciation! How might you discover or experience visual delight?

❏ Paint—watercolors, oils, or bathroom walls—for yourself or maybe for someone you love.

❏ Take digital photos of objects you admire and share them.

❏ Look at art forms, in a museum or a book or outdoors.

❏ Visit beautiful places; take house and garden tours.

❏ Behold nature, whether tree or forest, flower or bouquet.

❏ Take a course at a local botanical garden.

Hearing: sound and music. Do you groove on the music piped into your favorite stores? Do you love eavesdropping on other shoppers at the mall? Do you love the noise of the city street when you're out window-shopping? What other sounds could fill your ears and lift your soul?

❑ Sit outside in springtime and listen to the birds.

❑ Listen to a free public lecture.

❑ Volunteer to usher for a benefit performance.

❑ Sip something at an outdoor café and listen to the street sounds.

❑ Sing a song from your childhood.

❑ Play, really *play,* a musical instrument.

❑ Go to a pond at night and listen to the frogs and crickets.

Emotion. Emotions, both positive and negative, charge and direct a lot of overshopping behavior. When we feel nostalgic, when we don't feel connected, when joy is absent, when we feel like celebrating—in these and a great many other emotional situations, we may shop. Instead of shopping in response to your emotions, practice targeted self-kindness: find alternative activities that meet the emotional needs behind your overshopping impulses. What emotionally satisfying alternatives to shopping might work for you?

❑ See a deeply human, moving film, an old classic perhaps.

❑ Spend time with a favorite animal.

❑ Volunteer to help someone who really needs your help.

❑ Attend an event or a performance that promises to be joyful.

❑ Learn by heart and recite a favorite poem.

Intellect. While you may not think of shopping as an intellectual pursuit, the puzzle-solving aspect of shopping motivates and energizes some people. It's an active pleasure for them to sort through an infinite number of choices, factoring in variables such as style, value, and utility, zeroing in on what says, "This is me." But there are so many other ways to experience cerebral delight, so many other puzzles to solve! What nonshopping joys of the mind can you suggest for yourself?

❑ Use the internet to improve your skills in chess or Scrabble.

❑ Take a leadership role in an organization or a club you belong to.

❑ Read a challenging book and talk about it with someone.

❑ Take lessons and learn a new language.

❑ Learn to knit, draw, meditate.

❑ Write anything, from a diary to a Wikipedia entry.

Discovery. Discovery is a particular kind of intellectual pleasure, one that drives a good deal of overshopping. After all, there's always something "new" out there; something different, something unexpected that can grab your attention (and suck the money right out of your wallet). Do you fall for the latest, hottest thing? Do you frequently recheck your favorite stores or Internet shopping sites for what's "just in" and not yet found by others? If so, how can you be kinder to yourself and, at the same time, feed your curiosity and/or relieve your boredom?

❑ Go to a workshop on a cutting-edge topic by a leader in the field.

❑ Take that course you've been thinking about.

❑ Experiment with something artistic or technical.

❑ Look into a controversial issue in politics or some other social field.

❑ Engage in a community service activity or hobby that's new to you.

❑ Go into the woods looking for edible mushrooms or wildflowers.

Spirit. Are you overshopping mostly to distract yourself from feeling empty or hollow? Spiritual self-kindness helps connect the self to the universe, helps us to see ourselves through a lens less clouded by the storm and stress of everyday immediacies. This may be the most difficult type of self-kindness to design and enact, but give yourself every chance to discover unexpected resonances inside you. Remember the words of Walt Whitman: "I am large, I contain multitudes." If you get stuck, you might fast-forward to the Spiritual Needs and Hungers Questionnaire in chapter 9. In what ways might you give yourself this important form of self-kindness?

❑ Personalize a mantra.

❑ Pray, meditate, or practice a period of silence.

- ❑ Experience the life force that flows through you.
- ❑ Walk in nature or a garden, or quietly watch the sunrise or sunset.
- ❑ Sit outside in the evening and really look at the stars.
- ❑ Think about what you're grateful for and lovingly count your blessings.

Self-Care

In our contemporary world, where many of us juggle several roles, self-care often trails well behind a long list of other responsibilities. So it's critical to remind ourselves that self-care is the base from which we care for others, the vital bud that flowers into generosity; this is precisely what we mean when we say, "Charity begins at home." Self-care is *not* selfishness, a fixation on self to the exclusion of others. It's a proper attention to personal needs so that the self can flourish, not in isolation but extending outward.

Overshoppers are often woefully deficient in self-care. While it's usually most obvious in finances, other important areas are also relegated to the back burner (or taken off the stove altogether) because of the time, the money, and the mental and emotional energy taken up by shopping. Do you procrastinate about making doctor's appointments, neglect health issues, forgo regular checkups, diagnostic tests, or prescription medications because the money for these has gone to things you've bought obsessively? Have you allowed your shopping addiction to so damage your supportive human web of family and friends that it feels as if there's no one to help you with your recovery or turn to in an emergency? Does the sheer amount of clutter in your home prevent you from having people over and perhaps even present a serious risk to your health and safety?

Self-care differs from self-kindness in that you don't always experience its benefits immediately. Brushing your teeth may not *feel* as kind to yourself as taking a hot bath scented with fine oil; but while you're brushing them, if you imagine a future with strong teeth, healthy gums, and a broad, relaxed smile—free of pain and dental bills—you can actually experience some of the good you're bestowing on yourself. Part of recognizing and celebrating your worth as a human being is seeing that your teeth are properly attended to, your meals are nutritious, your home is safe, and your future is provided for. Self-care is as central to stopping overshopping as self-kindness. It *prevents* bad things from happening to you—your car being stolen, your house getting broken into, you being mugged or getting sick. Self-care means never incurring outrageous late fees for missed deadlines, not because you didn't have the money but because you didn't open your mail in time.

So how can you begin to take better care of yourself? The trick is to give up the habit of *reacting* to your needs. Instead, each day act as your own loving caregiver. *Anticipate* your needs. (You don't wait to buy Band-Aids until your child cuts himself.) Doing this preventive self-care may not give you the instant gratification that shopping does, but you'll be in control of your life rather than at constant risk of being caught short—and that feeling of control will buoy you, giving you confidence in the present and excitement about the future. This change is not unrealistically difficult, although at first it may appear that way. On any given day, the time you'd otherwise spend overshopping can provide you with a quieter but far healthier gratification: clean and folded laundry, or a living room you want to sit in rather than close off, or timely renewal of your car registration, or a closet or cabinet organized and arranged so that you can see what's in it, or a delicious meal that you've cooked rather than bought.

Now take a deep breath—and then an honest look at the basics of your physical comfort, health, and safety. How well are you doing in these areas? What aren't you taking care of? Would it be a good idea to . . .

- ❏ write a list of emergency contacts and post them on your refrigerator?

- ❏ check your burglar or fire alarm system, or relearn how to work them?

- ❏ contact an attorney or accountant on a matter you've procrastinated about (for example, filing quarterly taxes or updating your will)?

- ❏ make an appointment to improve the safety of your car (such as bad brakes or bald tires)?

- ❑ remove physical hazards from your home (chemicals or loose wires) or health hazards (dust, mold, or pests)?
- ❑ spend some time every day keeping your car/office/home clutter-free?
- ❑ exercise for at least twenty minutes several times a week?
- ❑ prepare a healthy meal for immediate or future use?
- ❑ make a medical or dental appointment, whether routine or in response to symptoms?
- ❑ drink at least forty-eight ounces of water a day?
- ❑ take daily vitamins and medications as prescribed?
- ❑ get more sleep?
- ❑ practice safe sex?
- ❑ set up a retirement account?
- ❑ open the mail and process it in a timely manner?

JOURNAL TIME

Acts of Self-Care

Start a page in your Shopping Journal for Acts of Self-Care. On it, list the most important activities you've checked above and any other important ones you've thought of. This will give you a list of things you could accomplish in anywhere from a few minutes to a few hours—perhaps the same amount of time you spend shopping on any given day. (Beware of the part of you that will say you can't do these things, that you don't have the time or money, or that they don't or won't matter anyway. Listen instead to the small, quiet voice that knows better and can see through these excuses.) You might want to make a copy of the list for your bulletin board and refrigerator, too. You'll now have a handy reminder of several ways to care for yourself instead of shopping. One word of caution: Don't think of these as things you *should* do but rather as things it *makes sense* to do. Think of them as caring gifts for the happier, healthier, safer version of yourself that you're becoming.

Self-Respect

Self-respect is having the proud feeling that you matter. It's the natural outcome of holding what you see with acceptance and compassion. People who've suffered abuse as children or young adults internalize the negative messages they've heard from others; they lose self-respect and don't acknowledge their own worth. *Compromised self-respect must be reclaimed—and it can be.* The wonderful American poet Galway Kinnell tells us this, unforgettably, in "Saint Francis and the Sow":

> The bud
> stands for all things,
> even for those things that don't flower,
> for everything flowers, from within, of self-blessing;
> though sometimes it is necessary
> to reteach a thing its loveliness,
> to put a hand on its brow
> of the flower
> and retell it in words and in touch
> it is lovely
> until it flowers again from within, of self-blessing.[1]

Self-kindness, self-care, and self-respect are powerful, intricately interrelated ways of relearning the loveliness of ourselves, so that we flower again from within. They help counter the negative messages from which overshopping has been an unsuccessful attempt to escape.

NEEDS: LOVE AND AFFECTION, BELONGING, ESTEEM, AND SELF-ACTUALIZATION

All human beings have the same life-sustaining needs, some of them physiological, others psychosocial. Abraham Maslow, the father of needs research, developed a hierarchy of these in the 1940s, and it's still the gold standard. Maslow's work interests us here primarily because it usefully organizes the myriad shades of psychosocial need—the kind of need, as we've already seen, that overshopping is a doomed attempt to meet—into four general areas: love and affection, belonging, esteem, and self-actualization. It's these four areas that we now investigate, because when you identify the specific needs that drive your shopping behavior, you can tailor healthier, more fulfilling alternatives, ones with infinitely more upside potential.

Love and Affection

A deficit of love and affection plays itself out in the overshopping arena in several ways, but compulsive gift giving is the most common. Remember Eileen, the woman in chapter 4 whose Weigh-ins we followed for a week? We heard two or three times during her workweek that she was treating coworkers to breakfast and lunch when she couldn't afford to and buying an excessive amount of candy from a coworker who was selling it for her daughter. She commented on her own behavior:

> I brought something back for my secretary to eat, which she'd asked me to do. I paid for her lunch, which she *didn't* ask me to do; but I tend to overdo it because I want to be liked and thought of as generous. I didn't have to do this.

> I bought $50.00 of candy from a coworker, who was selling it for her daughter and for a good cause. I did it to be nice, but I could have bought one box and then used the extra money to pay off more of my debt. Again, this is me: one thing I seem to do with money— something I need to stop doing—is trying to buy love.

Instead of overshopping, here's a little starter list of things you might do to meet your need for love and affection:

- Choose to sit with and pet a beloved animal.
- Plan an activity that brings you pleasure. You might ask someone, in advance, to do it with you.
- Talk about your hurt to a caring listener. Let yourself cry and be held.

- Communicate with someone with whom you've lost touch.
- Arrange or buy some flowers and give them to someone.
- Tell someone you're sorry and offer to make amends.
- Handwrite a note or card to express appreciation or thanks.
- Tell someone everything about why you love them.
- Hug or hold hands with someone, or kiss, or make love.

JOURNAL TIME

Overshopping and the Need for Love and Affection

Now it's your turn. The following questions are designed to help you think, in a deeper way than you normally would, about three things: how the need for love and affection is expressed in your overshopping, what kind of alternative to shopping you could tailor to meet it more positively, and what would have to happen in order for you to actually commit to that alternative. This is important stuff. Tailor-made alternatives, which are designed not to distract you from your underlying needs but to nourish you by feeding those needs, are far more enduring than the quick fix of shopping. So take plenty of time as you do these exercises and allow yourself to be creative: this work is simultaneously a *diagnosis* of your overshopping illness and a first *prescription* for its treatment. Write out your answers in your Shopping Journal. (If you need more inspiration for tailor-made alternatives, refer back to the "Self-Kindness" and "Self-Care" sections.)

1. On a 1 to 10 scale, how much do you think your need for love and affection is a factor in your overshopping?
2. How and when do you think it expresses itself in your overshopping behavior—either specifically related to a particular person or persons, or more generally?
3. What healthier alternative can you tailor to meet your need for love and affection?
4. How would doing that enhance your life and be in alignment with your vision?
5. What's the cost of not doing this?

6. In addition to yourself, is there anyone else you'd need to enroll to bring this about? If so, who is it and what role would that person (or persons) have to play?
7. What would have to happen for you to be willing to give this a try?

Now make a commitment to enact this alternative. Talk to your Shopping Support Buddy about it, and then go do it! Afterward, process how it went with your Shopping Support Buddy and/or by writing about how it went in your journal.

Belonging

The need to belong, to feel *a part of,* rather than *apart from,* often kicks in at the same time as our need for love and affection. Whether it's to a work-related group, a family group, a peer group, a neighborhood, or some other collection of souls, human beings crave inclusion. And in order to be part of the group, quite a few of us buy things we can't afford: sneakers, clothing, flat-panel TVs, a country club membership, a car, or a house. (This is the stuff of social pressure, material you'll read about in the next chapter.) Are you one of these people? Fill in the blanks and try this on for size: "...'s got ..., and I want it, too. Do I need it? Of course not!"

Not surprisingly, the needs for love and belonging overlap in places; overshopping is often an expression of more than one need. Let's suppose, for example, that you frequent stores and overbuy out of a craving for the easy personal attention of salespeople, the ready rapport available when buyer and seller become joined (albeit only briefly) in the pseudoconnection of transaction. Underneath this urge, in all probability, are feelings of loneliness and isolation. What you're *really* shopping for isn't the merchandise but the connection, support, or affection; you yearn to feel attached, to belong, to be accepted. There are components of both kinds of need, for love and for belonging, to this overshopping.

Here's a short starter list of alternatives to shopping that might address your need for belonging:

- Go to a club or community meeting. Share and get support.

- Volunteer your help or expertise; we always feel more connected when we give to somebody else.

- Ask to be included in an upcoming celebration or other event that people would be surprised you wanted to attend.

- Volunteer your time and talent to an organization or an event.

- Invite a group of people you've wanted to be a part of to do something with you that doesn't cost money.

- Join a committee or lead a group in which you don't presently take a leadership role.

- Attend a conference in your field or area of interest and connect with some of the people there.

JOURNAL TIME

Overshopping and the Need to Belong

It's your turn again. Carefully and creatively answer the same questions you already have about your need for love and affection, but this time answer them about your need to belong. Again, make a commitment to enact the alternative that you've come up with. Talk to your Shopping Support Buddy before and after you do it, and write in your journal about how it went.

Esteem

Our need for esteem has two faces, one looking inward, the other, outward. We need both *self-esteem,* our own considered approval of who we are, and *the esteem of others,* the approval of the village. When we're feeling low on either of these essential components of self-worth, we feel insubstantial and empty—and compensatory overshopping often results. The remedy, here as above, is to recognize what you're really shopping for and then hatch a well-grounded plan for getting it.

This is a little tricky with esteem needs, because there are so many shades of them. Do you want "acknowledgment," "applause," "respect," "acclaim," "eminence," or "veneration"? Do you desire "to be heard," "to have authority," "to be deferred to," or "to dominate"? These distinctions are worth thinking about, because focusing in on the shade of your need will help you to precisely tailor your alternatives.

Both faces of esteem need are connected to overshopping through the myth of magical transformation. When our needs for esteem are frustrated, we feel inadequate, inferior, hopeless, and helpless. Then we're particularly vulnerable to the culturally dispensed falsehoods that augmenting what you own can make other people see you differently or can actually transform you. But buying into this myth will cost you a pretty penny, both financially and emotionally. Instead, you'll do far better to invest yourself in the kind of activity, experience, or relationship that can genuinely meet your esteem needs, that can draw you closer to what you're missing—deeper and more fulfilling relationships with family, friends, and self.

Self-Esteem
Here's a tickler list of possible ways to genuinely meet your need for self-esteem:

- Wear something you already own that you feel and look great in.

- Take on a personal challenge you've been putting off.

- Become passionate about a cause and do everything you can to champion it.

- Teach a class, mentor someone in your field, or become a Big Brother or Sister, either officially or informally.

- List your strengths and assets as a person.

- Say no. (Tell someone you're no longer going to do something you don't want to do anymore.)

- In front of a mirror, practice saying something that you've been afraid to say.

JOURNAL TIME

Overshopping and the Need for Self-Esteem

Now carefully and creatively answer the same seven questions you already have about your need for love and affection and your need to belong, but this time answer them about your need for self-esteem. Make a commitment to enacting the alternative you came up with. Talk to your Shopping Support Buddy about it—and then do it! Afterward, write about how it went.

THE ESTEEM OF OTHERS

Here's a short list of possible alternatives to shopping that might meet your need for the esteem of others. After this list, you'll again be asked to tailor your own.

- Perform or speak or display your work in public. (Don't hide your light under a bushel.)
- Seek the company of someone who admires or respects you.
- Make your boss look good. Defend those you supervise.
- Teach someone to do something you do well.
- Be the best spouse or parent you can possibly be.
- Lead by example.

JOURNAL TIME

Overshopping and the Need for the Esteem of Others

Once again, thoughtfully answer those same seven questions; but this time, answer them about your need for the esteem of others. Again, make a commitment to enact the tailor-made alternative. Talk to your Shopping Support Buddy about it before and after, and write about how it went.

Self-Actualization

The need for self-actualization, for "doing what we were born to do," is the last general area of psychosocial need we'll consider here; as Maslow puts it, "A musician must make music, an artist must paint, and a poet must write."[2] It's this need that drives us to learn, understand, and seek meaning; to search for beauty, balance, and form; to work toward personal growth and peak experiences. Self-actualization is a form of autonomy, for as much as we need to be connected with others, we need as well to act independently, to be at the helm of our own ship. When that need is stifled, when freedom of self-expression is closed off, a tense, edgy restlessness ensues—and sometimes this leads to overshopping.

A woman I worked with in therapy overbought clothing, jewelry, and accessories. Much of the thrill for her was in creating novel outfits and combinations. Yet her creativity was costing her family so much that it was unclear how she and her husband would be able to pay their sons' college tuition. When we managed to separate the needs braided into her overshopping, it became clear that while there were certainly esteem issues, the fundamental issue was her restlessness, a feeling of being insufficiently stimulated. Her recognition of this led her to rediscover an old joy, sculpting—and the more she sculpted, the less she needed to spend on creating artistic looks for herself.

Remember the "Why Do You Overshop?" vignette about Suzanne, who felt hopeless about being heard by her dentist husband? She recognized her overshopping habit as a rebellious response to the power disparity in their relationship; she realized that she felt a deficit of both love and esteem. Beneath these, however, she saw another deficit, an inability to self-actualize. Out of her awareness came two nicely tailored alternatives to shopping, two activities that directly addressed her needs for autonomy and competence: first, to write an unsent letter to her husband, which would focus her thoughts and help her to express her feelings; and second, to take up kickboxing, a healthy outlet for some of her anger.

Here's a final starter list of activities, this one of things you might do to legitimately meet your need for self-actualization:

- Take a course in something you've been wanting to learn.
- Investigate a spiritual or religious practice that you've been curious about.
- Take a hike and gather the most beautiful leaves, seedpods, and cones you can find.

- Practice noble silence.
- Express a dissenting opinion. Stand up for something you believe in.
- Watch the sunset from a beautiful location.
- Talk about your hopes and dreams with someone close to you.

JOURNAL TIME

Overshopping and the Need for Self-Actualization

Now, one last time, answer those same seven questions, but this time about your need for self-actualization. Again, make a commitment to enact the alternative you've chosen. Talk to your Shopping Support Buddy before and after you do it, and write about how it went.

JOURNAL TIME

Tailor-Made Alternatives

You've now worked with five important needs—love and affection, belonging, self-esteem, the esteem of others, and self-actualization—that underlie overshopping behavior, and you've identified and begun to use healthier alternatives to meet these needs. This is the moment to reinforce what you've done and give yourself a reminder whenever you're caught in the throes of an overshopping impulse by creating a list in your journal of the Tailor-Made Alternatives you've come up with. Add to this list whenever you discover further alternatives.

FULFILLMENT AND HAPPINESS

"No two daisies are alike," the very wise old woman tells her young charge in the classic movie *Harold and Maude,* and she elaborates: "See, some are smaller, some are fatter, some grow to the left, some to the right, some have even lost some petals. All *kinds* of observable differences. You see, Harold, I feel that much of the world's sorrow comes from people who are *this* [she points to a particular daisy], yet allow themselves be treated as *that* [she gestures to a whole field of daisies]." Maude's observation perfectly introduces this section.

Each of us has a unique complement of gifts, of natural, signature strengths; if we fail to identify and use these for recovery, we're apt to be stuck with only ineffective generic solutions to highly individualized problems.

To say this another way, when you recognize your gifts, your unique constellation of human talents and virtues, you are gaining leverage on your life. Once you do that, you can lean on those strengths, maximizing your power to change things.

But important as it is to own and celebrate your strengths, many people have a hard time doing it. Perhaps it's the result of years of putting yourself down, behavior you most likely learned as you grew up (whether directly, by actually being put down, or indirectly, by being neglected or abused). Whatever the case, if this sounds like you, step back from your negative self-image and try to see a different, positive reflection.

Character strengths are the means by which virtues get expressed and can be nurtured throughout life, with consequent benefits to health, relationships, careers, and addictive behaviors. Research tells us that happiness can be cultivated by identifying and using many of the strengths and traits that people already possess—including kindness, originality, humor, optimism, and generosity. Using our signature strengths inoculates us, to a certain extent, from misfortune and negative emotion, and makes positive emotions much more likely to occur. A particularly exciting way to look at these signature character strengths has been developed by the Values in Action (VIA) Institute.

EXERCISE

Activating Your Gifts

The following is a list of the twenty-four character strengths—they're also your gifts—delineated by the VIA. Read and then choose one of the following two options: (1) register at www.viastrengths.org and take the free online signature strengths survey (the whole process takes about thirty minutes and will immediately provide you with a report of your five dominant strengths and a description of each of those strengths), or (2) simply circle the five signature strengths you believe are your most dominant. You might even want to make your own choices *and* then take the survey. Afterward compare your self-report with the survey report.

Creativity, ingenuity, originality	Zest, enthusiasm, energy	Modesty, humility
Curiosity, interest in the world	Capacity to love and be loved	Caution, prudence, discretion
Judgment, critical thinking, open-mindedness	Kindness, generosity	Self-control, self-regulation
Love of learning	Social intelligence	Appreciation of beauty and excellence
Perspective, wisdom	Citizenship, teamwork, loyalty	Gratitude
Bravery, valor	Fairness, equity, justice	Hope, optimism, future-mindedness
Industry, diligence, perseverance	Leadership	Humor, playfulness
Honesty, authenticity, genuineness	Forgiveness, mercy	Spirituality, sense of purpose, faith

It's time now to put your five signature strengths to work for you, to think of ways they can assist you in recovery from overshopping and begin to help you live a better, happier life. Linda's story may help you get started.

Linda is a forty-five-year-old trainer in the human relations department of a hospital. Years of overshopping have resulted in approximately $40,000 of credit card debt, a lot of friction with her partner, and the humiliation of not having any money to contribute toward her son's college tuition. Linda's five most prominent gifts are these: fairness, equity, and justice; kindness and generosity; forgiveness and mercy; social intelligence; and humor and playfulness. Here's how she plans to use them in her recovery and en route to a better life:

FAIRNESS, EQUITY, AND JUSTICE
I'm going to begin doing some research into becoming a mediator.
It's something I've thought about for a while. By doing so, I'll challenge

myself, stay out of the stores, help people, and probably feel a lot more competent.

FORGIVENESS AND MERCY

I think I must have scored high on this strength because of how forgiving I am toward other people. To stop overshopping, I'm going to need to turn this toward myself. That'll help me stop beating myself up, stop second-guessing myself so often. I'll start giving myself the benefit of the doubt and work on developing more compassion for myself rather than judging myself so harshly.

SOCIAL INTELLIGENCE

I can do some fulfilling volunteer work, where my people skills will be valued. I can also go to Debtors Anonymous, where I'll interact constructively, which always makes me feel good. The better I feel about myself, the less I'm going to feel like a slave to fashion and the less I'll worry about what other people think.

KINDNESS AND GENEROSITY

I can become a Big Sister and help shape a young girl's life, giving her a positive role model and exposing her to ideas and experiences she wouldn't have otherwise. Now that my son is grown up, it'll also help fill up my empty nest. It's a great thing to do on Saturday afternoons, which I now spend shopping.

HUMOR AND PLAYFULNESS

I can use these for everything! I don't think I ever realized how much a part of me these gifts are. Now I need to learn to be playful and humorous when it comes to stopping overshopping. My Shopping Support Buddy and I made a chart with little empty shopping bags instead of stars I earn for following through on my goals for the week. Maybe I'll suggest that a certain number of empty shopping bags be redeemable for the activity reward of an evening at a comedy club.

JOURNAL TIME

Putting Your Signature Strengths to Work

That's Linda's plan. Now make one for yourself. First, list your five signature strengths on a page in your journal. Next, write down a short plan to build on and develop these strengths. Complete this idea for each one, just the way that Linda did above: "I can use my [signature strength] to . . . , and, by doing so, I'll . . . ." After you've written out your plans, notice the scale of the activities you're planning. If any of them seems too large or too general, like "Do some fulfilling volunteer work, where my people skills would be valued," write down a *next step* you could take toward that goal, something that you could accomplish within a maximum of two hours: maybe "Call the Red Cross and find out what volunteer openings they have available right now," or "Go to the community center and observe the after-school program to see if volunteering there might be a good fit." Anytime you take one of these next steps instead of going shopping, you'll be further along the road to a richer and more satisfying life.

INNER STRENGTH AND MEANING: AFFIRMING YOUR TRUE SELF

Whether you consider your overshopping to be a powerful negative habit or see it as an addiction, overcoming it is a strenuous process, one that calls for all your resources. Like an athlete who trains for an event, who builds capability by daily exercise, you can train to stop overshopping. The muscles you need to develop, though, aren't physical ones. Rather, you need to develop psychological balance and emotional calm. The strength-building regimen that follows will help you do this. This technique, one with many modern variants but roots in ancient religious and spiritual traditions, will help you build inner strength and meet your authentic human needs.

Research has documented the power of positive thinking. Over and over, in area after area, optimists do better, feel happier, and live longer than pessimists. There seems to be a law of attraction: what you *think* about, you *bring* about. A particularly powerful way to tap into positive thinking derives from the language and traditions of the Buddha. In Sanskrit, *Metta* means "loving-kindness." A strength-building regimen in the Buddhist tradition is to express Metta, loving-kindness and compassion toward yourself, in the form of positive statements that we'll call *Metta Tags*. These affirmations counteract negative messages you've been programmed with, either from your early upbringing or from negative life experiences later along the way. They can help you to affirm your deepest convictions and clarify your immediate and ultimate goals.

You solidify your convictions and strengthen your determination when you make positive statements that describe *what you want to believe* and *what you want to become.* You draw a clear and detailed inner map that charts the course for your life. When, with belief and optimism, you affirm a change you wish to make, when you picture it vividly and verbalize it as though it's already happened, you help it come to pass.

Metta Tags are written or spoken *as if those changes have already happened.* If, for example, you want to work out three times a week instead of shopping, you can encourage and affirm that change with a Metta Tag. Write out—and say aloud to yourself several times a day—"I go to the gym three times a week, and I control the urge to shop." For extra impact, you might want to place yourself in front of a mirror, standing tall and looking at yourself as you repeat the statement. Keep repeating it until you experience yourself believing it, *living* it. Doing that with the following Metta Tag has proved invaluable for me and for several people I've worked with: simply say your name—let's suppose it's Maria—and follow it up with, "I love you just the way you are." Repeat this affirmation—"Maria, I love you just the way you are"—until you can let go of some of the feeling that saying it evokes. Continue using this Metta Tag over time, first *noticing* the feeling, then refraining from doing anything to blunt or hide it, and finally allowing yourself to really *feel* it. Do this and you'll grow in self-acceptance.

The more your Metta Tags are tailored to suit your individual needs, the more powerful they will be at helping you build strength and make the changes you want to make. Important reminders of your capacity to change, Metta Tags will increase your self-confidence and your follow-through on goals. You can also use them to reward yourself for your progress and to reinforce it. Here are some examples:

"I only shop when I'm calm and in control of my emotions."

"I actively develop peace, calm, and order in my life."

"I provide for my future."

"I cope with negative feelings in more effective ways than buying."

"I take good care of myself."

"I transform self-destructive behaviors into constructive ones."

"I'm grateful for who I am and what I have."

Jerrold Mundis, in *How to Get Out of Debt, Stay Out of Debt, and Live Prosperously,* suggests a particularly intriguing way to create Metta Tags. He recommends writing them in first, second, and third person—"I shop mindfully," "Julie, you shop mindfully," and "Julie shops mindfully"— and after each instance jotting down whatever comes to mind. The idea of the three voices is to get the positive attitude into your subconscious in the same ways that the negative attitude it counteracts originally got there: through what you told yourself, through what others told you, and through what you heard.

JOURNAL TIME

Metta Tags

Create a page in your journal for your Metta Tags and write yourself a few. Make sure to keep them simple, positive, and in the present tense. Add to—or revise—this list whenever something appropriate comes to mind or your wants, needs, feelings, and thoughts change. Say them to yourself, silently or aloud, every day. They're particularly helpful in high-risk situations, when you have the urge to shop, or to congratulate yourself when you've successfully resisted the urge to shop.

Don't underestimate the power of creating and using Metta Tags. Affirming your true self not only helps you recover from the effects of negative messages from your past but will also inoculate you against current negative influences in your life. Using your Metta Tags will help build the motivation and inner strength to stop overshopping. And they can help you at a deeper level, too, now and in the future—to live in accordance with your highest, truest values, to be the self you want to be.

INSTEAD OF SHOPPING

If you've done the serious work needed to get this far in the book—tough, introspective, and eye-opening—you've come a long way toward uncovering and articulating the authentic human needs that underlie your overshopping behavior. You also have some ideas about what to do *instead of shopping:* your tailor-made list of healthy alternatives stands ready and waiting in your Shopping Journal. You're ready now to begin feeding your true inner hungers. You're ready to take action, to develop the habit of getting what you *really* need, what you're *really* shopping for.

Next time you have the urge to shop—and whenever you have it from now on—*before you shop, decide what you're really shopping for.* Open your journal to a blank page and answer the questions you've been asking yourself when an urge strikes: How does your body know it wants to shop? What negative and positive thoughts and feelings go along with it? What do you think is triggering you? What do your heart and head say? Now add this further step: pinpoint, in a word or two, what you *really* need. (Is it some shade of the need for love and affection, or to belong, or to feel self-esteem or the esteem of others?) Once you've pinned down the need, write down one or two of the tailor-made alternatives you came up with to meet it—alternatives that will enhance your life rather than erode it. *Then* make your decision. Either proceed to the healthier alternative or decide to shop. If you do decide to shop, be sure to ask yourself—*and answer*—the questions on your Reminder Card.

The urge or pressure to shop can be sharp and strong; it can feel almost impossible to bear or oppose. But it can be borne. It can also be usefully deflected, redirected, or transformed. Do something instead of shopping, and you're taking control of your habit and your life. Do something instead of shopping, and you'll eventually notice that the urge has diminished—or dissipated entirely. And every time you do that, you're reinforcing your power to resist subsequent urges. When you do something instead of shopping—when the replacement is a more authentic activity, one more likely to give you what you really need—you're building important new muscles, building inner strength.

And you're going to need inner strength. As we're about to see, there are powerful external forces working to shape your behavior to their purposes, an entire culture of consumption beating incessant drums for shopping. There are ingenious ad campaigns single-mindedly focused on selling you something, anything, and they're extraordinarily effective at making you want things you don't need. They're so clever that they may fool you into thinking you *need* everything you want. These messages don't encourage you to play or take care of yourself or connect with others. They don't urge you to develop your gifts or live according to your ideals. Those are experiences you have to create for yourself. But when you do, those experiences—unlike shopping!—provide the kind of satisfaction that lasts a lifetime.

6 | Countering the Pressure to Consume

But you still need to do *some* shopping, right? You still need to supply yourself with necessary goods and services, even if you've already begun to build a life full of gratifying, shopping-free activities. So you're going to have to learn to handle the hype, the manipulation, the pressure coming at you from all sides: from stores, the Internet, television commercials, catalogs, magazines, TV shopping channels; from the multibillion-dollar marketing and sales industry; from friendly salesclerks; from your own family and friends; and from "the Joneses" next door (or wherever they are). Your shopping challenge is to stay calmly centered, clear about your own agenda and focused on it. This chapter offers specific, proven techniques to help you do this, to shop without *over*shopping by anticipating, preparing for, and countering the pressure to consume.

DEMAGNETIZING: RESISTING THE PULL

Ours is a culture of consumption, one in which the swirl of buy-messages generates a kind of magnetic field, a climate that predisposes us to desire an excess of material things. Unless you do something active and conscious about this, you'll be a prisoner of that desire, powerfully drawn by invisible forces into behavior that makes no logical sense and negatively impacts your life. How can you demagnetize? How can you counter the pull to buy, buy, buy, more, more, more, now, now, now?

First, be acutely conscious of the existence and strength of the pull. Recognize how and why it resonates within you. Second, keep your distance. Reduce your exposure to buy-messages. Avoid them whenever you can. Third, find and strengthen your own center of gravity. Ground yourself in *your* priorities, *your* values, *your* goals—and create a solid *plan* for your next shopping trip. Fourth, when you do shop, slow down and shop *mindfully,* so you don't get carried away. Finally, if you need to, reach out for someone who can help pull you out of the worst of the storm until you can get your bearings.

We'll now take a look at some of the techniques that marketing geniuses use to get us to buy, to *move* us toward making a purchase. We'll first look at the overall attempts to whip up your acquisitive desire, then at how this is accomplished in each of six strong shopping magnets: malls and stand-alone stores, Internet shopping, TV commercials, magazine ads, catalog shopping, and TV shopping channels. You'll then custom-build a page in your Shopping Journal to help you keep your distance, to resist the pull of particular venues that tend to draw you in.

Shopping versus Recreation

A great many women view shopping as a form of recreation—if asked to choose, they prefer shopping to seeing a movie or eating a meal in a restaurant. Most men see it as work and don't expect it to be fun. Men, however, don't equate the considerable time they spend browsing in book, record, or computer stores—or on the Internet—with the time women spend in clothing, jewelry, and shoe stores. Whatever your gender, suffice it to say that in order to stop overshopping, your recreational outlets cannot also be retail outlets. The "thrill of the hunt," the acknowledged (or disavowed) excitement of shopping, tugs you into a powerful magnetic field, designed to cloud your judgment and extract your money. To stop overshopping, you need to stay centered, resistant to every attempt to whip you into a buying frenzy. You need to pass up those wild rides on the consumer merry-go-round and instead use a different vehicle to satisfy your basic needs for stimulation, activity, attachment, affiliation, and self-expression.

So far in this book, we've focused on the ways that negative emotions can trigger the urge to shop, but *positive* emotions, too, can trigger overshopping—and marketers know it. "Go ahead, live a little! You deserve it!" the ads proclaim, seizing upon your urge to celebrate after finishing an exam, getting a raise, having a birthday, or simply making it through a day at work. Unexpected or sudden good luck, such as an inheritance or some other windfall, often triggers overshopping, as many a lottery winner has discovered too late. In fact, whenever you're feeling optimistic, confident, or joyful and you head out to the shops or surf over to eBay, you're at increased risk of overshopping: you're already excited, you're already *moving* toward the black hole of shopping, so you're an easier target for marketing lures when you get there. And it doesn't take a winning lottery ticket to trigger a binge. It might be nothing more than your monthly paycheck, which, after a week or two of forced restraint, leaves you feeling free to indulge your pent-up desires.

Even when shopping is prompted by mundane necessity—a run in your stockings or a shortage of toilet paper—you can still get caught up in a buying frenzy. You may discover more appealing items as you approach the point of purchase; stores are carefully arranged to promote this possibility. And once your adrenaline starts to flow and your breath quickens and your heart begins to race, rational considerations fly away, and shopping all too easily escalates into overshopping.

If shopping even *starts* to feel like skydiving or safari hunting or great sex, you're gravitating toward dangerous overshopping territory. Does this mean you need to completely let go of shopping as the way you get your thrills? If you genuinely want to stop, yes it does. If you crave excitement, go ahead and take up skydiving (or whatever else you may find thrilling)—but give up getting it from shopping. This may amount to a profound change of habit, and you'll certainly have to make a substantial attitude adjustment. But it's a crucial step toward stopping overshopping.

Consumer research—notably, Paco Underhill's eye-opening and readable books, *Why We Buy* (2000) and *The Call of the Mall* (2004)—has demonstrated a very strong correlation between how much time people spend *browsing* and how much money they actually *spend*. If you're going to stop *over*shopping, I strongly recommend that you reduce the amount of time you spend shopping. This extends to "near-shopping experiences"—a morning walk "for exercise" in the mall before the stores open, for example, or a slow sashay past shop windows on the way to or from work. Until you've kicked the habit, no driving past your favorite boutiques on the way home instead of taking the expressway, or "just looking" on your favorite Internet shopping sites.

For someone working to stop overshopping, "just looking" makes about as much sense as "just hanging out at the bar" does for someone trying to stop drinking. Temptation, right there under your nose, is too hard to resist. Marketers, remember, make their living using every subtle and not-so-subtle trick to excite your acquisitive desires, and they're particularly skilled at bypassing your rational mind, making a beeline instead for the more visceral appeal of your five senses. If you vastly reduce your time "just looking" at beautiful store displays, glossy magazines, and catalogs; "just listening" to the radio's catchy jingles; "just touching" the soft fabrics or the sleek power tools; "just smelling" the perfumes and candles; or "just tasting" the delicious free samples, you'll vastly reduce the power these marketing magicians have over you.

Six Powerful Shopping Magnets

When you shop, keep in mind that the huge, psychologically sophisticated, and extremely well-financed advertising industry has been pitching products at you from the cradle onward. And, good as they were already, they've gotten even better over the past couple of decades, now applying the insights of modern social science to their armaments of persuasion. Not only is advertising inescapable—it's on television and in magazines, on the Internet and at the ballpark, on the highways and on our clothing, in public restrooms and school lunchrooms—it's also subtle. Rather than simply displaying the virtues of a product, it stirs up your fears and desires. *Advertising promises you a feeling and hooks a product onto it.* Growing up, we imagined that its purpose was to inform, to spread news and information about products and services. In truth, most advertising has a sole and single-minded objective: *to create in each of us the desire to buy what we don't need.*

Think about which venues, or which particular stores or sites within each venue, are your danger zones. Strategies for resisting the six primary shopping magnets are offered below. These are neither complex nor difficult; they're mostly common sense. As you read, check or highlight any that might be particularly helpful.

And, remember, whenever you get near a shopping magnet, *notice* the pull. Stand back and observe what the magnet is doing to you. You may tell yourself, "I'm buying this conditioner because I want my hair to look like that model's in the commercial." But experience tells you otherwise: how likely is it, really, that science has just taken a great leap forward in the Clairol laboratories? Rather, you buy because, subconsciously, you want more than her hair: you want her beauty, her figure, her poise, her confidence—and that attractive man who's striding toward her. You're buying the *context*, not the content, the person who's *connected* with the product rather than the product itself. This was made particularly obvious in those psychologically transparent ads for basketball sneakers, where a charming variety of on-court, would-be Jordans proclaimed, "I wanna be like Mike." You *know* better than to hope for serious airtime from a change of shoe, but the identification with His Airness has sold an awful lot of Nikes. You like Michael Jordan; you love what he does; you buy "his" sneakers. This reaction is entirely human. See it clearly and be compassionate with yourself. Then do whatever you can to steer clear of the danger.

Malls and Stand-Alones: What's in Store?

A mall may be the hardest test of your shopping recovery. Malls are extremely stimulating, often appealing to all of your senses simultaneously. There's a whole science of "atmospherics," a careful psychological design for eliciting emotional reactions that incline you to buy. You're also led toward spending by the examples all around you, lots of other people festive with purchases.

- As soon as you enter the mall, notice how your attention is being manipulated. Is there a particular scent or a particular display, a model giving out free samples, music that's attracting you to a certain store? What appeals are being made to your five senses? Is there anything in the "atmosphere" that seems to be triggering particular feelings or thoughts?

- The stores—and the mall space as a whole—are designed to keep you there as long as possible. Have you ever noticed that there are no clocks around? No surprise! The longer you're there, the more likely you are to "happen upon" something that appeals to you. So limit the amount of time you spend in any store. At the very least, bring a watch with you. Setting an alarm on your watch or your cell phone can keep you from getting lost in excessive browsing.

- Limit the number of stores you visit. The more stores people visit on a given day, the more things they buy and the more money they spend. Thus, although comparison shopping may seem prudent, it can actually weaken your resistance to overshopping.

- Beware of displays that almost require you to ask for sales help. Shoppers who require sales help are more likely to buy than those who shop on their own.

- If you have a choice between a handheld basket or a cart, opt for the basket. You'll buy less. Also, find out about the store's return policy, and leave any store that will give you only store credit if you return something.

- Consider hold and layaway, two strategies that can protect you from your more ardent urges. Both offer you the chance to disrupt mall magnetism, to step back and make a considered and sensible decision. But beware: if you choose either of these options, don't let the incompleteness of the transaction gnaw at you, like a tune you can't get out of your head.

- Above all, don't get "on a roll." Research verifies what you know from experience: *once you've made an initial purchase, your resistance to additional buys drops sharply.* So take a break, slow down, and, if possible, leave the store (or even the mall) after your first purchase.

Internet Shopping: Happiness Is Just a Mouse Click Away
Online consumer spending is at an all-time high, and there's no end in sight. Online retail in the United States reached $175 billion in

2007 and is projected to nearly double by 2012. Already, 83 million Americans have bought online.[1] As accessibility broadens and marketing strategies improve, the substantial natural advantages of Internet sellers come to the fore. To begin with, no other kind of shopping so insulates a buyer from the traditional feel of payment, where you must always take out and hand over something you have with you—cash or a check or a credit card. On the Internet, you simply click a mouse, an action so simple and habitual that it can easily feed denial about spending.[2]

Internet vendors have a unique ability to target you in their marketing. They've kept track of your previous purchases and developed sophisticated software to categorize them, so they present you with choices tailored to your tastes, things you're likely to want. In addition, the Internet makes a limitless variety of goods available to you, day or night, rain or shine, dressed or in your undies—often with warm, live, 24-7 online support available from a sales associate. And because Internet sellers have a much lower overhead than traditional retailers—the Net, after all, is their "store"—online goods are often very temptingly priced. And there's more! With the auction sites, all these advantages are married to the competitive spirit, the desire to "win" by vanquishing the competition in a bidding war. Under the pull of this hypermagnetic field, rational decisions about buying are formidably difficult.

Here, as elsewhere, caution and realism must be the watchwords. Know your danger zones. If, for example, brick-and-mortar stores are your most powerful shopping magnets, because you adore the *feel* of fine clothing, then Internet shopping, which can't (yet!) appeal to your sense of touch, may be better for you. If, on the other hand, it's great deals that set your adrenaline flowing, the Internet may be too tempting.

Here are some tips for overshoppers who use the Internet:

- *Do what you can to keep uninvited Internet retailers from finding you or learning about you.* Upgrade your spam filter and block pop-ups. Change your browser settings to restrict cookies (small coded files that websites write onto your hard drive to keep track of the pages you've visited). Unsubscribe from sites or lists that entice you to shop. Don't give your e-mail address to Internet vendors, who will pass it on to "retail partners" so that they, too, can solicit you. Always choose the highest privacy option from any vendor you do business with: check off the option *not* to share your info with other vendors who might send you "notices of upgrades or special offers."

- Don't just get on the Internet and start browsing. Shop for something specific, and, before you do, allocate a reasonable time for the process and set a reminder timer. When it goes off, so do you!

- Remove all shopping milieus from your "favorite places" directory and avoid "bookmarking" temptations you happen across. If you must keep a list of Internet shopping sites, make it a written list, something you can't simply click on. *Slowing down the process will help you stay mindful.*

- As with brick-and-mortar shopping, beware of getting on a roll. Internet marketers know very well that once you've made a purchase, your resistance to further buying drops sharply. That's why, after you've bought the book you're looking for on Amazon.com, you see "Wait! Add $12.03 to your order to qualify for FREE Super Saver Shipping!" You *should* wait: take a deep breath and then finish checking out. Don't "save money" by quickly and impulsively adding two or three more books you hadn't intended to buy.

- You probably won't be able to eliminate every Internet lure. But you *can* train yourself to ignore the ones that sneak through. Make it your personal policy *never* to respond to them. And don't fall for that "limited time only" gimmick. There's no "once-in-a-lifetime buying opportunity" on the Internet—and even if there is, let go of it. You don't need it. You can't afford it. Ten to one you won't even miss it.

TV Commercials: Promises, Promises

If you think that TV commercials are harmless or that you simply "tune them out," think again. Sitcom, drama, or news program, nearly every show is so regularly interrupted by buy-messages that we spend, on average, *one year of our lives* watching television commercials. Though they're the most familiar of all advertisements, familiarity does not render them ineffective. We may channel surf through them, chuckle knowingly at their impossible claims and situations, and consider ourselves immune to their influence. Yet still they tug at us, subliminally tuning in to our desires and anxieties. The flashy or funny images, the catchy jingles and slogans—these stick to and crowd our minds. We become preoccupied with getting what we've been promised.

To resist TV advertising:

- Don't watch the commercials. Use a product that enables you to delete them, for example, TiVo.

- If you do watch a commercial, examine its credibility and analyze the allure of its approach. Consider text, subtext, and sales techniques—and don't allow your buttons to be pushed.

- Be alert to envy. Many ads present people in very appealing settings: driving a luxurious car or wearing a sexy outfit. Don't confuse the product with the context; *you can't buy the feeling the ad promises.*

- Be alert to anxiety as well. Some ads make you fear that if you don't use the product, you open yourself to rejection, humiliation, disease, mental illness, even death. Evaluate these implicit claims rationally.

- Never allow yourself to imagine that magical transformation is just a purchase away.

Magazines: Words and Pictures, Tailored to Suit
Because magazines target very specific audiences, their ads are particularly seductive; they're already tailored to your interests, whether high fashion or homemaking, stereo equipment or sports accessories. All those glamorous and sophisticated things you see, beautifully presented, are intended to spark deeply acquisitive feelings. They can also stir up envy or anxiety. Next to the high-fashion models pictured or the talented people interviewed about their perfect lives, you may feel inadequate, in need of "fixing"—and ripe, therefore, to be sold supposedly transforming products. Indeed, a well-known research study

found that 70 percent of women felt depressed, guilty, and ashamed after looking at fashion magazines for a mere three minutes.[3]

- If magazines are a danger zone for you, *don't read them;* the best defense is a good offense. If you subscribe to a magazine devoted to a particular product or activity that you overbuy, let your subscription lapse until this problem is well behind you. Better yet, cancel your subscription and request a refund for the unused portion.
- Keep your guard up. Most magazines exist only because advertisers pay for space there. Even "editorial" copy is often a glorified advertisement, clearly slanted in a direction that promotes the purchase of products advertised on nearby pages.
- Notice how carefully the contents, layout, and sequencing of the articles and ads are calculated. For example, directly following an article about the newest fad diet, you're apt to see an ad for a "proven" anticellulite cream. The designers want you to think about purchasing a product while you're feeling vulnerable and "in need of fixing."
- The environment you see in magazines is carefully assembled to call up longings for your ideal self, that self you'd like to become, the one you'd like others to see you as. Don't fall for the old magical transformation myth.
- Don't get hoodwinked by the allure of "newness." Newer is often *not* better. And more often than not, the great new thing (whatever it is) is merely something old that's been recycled.

Catalog Shopping: Stories That Sell

A catalog is a book of advertisements, a directory of things to buy effortlessly: with no cash and little energy expended you can order twenty-four hours a day, in your pajamas, with the promise of overnight delivery that's often free. And a truly effective catalog is more. It's a special kind of narrative—an open story with room for *you* in it. Whatever the story, whether it's the adventurous outdoor life of L. L. Bean or the warm southwest elegance of Sundance, the allure and the danger of such a catalog go hand in hand: first, that you'll be drawn to the story, and second, that you'll buy products to better fit into it.

This is the art of catalog design: to make the story as appealing as possible, text and graphics combining to portray people doing the kinds of things you'd like to do, feeling the way you'd like to feel, looking the way you'd like to look. Don't get caught up in this fantasy; always remember that what's being sold to you is a *promise* thinly disguised as a *product*. The feelings that go along with that promise simply aren't for sale. Forget this and you'll buy impulsively, almost always a guarantee of unwanted goods or costly returns.

- Stop catalogs from reaching you! Keep an ongoing list of all publications coming to your home for one month. At the end of the month, sit down, call the toll-free catalog numbers, and cancel. Repeat the process two months later.
- Remove yourself from consumer lists. Here are some resources to get you started: www.consumeraffairs.com, an independent source of consumer news, information, advocacy, and assistance; and www.the-dma.org/consumers, the Direct Marketing Association, where you can remove your name from lists used by telemarketers and direct-mail marketers. Also worth looking into is the website of the Privacy Rights Clearinghouse: www.privacyrights.org/fs/fs4-junk.htm.
- If any catalogs do appear in your mailbox, throw them out, unread, unopened. Don't even glance. There are far more fulfilling forms of entertainment, much more useful reading material.
- In general, avoid phoning in catalog orders. Sales staff or "personal shoppers," as some marketing genius has dubbed them, are trained to encourage additional sales with professional telephone warmth, personalized orders, and "special offers." Be aware and don't get lost in the moment! If you do call to place an order, have a prior, carefully thought-out, handwritten list in front of you. Ignore all sales plugs.

TV Shopping Channels: "Friends" in Your Home

Recent research makes definite and demonstrable what we already suspected: that QVC and other such channels are enabling and encouraging compulsive shopping.[4] For an overshopper, these channels are simply too seductive. *Don't go there. Stay away.* These are not retail stores, where, at your leisure and with sales pressure you can limit, you're able to compare one thing with another from an abundance of merchandise. More important, they're not brief interruptions, like magazine or television ads, where whatever buying urge an ad may generate may begin to dissipate when the "primary" matter returns—when you go back to the article you're reading or the TV show resumes.

The shopping channels are uninterrupted, dedicated, intimate, high-pressure sales machines, staffed by professional pitchpeople who bring virtual evangelism to their craft. And their effect is significantly magnified by the carefully chosen images that accompany the pitch. As bracelet after bracelet, handbag after handbag, or CD collection after CD collection is offered, each one shining on camera as it never will in life, each one caressed by the pitchperson's voice, each "an amazing bargain," an "opportunity" passing you by *right now* on the television monitor, the psychological pressure to buy can become nearly unbearable. For the overshopper—and probably for most people—this is simply not a venue for intelligent buying decisions.

These channels rely particularly on the emotional connection that you begin to make with the pitchpeople on the screen and that intensifies as you watch, a psychological bond carefully forged of three elements. First, there's the intimacy of television, in which sellers seem right here with us in our living room or bedroom. Next, there's the presentation style, which magnifies that intimacy: sellers talk directly and warmly to us; they become, in effect, earnest and attractive friends. Finally, there's the accumulated impact of repetition: as offer follows offer, we lose the power of resistance; we don't, after all, want to continue to disappoint these new "friends."

So beware of the combined appeal of two all-consuming pursuits, the double whammy of shopping and television. Don't even think about it. Take the fail-safe way: have your cable company disconnect the shopping channels, or, if you use satellite, exercise parental control over yourself and lock them out.

If, despite my attempts to dissuade you, you *do* watch, take these warnings to heart:

- Don't fall prey to the ratcheting pressure tactics these channels employ, whether it's the ticking clock, the dwindling supply, or the "one time only, incredible bargain price." These are gimmicks, designed to excite you, contrived to make you want what you don't need.

- Don't for a moment suppose that the sellers are meaningfully connected to you. Paid salespeople aren't your friends. If they were, they wouldn't be trying to sell you costly and unnecessary items that are likely to leave you feeling lonely, guilty, or defeated.

JOURNAL TIME

Danger Zones

Now create a page in your journal for your danger zones. Under each one, write the three most important strategies you've checked off for resisting the pull and create one additional strategy that's particularly suited to your own needs and vulnerabilities.

The Recap

Many of the marketing gurus' most powerful techniques are common to nearly all forms of advertising or shopping environment: the stirring of our fears and desires, the feigning of the "special offer" or "once-in-a-lifetime opportunity," the excited announcement of something "new," and the appeal to the "smart shopper" with two-for-one or second-item-at-half-price deals are but a few. Similarly, certain simple and practical strategies can counter the pull of nearly any shopping magnet:

1. *Avoid your danger zones.* Stay away. Don't go there. If you've a decided weakness for Home Depot, Macy's, or Prada, change your route so you don't pass by the store. If the television shopping channels suck you in like a great black hole, cut them off. The stronger your overshopping urges are, the more important it is to avoid your danger zones.

2. *Reduce your exposure.* You can't avoid every danger zone, but you *can* reduce your exposure. If you need to shop for a particular item, go to a stand-alone store rather than a mall, where a hundred adjacent temptations beckon you. If the convenience and selection of catalog shopping makes it genuinely valuable for you, unsubscribe from all but a couple of tried-and-true merchants. Tame the Internet with spam filters and pop-up blockers.

3. *Choose creative, smarter alternatives for meeting your material needs.* You're sometimes going to need to shop, both as self-care and as self-kindness. If, however, you want a new outfit for a wedding this summer, and you've got credit card debt, and Loehmann's is your black hole of overshopping, go to another store instead—and perhaps take a Shopping Support Buddy, who'll help you get in and out without collateral damage. Better yet, *borrow* something and make it feel like your own with a special accessory you've already got in your closet.

RESISTING SOCIAL PRESSURE

An important part of shopping without overshopping is developing the capacity to recognize and resist the varied—and sometimes intense—social pressure to consume. This pressure, which we expect from salespeople, can also come from nearly anyone in your social world: neighbors and acquaintances, close friends, and your nearest and dearest family members. Social pressures are tugs on the strands of the human web that each of us weaves for ourselves; and like any spider, we want to keep our web intact. Resisting these tugs feels uncomfortable, awkward, even risky—and this is particularly true for overshoppers, who as a group have less self-esteem, less confidence in web repair, than other shoppers. Over the course of this book, as you get in touch with your unanswered needs and develop healthy ways to meet them, your self-esteem will grow, and with it will come increased security about your human web. Part of getting there, however, is preparation. In this section, we look at preparing yourself for social pressure—at anticipating and recognizing it, and then employing practiced techniques and strategies to counter it.

Salespeople

Any interaction with a sales professional—in a store, on the telephone, even the pseudointeraction on TV shopping channels—is social. And, make no mistake, market research has provided sellers with a great deal of information about how to use social interaction in order to sell. While many salespeople are genuinely nice people, they're not there because they're nice or genuine; they're there because they have a job to do. They're there because experience has shown that if they interact with you when you shop, you'll buy more. Period. Yes, it can feel so much easier to take something home than to risk feeling embarrassed or "high-maintenance" when a sales associate gives you that "You've-tried-on-all-these-garments, I've-gotten-you-the-right-sizes, and-now-you're-not-going-to-buy-anything?" look. But the salesperson is simply doing his or her job. *Your* job is to take care of yourself, not to please the salesperson.

Be particularly wary of the "upsell." Many of the salespeople you deal with are on commission—the more you buy, the more money they make. Therefore, they're highly motivated to get you to buy more than you came for. The "upsell"—"Suppose I could put you in a Camry for the same price as a Corolla?"—is the standard sales technique of enticing you with more quantity and/or quality than you planned to shop for, more than you needed or wanted. Upselling—which so often turns shopping into overshopping—is the primary reason many sales folk are there. It's the salesperson's job to sell you *more* than you came for.

Don't get friendly with salespeople. Whether or not they're on commission, sales associates may genuinely want to satisfy you and—charmer that you are—may truly enjoy interacting with you. But watch out for the schmooze factor! If you're enjoying the interaction, you're more vulnerable to overbuying. Beware of "joining" with the salesclerk, as if you're new pals. Friendly chatter about the weather—or about that folding travel bag—can lull you into feeling that buying what the sales associate wants to sell you is in *your* best interest. As with shopping magnets that are danger zones for you, limit your exposure to salespeople; avoid them altogether if you can. This doesn't mean you're unfriendly or rude. It means you're a recovering overshopper, wisely steering clear of temptation.

So don't engage in chitchat, don't accept help you haven't asked for, don't ask for help if you can avoid it, and don't ask a sales clerk to evaluate a product for you—or *on* you. Salespeople get paid to endorse the products they sell, and their inevitable enthusiasm will put you in the position of feeling ungracious if you don't then buy. If you must ask about a product's features, stick to the facts. Better yet, get the information from written sources ahead of time. (This is the kind of thing the Internet's great for—as long as you don't buy while you're there.) Never fall for "Aren't those just gorgeous?!"—or any other oohing and aahing. As with the television shopping channels, these are ratchets, upping the pressure. Walk out of the store or hang up the phone if you feel your overshopping urges stirring dangerously. If you genuinely want help with your decision making, take a trusted friend with you, someone who understands your goals and won't encourage overshopping.

Here are a few more tips on decreasing your vulnerability to social pressure from salespeople:

In General

- Conduct yourself in a straightforward, businesslike manner. Answer friendly greetings or questions with brief, polite responses, and then get on with your business.
- If you find it difficult to resist a salesperson's offer, sometimes pressure, to help you, practice saying "No thanks," politely but clearly, in front of a mirror. Practice until you're really comfortable with it.
- If a salesperson begins to call you at home, telling you that something's come in "with your name on it," or begins sending you notes or e-mails, tell the truth: that you appreciate the thought but are committed to saving money right now and would prefer not being tempted with calls or e-mails.

In Stores

- Ignore the staff when you walk in. If they say "Hello," say "Hello"—but avoid prolonged eye contact, don't turn your body toward them, and continue on about your business. In other words, communicate through your body language that you're there to examine merchandise and/or make a purchase, not to engage in social interaction.
- If they ask if you want help or in any way try to strike up a conversation, say, "Thanks. I'm just looking."
- If they persist, say, "No thanks. I'll let you know if I need anything." Repeat as necessary, "I'll let you know if I need anything."
- Never agree to a new store credit card, no matter what kind of discount comes with it.

With Telemarketers

- Don't listen to their spiel. Interrupt, politely but firmly, with this legally binding sentence: "I'm not interested, I don't take sales calls, and please remove my number from your call list immediately."

With Phone-in Catalog Salespeople

- Say, "Hello, I'd like to order these items," and state them clearly, reading from your prepared, written list.
- Answer friendly questions with one or two words only, then get quickly back to "I'd like to order these items." Don't listen to any of "today's special offers." They aren't "special," and they're not on your list.

"The Joneses"

Neighbors, coworkers, members of community groups you belong to—"the Joneses," those people who comprise your wider social network—can (and often do) exert pressure on you to buy what you neither need nor want. They're taking advantage, intentionally or not, of their social connection to you, of the obligation you feel toward them, of your wish to be accepted. This more than compensates for any wrinkles in their salesmanship, so whether they're selling charity raffle tickets, Avon products, or insurance, you're drawn to buy. You're *inclined* to buy; you want to cooperate with these people. Even if you'd never open your door to a salesman, uniformed little Jenny Jones gets in with her order pad. It'd be downright un-American not to buy Girl Scout cookies, wouldn't it? Watch out! Before you know it, you've upsold yourself: *"That's twelve boxes. Gee, thanks, Mrs. Pigeon!"*

Social sales pressure often catches us off guard, increasing our vulnerability to impulsive overbuying. Even when the requests are "for a good cause," they're sales pitches nonetheless. To be vigilant about overshopping, you've got to resist social selling. And to resist social selling, you've got to *prepare* for it. These tips may help:

- Plan and execute your charitable giving on an annual basis rather than on impulse. This gives you a tenable reason to say "no" to immediate requests. *"Thanks for asking, Bob, but I've already committed my charitable donations for this year. Let me put your materials in my donations file and see what I can afford next year."*
- Establish a personal policy for social selling, write it down so you remember it, and prepare yourself to invoke it. Practice it, so you can politely, clearly, and confidently deflect the pressure: *"Thanks, Michael, but I'm satisfied with the insurance I have now."* If he persists, *"Thanks, Michael, but I don't borrow money or buy goods or services from friends or neighbors. It keeps us friends, and that's important to me."* Or, *"Thanks, Jenny, but I really don't want any cookies. I'm on a diet, and I've promised myself not to buy sweets."*
- If you're genuinely dying for a box of Girl Scout cookies, by all means buy one. *One.* Psychologically, the first box is pivotal. After you buy it, the rest want to follow. Don't let them. Don't let yourself. This is a controlled release, not the bursting of a dam.

None of this is easy. Social pressure is an important ingredient in the glue that holds civilizations together. It's powerful stuff, and resisting it takes strength—particularly for overshoppers, who tend toward people-pleasing. *But you can do this.* And once you turn aside the first few thrusts, fewer will follow, and they'll be easier to parry.

Significant Others, Family, and Friends

If you overshop for significant others, family members, or close friends, it's important to ask yourself why. Simple generosity is the happiest answer—but simple generosity doesn't overbuy; it has an innate sense of proportion. So in all likelihood, either you're trying to gain power and control over the recipients—perhaps trying to "buy" or to hold on to their love, perhaps challenging them to reciprocate in a kind of test—or you're responding to their pressure. We talked about the first of these two motives for overdoing it with gifts in chapter 3. Remember Karen, whose lavish gifts eventually boomeranged, dissolving the friendship she'd so desperately wanted to maintain? 'Nuff said. You can't manipulate the feelings of important people in your life by overgifting them. It will ultimately make a good thing bad or a bad thing worse.

If you're pressured for gifts or donations—or sales, heaven help us (but it happens)—by significant others, family, or friends, you have to take stock. Consider both the scale of the request and the form of the pressure. If either seems inappropriate, it's reasonable to ask yourself how healthy the relationship is. Listen to the knowing voice inside you, and rephrase the questions on your Reminder Card:

- Why I am buying this for X?
- How do I feel about buying it?
- Does he or she need it?
- Do I need to be repaid in some way for this gift?
- Does X have room for this in his or her life?

Always keep in mind, no matter who wants what how badly, that your gifts and donations, like everything else in your recovery plan, should stand up to the cold, unpressured light of reason.

If you overshop not *for* somebody else but *with* somebody else—if a particular friend somehow spurs you into overshopping—this, too, can be a response to social pressure. That's why looking at *with whom* you shop may be as important as looking at *why* and *where*:

> Not a week went by that Eileen (you'll remember her from the Daily Weigh-ins) didn't get a call from her close friend Jill, out at a store, who'd whet her appetite for a bottle of perfume, a scarf, or a beach cover-up that "has your name all over it, and at a great price, too!" Jill would offer to put it on her credit card; Eileen could pay her back when she had the money. Reeled in by her friend's "generosity" in acting as personal shopper, Eileen almost always took this bait, despite her massive and mounting credit card debt. She experienced Jill's behavior as caring and didn't want to run the risk that she'd feel rejected. Besides, she considered Jill's taste terrific.

Jill's behavior here isn't caring at all, especially because she knows the extent of Eileen's debt and the pain she's in because of it. If you have a friend who encourages your overshopping habit, his or her behavior isn't caring either. Don't shop together anymore. Try to find a new axis for the friendship or give it up. Even if your enabler is a family member, find a way to stop shopping together.

Your Children

Children rate a subsection of their own, because, particularly when they're small, they get virtually everything from us. It's entirely natural, then, that they ask us for gifts. And they do—*more* than is entirely natural. The degree to which the multibillion-dollar marketing machine has seized control of the hearts and minds of our children is an appalling lesson in media savvy. Eighteen-month-old babies recognize logos, and children request brands as soon as they can speak.[5] By age three or three and a half, children begin to believe that brands communicate their personal qualities: they're "cool," for example, or "smart." All the bombardment—to the tune of $15 billion a year spent pitching products to children—hops children up on material wants. And we love our children. No surprise, then, that in a recent study, *half* the twelve- to thirteen-year-olds surveyed said they were usually successful in getting something they saw advertised, even if their parents didn't want them to have it.[6] But this type of "love" is costly. An abundance of research shows that placating kids with material rewards hinders their social and psychological development.[7]

How do you resist social pressure to overshop when it's coming from your own children? Apply to them some of the same tools and techniques you're applying to yourself. First, spend lots of healthy, constructive time together, and provide plenty of nonshopping alternatives for fun and learning. Then, limit their exposure to shopping magnets, so they're not as easily sucked in. In a sadly indicative recent study, 93 percent of teenage girls reported that shopping was their favorite activity.[8] Kids six to twelve now spend *five hours shopping for every hour they play outdoors.*[9]

It's reasonable and appropriate that your children ask you to buy things for them. But it's also reasonable and appropriate that some of their purchases be *planned,* especially large ones. Leave room for spontaneity, but make it general family policy not to buy anything the first time your child sees it in a store, unless you've talked about it ahead of time. Once kids are old enough, it's a good idea for them to write a list of the toys and other discretionary items they want, especially for birthdays and big holidays. You might post it on the refrigerator and have them prioritize their requests. Learning to plan, to prioritize, and to delay gratification is as important for your children as it is for you. When they're old enough, giving them an allowance and helping them to plan their own purchases is extremely valuable practice and works to ensure that your problems with overbuying don't extend into the next generation.[10]

Now *let go of guilt.* Your children don't need everything the marketing machine has dangled in front of them. They probably have an overabundance already. The average American first grader accumulates a staggering *seventy* new toys a year, along with an unprecedented number of other possessions. What your children need is *you.* Recent research shows that parents who spend less time with their children spend more money on them.[11] Instead of buying yet another thing when your child turns on the pressure, think about what he or she *really* needs and do what you can to provide *that*.

JOURNAL TIME

Identifying, Avoiding, or Deflecting Social Pressures to Buy

In your own life, where's the social pressure to buy coming from? Think about the material you've just read. Remind yourself of what you wrote in the Shopping Patterns Checklist and the You and Your Stuff Questionnaire. Look also at "Do You Overshop to Hold on to Love?" (in the "Why Do You Overshop?" section of chapter 1). Whose social pressure squeezes you into overbuying? Is there a general category, such as "the salesclerks at the big-box electronics stores," or a specific person, such as "my brother-in-law Phil"? Consider especially people with whom you have dual or multiple roles or relationships—if, for example, one of the salesclerks at the big-box electronics store is your brother-in-law Phil!

Start a new page in your journal for your particular social pressures. On it, note your three most challenging sources of social pressure to overbuy. Then write out a strategy for avoiding each source and a script—it can be from a few words to a few sentences—you can review to deal successfully with the pressure when it comes at you.

Practice your scripts aloud, preferably in front of a mirror, a few times. At first, you may feel awkward. You may think you're sounding rude, not at all the engaging and friendly person you want to be. *Keep practicing 'til you sound pleasant—and clear, assertive, and confident.* This page can then serve as a refresher when you anticipate encountering one of your sources of social pressure; review it and do a mental rehearsal before entering the social situation. If it's not possible to review it ahead of time—Michael Jones, the insurance salesman, corners you unexpectedly at a neighborhood picnic—review it afterward to see how you might have handled the situation better. Or congratulate yourself for how well you did!

In this chapter, we've explored two ways to be mindful. The first is to recognize the power of the psychologically sophisticated buy-messages we're all drowning in and then to arm ourselves with rational strategies for countering these messages. The second is to anticipate and prepare to parry another kind of pressure to buy, social pressure, wherever in our human network it may come from. These two specific ways to be mindful lead us strategically into the next chapter, where we take a more encompassing look at mindfulness and its importance in shopping.

7 | Mindful Shopping

Shopping without *over*shopping is possible; millions and millions of people do it every day. But as you know better than almost anyone, if you've gotten into the overshopping habit, it's not easy to break, especially given the reinforcement for buying that our culture constantly provides. Your challenge is to stay emotionally centered and *mindful*—of what you plan to buy; of what you can comfortably afford to spend; of what you're responding to; and, above all, of who you are and what really matters to you.

This book arms you with specific, proven techniques for shopping without overshopping. As you near the point of purchase, though, you're vulnerable to being disarmed—*unless* you adopt the self-caring stance introduced in chapter 1. First, be *calm:* shopping—at a mall, on the Internet, or even from a catalog—is almost guaranteed to stir up feelings. Do whatever you can to slow the rush, whether the feelings are negative or positive. Notice what you're feeling and thinking, the way you're responding to your internal and external environment, and then *acknowledge* your responses. *Reassure* yourself that you've all the tools and the skills you need to shop mindfully, that everything's going to be OK. Then *engage*! Go ahead and shop—mindfully. Buy what you planned to buy, where, when, and how you planned it. If somehow you slip up and overshop, look closely at how it happened, learn from the experience—and forgive yourself. Return the items you overbought—unless you're a compulsive returner—and plan, as specifically as possible, to shop more mindfully the next time. *C*alm, *a*cknowledge, *r*eassure, *e*ngage: think of this caring attitude toward yourself as *care*ful shopping.

SHOPPING WITH A PLAN

Ours is largely a culture of spur-of-the-moment, impulsive, recreational, *mindless* shopping; we typically put about as much conscious thought into it as we do into digesting. Advertisers and marketers encourage and exploit this, of course, because it's great for sales. But the truth is, we as individuals have *let* it happen. Literally and figuratively, the buck needs to stop with us.

Shopping hasn't always been mindless. Most of our country's founders, and many of the ethnic groups that subsequently arrived on our shores and settled the country, prided themselves on thrift, prudence, and vision in managing their affairs. Somewhere along the way, however, improvements in production and delivery gave goods a new and previously unimaginable variety, affordability, and availability—and shopping became a Great Adventure. We abandoned forethought or planning; we "headed out" (the phrase is apt!) to see what we might "discover." In the excitement, we lost our heads. Today, with the increased sophistication of the marketing industry and the ever-increasing ease of incurring debt, is it any wonder we're a nation of impulsive and compulsive buyers?

We've already talked about how important it is, if you want to stop overshopping, to let go of shopping as recreation. It's also essential to let go of shopping as Great Adventure. If you want spontaneous adventure in your life, by all means go for it. Follow the yellow brick road or hunt wild mushrooms in the woods behind your house—whatever you find exciting. But don't look for spontaneous adventure at the mall or on Internet auction sites, on television shopping channels or at any other commercial venue. *Plan* your purchases and *prepare* for the trip.

One further point: don't mix shopping with eating, drinking, or recreational drugs. These prolong your stay and loosen your resolve.

Planning Your Purchase

I strongly recommend that you set down in writing, in your Shopping Journal, a *plan* for each shopping trip you make, whether the trip's virtual or physical, whether you're sitting or standing. If you're shopping on the Internet or by phone, keep the specific plan open beside you; this will help you limit browsing and stay mindful. If you're shopping away from home, have your plan with you and review it before you begin.

What should a plan look like? It should specify the following things:

Identification of item and purpose. Compile a list of the specific item or items you intend to purchase. If you don't know the exact item yet, be as specific as you can about what you're looking for. Much better, for example, than "something to wear to Jamie's engagement party" would be "a dress for Jamie's engagement party that will work with my black suede pumps and bag." Not "a new computer monitor" but "a nineteen-inch flat-panel LED monitor." Jot down what you'll use each item for.

Necessity Score. Honestly assess how necessary each item is and assign it a Necessity Score between 0 and 1, the same way you do in the Daily Weigh-in. Keep in mind the practical questions that bear on necessity: How soon will I be able to make use of each item? Will I unpack it, remove tags and stickers, and install it in my life in a timely manner? Do I have the skills required to install or use it? Can I afford the time and money to maintain it?

Maximum $. Write down your ceiling, the maximum dollar amount you're willing to pay for each item on your list.

When. Build in a delay between making and executing your plan. Even a ten-minute delay between the time you make an Internet shopping plan and the time you get on the computer can help you calm down and shop more mindfully. For larger purchases, make it a day, a week, or a month. During the delay, consider whether you might need support—perhaps your Shopping Support Buddy, who'll remind you of your plan, either in person or by phone, at the critical moment. If so, be sure you've made arrangements for the contact.

Where. Write down where you'll shop, being sure to avoid the danger zones you've identified. For brick-and-mortar shopping, think through the route you'll take—to the mall, through the mall, and through the store—so you can avoid dangerously tempting departments. For Internet shopping, write down which sites you'll visit and/or which keywords you'll search. For catalog or magazine shopping, write down which titles you'll browse on a given day. Avoid side trips as much as possible; try to chart a direct course to your planned purchase. Be specific, accurate, and complete with this plan.

With/for whom. Consider shopping with a friend or family member who'll support you in not overshopping. Avoid overshopping "buddies" who are likely to egg you on; suggest other activities to do with them. Also consider *for whom* you're shopping. Overshoppers sometimes see tempting items that they can't quite justify buying for themselves but can allow themselves to buy for someone else. Right here in your plan, get clear about *what* items you're planning to purchase, and *for whom*. If they're for someone else, ask yourself whether that person really wants or needs what you're planning to buy, or is this, perhaps, a justification for you to buy it for yourself?

How long. Regardless of where you plan to shop, you need to limit browsing time: the longer you browse, the more you'll buy. But don't rush either; staying calm is crucial to staying on track. So give yourself a browsing interval that's long enough to calmly undertake the necessary searches and comparisons, and *too short* to permit wandering into temptation. If your allotted time expires before you complete your transaction, stop. If you're in a store, walk out. Observe, calmly and with compassion, how you feel about this "interruption"—you may be surprised at the intensity of your feelings. We'll explore this further in chapter 10, doing a "not-to-buy" walk-through.

Payment method. Cash, check, or debit card only! When using cash, it's a good idea to segregate your shopping money from your other funds; the pocket in your journal is a good place for it. Use a debit card for Internet or catalog shopping if and only if you feel secure about the venue. If you're going to shop at a mall or stand-alone store, consider loading your debit card and ID into your journal pocket and locking your wallet in your trunk. That way, you can't be tempted to "bury" something extra on a credit card or fork over cash you hadn't planned to spend.

Risk. When you've written out your plan, estimate your risk of overshopping. If the plan seems too risky, revise it. If there's still a substantial danger of overshopping, postpone the shopping trip until you feel more in control. When you do shop, be sure to keep your journal with you, and have a contingency plan in case the vibes to overbuy get too intense.

REGULAR PRACTICE

Developing Awareness and the "Mindful Pause"

Mindful shopping, the habit you want to develop, doesn't mean the absence of feeling but rather the presence and engagement of your mind. You *observe* what you're feeling and thinking, what your heart and head are saying. You pay attention to what your body and soul are saying as well. You notice how you're responding to your environment. You remember what you're shopping for, and you stay on track. You remember how much you intended to spend, and you limit your purchases to what you can comfortably afford. You act on *your* agenda, unswayed by advertisers' or salespeople's agendas or tactics aimed at pulling you off course. Your purchasing decisions lock into the grander plan of who you *are;* they aren't based on anyone else's ideas or even on your own fantasies of who you might *become*. Mindfulness helps you make decisions based on conscious choice rather than impulse. In chapter 9, we'll look more closely at what it takes to become mindful. For now, when you shop, just practice paying attention to your bodily sensations, your emotions, your thoughts, and your actions.

Stay self-aware, for example, as you enter a mall. You may immediately have disturbing thoughts and feelings and a strong urge to overshop, or that may happen when you begin to shop. Notice any "justifiers" running through your mind, begging for "permission" to make purchases you don't feel quite right about (consult your Shopping Patterns Checklist if you need a refresher on these). Notice if your heart pounds or your breath quickens or your palms sweat; notice any tension or elation. The more attuned you are to what you're feeling or thinking or doing—the more clearly you observe yourself—the easier it will be to redirect some of your needs and desires, and the more likely you are to resist overshopping when you shop.

A particularly critical step here is the *Mindful Pause*. The time you've taken to think about and write down your purchasing plan constitutes the first of two opportunities to slow down and mindfully consider a purchase. After you've found an item that you want to purchase—but before you pay for it—take a Mindful Pause. If you're in a store, walk away from or put down your item(s), or have the salesperson or the person you're shopping with hold it, and then find a place to sit. Slow down; take a few full, deep breaths; center yourself. If you've been Internet shopping, sit down in a peaceful place away from the computer. You may need strong resolve to take even this short break; the prevailing winds to buy can blow with gale force. But the pause costs you nothing—and it preserves all your options. It interrupts the *automatic* buying response, giving you the choice to buy or not to buy, helping you become aware that you *have* a choice. In these few moments, take internal stock. Look at your Reminder Card and ask yourself and answer the questions:

1. *Why am I here?* Are you here to execute a planned purchase, or did you get pulled off course? What brought you to this point? Are you trying to get away from someone or something? Is your urge to buy an attempt to move toward some desired state?

2. *How do I feel?* Shine the spotlight of your self-awareness onto your bodily sensations and your emotions. What bodily sensation, feeling state, and thought have prompted you to want to buy this?

3. *Do I need this?* Keep in mind the difference between wants and needs. Don't be tempted to buy anything that you or someone else *might* need or want someday for some reason; if you don't know who it's going to and when, don't buy it. If an item you're considering wasn't planned, how necessary do you think it really is? Listen for "justifiers," especially the ones you identified previously in the Shopping Patterns Checklist. Overshoppers who kick the habit often arrive at a key phrase, such as a Metta Tag, to counteract self-justifications for overbuying—for example, "I can live without this," or "I know what I really need. This ain't it."

4. *What if I wait?* OK, let's say you've found an item you'd definitely like in your life and might even need. Do you need it *now*? Will you feel the same way tomorrow? Next week? Might you change your mind altogether? Give it a bit more time. Consider the possibility of not allowing yourself to buy anything the first day you see it.

5. *How will I pay for it?* Think of this question in both narrow and broad terms. Cash, check, or debit card, to be sure, but not that alone. Have you the time and energy to add this to your life? Are

there important hidden costs—maintenance over time, the tension it might cause at home? If you buy this now, what might you have to do without?

6. *Where will I put it?* Be really honest with yourself here: Have you space for this in your home and in your life? Are your closets, your workroom, your playroom, or your storage locker already bulging with stuff? Do you have a clear idea of where you'll store it? Can you commit to a date in the near future when it will be fully installed and in use? If it's a gift, do you know when you'll give it? Will it get used as intended? Even a single "no" means you don't have space for it: you're overshopping. Wait until you're ready to give it a good home.

Taking a Mindful Pause before each purchase on any given shopping day can help you stay off of the consumer merry-go-round. With practice, you'll gain more self-awareness and self-control; until then, purchase just one or two items per shopping excursion. Initially, you'll probably need a long Mindful Pause, long enough to center yourself and fully consider the Reminder Card questions. When you can more easily shop without overshopping, a shorter pause should work.

JOURNAL TIME: REVIEWING YOUR PURCHASE

After you've finished your shopping—either immediately afterward or when you get home or that night, at the latest—take the next step on the path to mindful shopping: reviewing your purchase. Your job was to create a viable plan and execute it, taking a Mindful Pause before the purchase. How did it go? How closely did your experience match your plan? In your journal, answer these questions and explore any difficulties you had in following through.

If you overshopped, write down what you bought, giving each purchase a Necessity Score and specifying what you paid for it. Did you identify your trigger? Your underlying need? Did you think about an alternative activity? Did you plan your purchase and take a Mindful Pause before buying? Write a sentence or two about how your plan went awry. Now try rewriting the script. What else could you have done with your time and money? How might this story have had a happier ending?

WHEN THE DEED IS DONE:
RETURNING, RESELLING, AND RECYCLING

You meant to stick to your plan today—but a brown beret sang to you from the hat tree as you walked into Talbots, and a butterfly stick pin flitted across the counter at Zales, and all the salt spreaders at Home Depot were calling you. Maybe you got caught up in the moment, then got home and realized you'd bought something you can't afford, don't need, probably won't even use. You've made a mistake, and you're stricken with remorse, guilt, or anxiety. Perhaps your pursuit of the perfect thing—multifunction printer/scanner/copier, animal-print bathrobe, whatever rainbow of perfection you happen to be chasing—has seduced you. Perhaps the endless choice in everything from blue jeans to blue cheese has dazzled and baffled you. Maybe you were browsing or surfing because, you now realize, you wanted activity, distraction—not the item itself. What now? Do you wave the white flag and shove your MasterCard bill even farther under the pile? Do you pull the mathematical wool over your eyes, dump a few old things, and then argue that as long as one thing goes out when another comes in, you're not *really* overshopping? No! *Return* anything you can. *Resell* or *recycle* anything you can't.

Returning

The return has two faces. As an occasional correction to an occasional mistake, it's terrific—clean, final, redemptive. And if you overshop but rarely take things back, then *forcing* yourself to return may be the best way to own up to your problem. Instead of letting yourself off the hook with "Oh, well, too late now. I bought it; I may as well keep it," you recognize that you've overshopped, you reflect on it—and then you take the trouble to rectify it. This process, "doing the non-habitual," is the fourth *R* of Pema Chödrön's prescription for getting unhooked, first introduced in chapter 2. Even if you've missed the first *R*, refraining from buying it in the first place, this kind of returning can help you detach from overshopping. (Be warned, though: because returns cost stores money, their policies are tightening. And these days, stores use sophisticated software to track returns as well as returners; they're on the alert for both fraud and abuse.)

Tips on Returning
- Keep all tags intact and save your receipts in an orderly way. The pocket of your Shopping Journal is perfect for this purpose.
- If you know you might return it, acknowledge this up front. Tell the salesperson that you want to take it home and try it out. If you then return it, you can feel more comfortable about doing so.
- If you're taking it home to try it out, pay with cash or a debit card, not a check. Checks take time to clear, delaying the return and clouding your decision.
- Never use returning one item as a justification for buying another. When you've made your return, don't look back—or at anything else that day. Walk out of the store, empty of hand, full of heart.

Compulsive returning is the other face. As a *habit,* returning is not a solution to overshopping but an extension of the problem. The compulsive returner fails to understand that in shopping, as in physics, material things and energy are related. She may undo the financial consequences of impulsive buying, but at a high price in time and energy. It's not unlike the high cost of credit card debt, in which you end up paying double, triple, or worse for the items you've charged. With compulsive returns, you end up spending two, three, or more times the energy and hours. And these resources are far more precious than your money—they're irreplaceable.

Habitual returners combine two seemingly contradictory tendencies: they're highly impulsive, yet they have a great deal of difficulty making up their minds. In addition, they're often in denial, completely out of touch with the huge expenditure of time and energy their habit costs them.

Are You a Compulsive Returner?
- Could you reasonably call the trunk of your car "the halfway house," because there's always a lot of stuff in it, either on the way home from the store or on the way back to it?
- Do you habitually have shopping bags or packages lined up in your closet or by your front door, ready to be taken or mailed back to the place where you bought them?

- Do you frequently buy things you don't need, won't use, or can't afford (swept up by the chemical "high of the buy") and then, when you get home and come to your senses, feel guilt and remorse and rush to return them?
- Do you perennially "trade up," returning a purchase you've made because you've found something a little more perfect?
- Do you time a return so that the salesperson who helped you buy won't be there to see it? Do you ask someone else to do the returning for you?
- Do you deny problem shopping, since the net effect of regular returns makes it seem as if you're not buying that much?

If you recognize yourself in the questions above, having said "yes" to at least a couple of them, your road to recovery may well begin with letting go of returns. Making it a personal policy *not* to return can compel you to face up to your overshopping—and help you *prevent* it, instead of squandering time and energy trying to *undo* it. And when you *do* shop, this policy will force you to be more decisive and will lead to better decisions. If you can't make up your mind—if you think you might wind up wanting to return the item—don't buy it! Leave it there! (You can always come back later if, upon reflection, you're really sure you want it.) Above all, don't kid yourself. Compulsive returning *is* overshopping. You're merely *dis*charging your *batteries* instead of *charging* your *credit card*.

Reselling

While you're working to stop overshopping, you need to deal with the consequences of having overshopped previously. If there are items you need to unload, mistakes you need to get free of—whether to recoup some of your money, to rid yourself of clutter, or just to pare down—reselling can be an option worth considering. See craigslist (www.craigslist.org), iSoldIt (www.i-soldit.com), and Yahoo.org Classifieds (http://classifieds.yahoo.com).

But, as with returning, there are two faces, the occasional and the compulsive. The occasional resale makes for good riddance and puts some money in your pocket (though, in general, it's substantially less than you originally spent). Compulsive reselling, on the other hand, is just compulsive shopping from a different angle: more time and energy poured into commerce, less of both available for your real life.

Tips for the Occasional Reseller

- Know that, as a reseller, you'll generally take a loss. You're unlikely to be able to pre-sent the item in as attractive a setting, to as willing a buyer, for as high a price.
- Internet auction sites may be a viable way to go, but don't do it yourself. Let drop-off establishments such as iSoldIt or eBay do your selling. Yes, they take a commission; that's their business. *Your* business is to get away from all this buying and selling. And go for sure sale and lower price rather than risk getting the item back by going for top dollar.
- Drop the item off and *let it go*.
- Don't ignore traditional vehicles for reselling—an ad in the classifieds, postings on bulletin boards, a garage sale.

Keep an eye on your motives. Occasional reselling to unload is reasonable behavior. If it slides into something else—the excitement of commerce, a way to meet social needs—step back and find a healthier way to meet those needs.

Recycling

Recycling is a third vehicle for unloading. When you recycle, you give things away, either to those who may value them or to those who may need them. Recycling clears your space (both physical and emotional) and is friendly to the planet. Recycled items get reused rather than thrown away, and you get to feel legitimately good about your generosity. Giving things away can reinforce your decision to buy less in the future.

Tips for Recyclers

- When you give it away, *let it go*. Give up any emotional attachment to the gift. Release it like a bird from your hand and smile as it flies away.
- Recycle to people you know only when you're sure you've found an ideal match. Seeing someone who matters to you

cherish something that was yours brings a special joy to your heart. But don't put both of you in an awkward position, the recipient for hating your sweater, you for having given it to an ingrate.

Consider giving to charity fund-raising auctions, the Salvation Army, or an organization such as Goodwill—and taking the tax deduction that goes with it. Look at local charities you can find in a phone book or with a search engine, or try Freecycle (www.freecycle.org).

Letting Go

We all make mistakes. Wise people learn from those mistakes, forgive themselves, move on—and do better next time. If you've made a purchase you regret, calmly acknowledge the mistake and then get on with your life. Do what you can to rectify it, and learn from the experience. If you've put something on layaway and realized you shouldn't have, *let it go:* don't throw good money after bad. Mindful returns, resale, and recycling all have their place. And sometimes, you simply have to let things go or throw them away. Getting stuff out of your possession can help you flush the guilt along with the stuff.

Consider all of these vehicles for unloading like the training wheels on a bicycle. As you overcome your shopping demons, as you gain control and make better shopping decisions, the need for them will fall away—and you'll speed along through your life with less friction and more fulfillment.

REINFORCING YOUR PROGRESS BY REWARDING IT

A fundamental principle of psychology is that rewards reinforce behavior. Confront a mouse with two identical doorways: to the left, he gets nothing, to the right, a tasty food pellet. Very quickly, he turns unfailingly to the right. Although we're not mice, we sure want the cheese. So the same principle applies to us: reward a behavior and you reinforce it, making it more likely to occur again. Whenever you choose the right doorway in your struggle with shopping, whenever you take a step in the right direction, reward yourself. This will give a positive flavor to your choice and make the right move likelier the next time.

The trick here is to find rewards that don't undermine your goal. Sadly, our consumer culture has taught us to equate rewards with tangible, material things. But rewards come in many nonmaterial shapes and sizes as well. And since research shows that we're happier having experiences than we are getting stuff, this is actually a double dip. Here, we'll look at two kinds of rewards, what we'll call kudos and playdates. Each offers you a chance to feel good about yourself and enjoy the moment while at the same time making the future more promising.

Kudos

For our purposes, kudos are congratulations or affirmations, positive statements about yourself that you think, write down, or say to yourself—preferably in the mirror—and give yourself a chance to *believe*. This last is critical: it's important that your kudos not be mechanical, mere lip service; you must own them, accept them, *revel* in them. Because overshoppers often have a problem with self-esteem, accepting your own congratulations may take some practice. But the result is more than worth the effort. You're celebrating your power and control when you look yourself in the eye and say, "I stayed out of the stores after work today, even though my boss went ballistic and shopping's my usual salve for that kind of wound. It wasn't easy. I'm very proud of myself. This is beginning to work!" You're enjoying an important victory, and you're making the next victory more probable.

There are many kinds of kudos. You can celebrate what you've done: "I listened to a twenty-minute meditation tape instead of browsing online this afternoon. So much better for me! I felt relaxed and calm, much more in control. . . . *Yes!*" Celebrate what you already are or are in the process of becoming ("I'm a deeply caring parent," or "I'm learning to manage my money wisely"). You can celebrate your capacities ("I'm able to take on strenuous challenges like a shopping addiction") or your wisdom ("I'm grateful for all that I have," or "I recognize that inner wealth is the kind that counts"). Add to your Metta Tags page any new kudos that feel particularly good.

Wonderfully convenient, kudos are always available and can be given immediately after you resist a trigger. Getting them not only feels good but, to reiterate, also reinforces your progress. Fully *receive* your kudos; bask in their warmth.

Playdates

Playdates are pleasurable activities, free or affordable, that you give yourself for having broken the chain between trigger and purchase. A playdate can be anything from a movie to an afternoon of bridge, from a morning at the museum to an all-day hike in the country, from a ride on a ferry to an evening of stargazing. It needn't happen immediately after you've successfully resisted a trigger, but it should celebrate that resistance. You might say to yourself, "Today I got my credit card bill, and there wasn't a single new purchase on it. I deserve to take a vacation day to look at fall foliage." And then go and do it!

Some playdates will reward your progress almost immediately. You pass the jewelry store, catch your breath at a blue sapphire bracelet in the window, pause and take stock—and then walk on. Since every success is important, you celebrate with a detour to the community garden in your neighborhood.

Many of the acts of self-kindness and the tailor-made alternatives to overshopping—activities that fulfill the needs you're *really* shopping for—make fabulous playdates. As alternatives to shopping, those activities are meant to keep you from buying, to healthily distract you from the urge and still more healthily fulfill the authentic human need that underlies it. Playdates are activity rewards for not having bought, for having taken steps in the right direction. Indeed, what starts out as a tailor-made alternative often morphs into a playdate.

It's vital to remember that overcoming a shopping addiction is no small matter; it's a very big deal. Every move you make toward that end deserves a reward. Celebrate your progress with kudos and playdates. They'll warm your heart as they solidify your progress.

8 | Enlisting the Body and the Heart

In this chapter and the next, we focus on the four central resources of every overshopper: body, heart, mind, and soul. Here we look specifically at the ways that body and heart can guide—or misdirect—us in the struggle against compulsive shopping. (We'll look at mind and soul in chapter 9.) We start with the oft-ignored wisdom of the body, our natural radar system, and then turn to the emotional precisions of the heart.

THE LANGUAGE OF THE BODY: PHYSICAL SENSATIONS

Why start with the body? Because here is where the unvoiced expressions of heart, head, and spirit reside, where half-formed emotions, thoughts, and longings assume a presence, if not a shape. There is a body wisdom, born of everything we've ever experienced. If heeded, it helps us to do right by ourselves.

This is far less mystical than it sounds. The body is many things: a remarkable engine for physical action, a complex network of perceptual sensors, a seat of deepest pleasures. It is also a source of essential information, a guard always on alert, signaling us when something needs attention. But body wisdom is often drowned out by the noisier calls of heart and head, so we begin this chapter by focusing on this quiet ally. Noticing body sensations—and expanding your awareness by doing so—can clue you in to shopping impulses and reduce their intensity. Attention to the body, like attention to thought, feeling, and spirituality, can help you eliminate harmful habits.

Of course, attending to the body means bringing the mind to it, focusing your head on what your body has to tell you. To do this, to pick up the body's radar, you must bring your mind wholly to the present moment. If the mind is busy ruminating about the past or the future, it's unavailable to the body; it's off-line. Tuning in to the body, noting and releasing its tensions and processing whatever feelings and thoughts accompany them—that mutes the background noise and gets you fully in touch with yourself.

Let's sum up this body talk more directly: paying attention to your body is essential to your recovery from overshopping. The body remembers all your past experiences, including every associated thought, feeling, and action; and the overshopping impulse is often a way to avoid experiencing some of the more unpleasant thoughts and feelings stored there. Until you allow yourself to become aware of these thoughts and feelings and actually experience them, you cannot release them and you remain enslaved to them.

A metaphor may be useful here. Imagine the body as a refrigerator. Ideally, you use what's inside the refrigerator in a timely manner, during its proper shelf life. Suppose, however, you leave some things in the back of a bin or behind some bottles and forget about them. After a while, they begin to spoil; perhaps you notice a slight odor of sour milk as you pass the fridge. Here you really need to take action: open up the fridge and clean it out. But maybe you're busy, eating out a lot, not cooking, and you're able to cover up the smell with room deodorizer. Another week goes by, and now worse odors seep from the fridge. The room freshener doesn't cover them anymore, so you stay out of the kitchen. The worse the odors get, the less you want to deal with them. You order in food for all your meals, or you eat out. More time passes, and eventually your whole place is affected. The smell is everywhere and overpowering. You're sleeping poorly, you can't have friends over, you don't want to live there anymore.

The point here is straightforward: passively keeping the door closed on our experiences, being unwilling to work with what's inside, has active consequences. The stuff we'd rather not deal with affects our lives adversely. We need to clean it up, or else we're forced into more and more negative, even crippling, compromises. If we want to reclaim our living space, we have to open the refrigerator door, look at what's inside, toss out the stuff that's rotten, and make room for fresher, healthier things. How do we do that? By sitting quietly or moving our bodies mindfully. When we do this—without distracting ourselves with the external input of music, reading, cell phones, or television—when, in short, we stop running from whatever it is we're running from, then our bodies can begin to process the feelings and thoughts that reside there.

But connecting with your physical sensations is not always easy. At first, it may be difficult to identify exactly what's going on in your body, or to locate it specifically, or to distinguish a physical feeling from an emotional one. Our minds have a way of distracting us from our bodies. This may have been an important protective mechanism when we were growing up—especially for those of us with a history of emotional, physical, or sexual abuse or trauma—but the mechanism is now a handicap. It tells us to run away from our own experience, to hide in the bramble bushes of overshopping, to deafen ourselves to what the body is saying, even if it means getting pricked by thorns.

EXERCISE

The Body Scan

The Body Scan, an age-old process designed to help you connect with your physical sensations, is a way to begin overcoming this escapist mechanism. It helps you to hear what your body is telling you. And this, along with the other tools, skills, and strategies you're acquiring, makes it possible to deal with troubling feelings, thoughts, memories, or images in a far healthier way than by overshopping. The text of the Body Scan, along with a figure for recording your experience of it, follows. (Make photocopies of the figure, use a fresh one for each scan, and record your observations underneath it.) Either have somebody read you the scan as you do it, or download the audio file of my voice guiding you at www.stoppingovershopping.com/audiofiles. Give yourself twenty-five minutes of uninterrupted time to do the scan and then respond to it.

Sit comfortably on a chair or lie down, whichever makes more sense to you. If you lie down, you'll want to have a mat or rug to protect you from the hardness of the floor. The point is to be comfortable and relaxed. Just keep in mind that it's easier to fall asleep if you're lying down, and you want to stay alert for this process.

Now allow yourself to take a deep breath down into your abdomen. . . . Take another deep breath, and now put your hands on your tummy and see if they move when you take a breath. . . . Take a deep breath down into your abdomen. Notice the expansion of your belly on the in-breath and how it flattens on the out. . . . Are your hands moving when you take a breath? Take a few more deep breaths, allowing your tummy to expand on the in and flatten on the out. . . . Good. Let yourself continue to breathe deeply, just like that. . . . Every so often, I'll remind you to check and make sure that you're breathing deeply.

Next, as I guide you, walk your way through your body with your mind. As you put your awareness into different parts of your body, you may feel different sensations: you may feel warmth or heat . . . cold or tingling . . . pressure, tension, ache, or strength—or perhaps no sensation at all. Allow everything you observe; there's no wrong way to do this. Whatever you notice is simply what you notice, and whatever you notice is good. You may have a particular thought or emotion about a part of your body. This is common. See if you can notice and allow whatever comes up—physical sensation, thought, or emotion. Simply let it be there as you observe and gather whatever information you can.

At some point in the scan, you may find yourself drifting off, your mind becoming sleepy. This is a normal response, a habit the mind has picked up: *not* to focus on the body. If you notice yourself drifting off, acknowledge it and make an effort to bring yourself back to the scan. Don't worry about what you may have missed while you were dozing. Just bring yourself back to whatever I'm saying.

Now let your awareness go to your feet. Notice them and pay attention to any sensations you feel there. . . . Then, let your awareness move from your feet into your ankles. . . . What's going on there? . . . Next, move your awareness up into your calves. What do they feel like? . . . Continuing up your legs, stop at your knees and put your awareness there. . . . Now move up to your thighs. . . . Feel the backs of your thighs touching whatever they're touching, the back of the chair, perhaps, or the floor. What do they feel like? And the fronts of your thighs . . . what sensation is there?

Now move your awareness up and notice your bottom. Feel how it feels. . . . Be aware of the part that's making contact with the chair, the couch, or the floor. . . . Notice the points of contact, and then move forward to your lower abdomen and check your breath. . . . Make sure you're still breathing fully and deeply. . . .

Next, let your attention move into your hips. . . . What do you notice there? . . . And now turn your attention toward your pelvic or groin area. . . . Are you still with me? What do you notice? . . .

Now move your attention up into your lower back. Take a deep breath— breathe three-dimensionally, as if you were inflating a balloon. Are your hands moving as you breathe into your abdomen? Invite this area to relax. . . . It's completely normal for your stomach to stick out.

Now allow yourself to move your attention farther up your torso. . . . Try to isolate your middle back and your upper back. . . . What sensations are there? . . . Now let's move into the chest and breast area. . . . Be aware of what you notice as you scan this area. Many of us unconsciously constrict our chests in an effort to protect our tender hearts. Notice if your chest is constricted, and, if so, allow it to fill and expand. As you breathe into your chest, let yourself notice what you feel.

Now let's move to your hands and see what sensations you notice there. . . . Focus your attention on your fingers first. What do you notice there? . . . Then, little by little, gradually walk your attention up your arms. . . . Notice first any sensation in your wrists . . . then move your attention up to your forearms. What's there? . . . What do you notice about your elbows? . . . And now move your attention into your upper arms. . . . What do you notice here?

As you continue, turn your attention to your shoulder joints. . . . Notice your shoulder blades, your upper back. . . . And now rest your attention on your neck. What does your neck feel like? . . .

Now let yourself focus on your jaw. . . . What do you notice? Do you feel clenching or tension, perhaps? . . . Now bring your attention into your throat. . . . What sensations do you notice? . . . Any thoughts? . . . Emotions? . . . Pay attention to your face: your mouth . . . your nose . . . your ears. . . . What sensations do you notice? You might pay special attention to the muscles around your eyes. Notice your forehead. What can you sense there? . . . When you focus on your whole head, what sensations are there?

And now bring your awareness to the top of your head. Let yourself imagine a fountain of white light coming into the top of your head, filling your whole body with healing energy . . . relaxing and neutralizing any bits of tension that may be lingering in your body. This unique white light filters out any negative energy. You're filled with this white light . . . surrounded by it. . . .

And now, bring your awareness back to your breath. . . . Let yourself take several deep abdominal breaths. . . . Lie or sit there quietly, experiencing the gentle energy of each inhalation and exhalation, one after the other, wave after wave. . . . And become aware of the wholeness of your body, skin and muscles, organs and bones, all functioning together miraculously: all of those parts intertwined, helping one another, giving you feedback about which areas hold stress and which hold comfort, telling you which areas feel more sensation and which feel little or no sensation. Thank your body for this information, this gift. It's so easy to forget to thank our bodies for all that they do for us, for carrying us through each day and bringing us so much pleasure. Then slowly, slowly, whenever you're ready, come back to the room and then open your eyes.

Congratulations on completing your first Body Scan! Often the hardest part is just showing up and doing it. Now it's time to record and expand upon your experience. On a photocopy of the figure on page 182, indicate the three areas that were the most significant for you as you listened and took a mental tour of your body. These might be areas where you (a) noticed but couldn't pinpoint sensations, (b) noticed and could identify particular sensations, or (c) noticed little or no sensation. They might be areas you had thoughts or feelings about, or areas you remember hearing mentioned but then become distracted or dozed off. Number and circle these significant areas or draw how the sensation looked or felt to you.

Once you've indicated each area, name it on your photocopy and make notes about what you experienced. The following questions might be useful prompts: What did you notice about the quality of the sensation? Did it

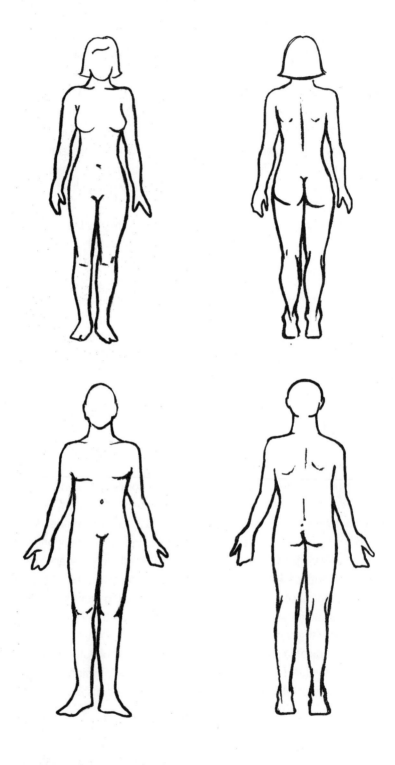

feel close to the surface, deep inside, or in both places? Which sensations did you notice more on the surface of your body, which deep inside? What kind of thoughts or feelings did you have about the sensations? Did the sensations change as you observed them? If so, how?

Keep in mind that anything and everything you experience during the Body Scan is valid. Also, know that your experience may be different each time and may change significantly. If you didn't get what you expected from the Body Scan, or didn't experience much at all, that's fine. Just work with what you *did* get.

JOURNAL TIME

Body Scan Follow-up

Now answer these questions in your journal about your experience with the Body Scan:

1. How did you feel after the Body Scan?
2. What was the overall effect on you?
3. What did you discover that could be helpful?
4. How will you use this when you have an urge to shop?

Do the Body Scan every other day for the next two weeks in order to get more acquainted with the language of your body. You may find that you can't answer some of the questions, but don't be discouraged if your body is talking to you in a way you don't yet understand. With practice, you'll begin to pick up more of your body's language. Listen with attention and acceptance to the messages your body is giving you. At the end of two weeks, take a look at the six or seven different sets of figures and questions, examining them as if they were different angles of a single subject. Although you may have different reactions each time, patterns will likely emerge.

Your ultimate goal here is to be able to do a quick Body Scan on your own at any time—when you have the impulse to shop, when you've been able to resist, or when you've actually shopped. Checking in with your body at these different points will open the refrigerator door. Taking the time to notice your body's sensations, signals, and needs will help you to control your overshopping: being aware of your bodily sensations can slow you down, give you information about what you really need, and reduce the intensity of the shopping impulse. Doing the Body Scan cultivates mindfulness and enhances your capacity to be present. It bears repeating that there is wisdom in the body; doing the scan will help you access that wisdom. Keep doing it, no matter what your experience is. Becoming fluent in the language of the body is a gateway to the language of the heart, which we now explore, and also to the language of the mind and the soul, which we explore in chapter 9.

THE LANGUAGE OF THE HEART: FEELINGS

The heart speaks the language of feelings, with an emotional alphabet that ranges from aching to zealous, with an infinite number of shades in between. Many of us have been taught to repress, deny, or distrust feelings or to mask, hide, or disregard them. Feelings, however, will come out; and if we don't express them in words, we're apt to express them through self-destructive behavior. (If you're this far along in the book, you've certainly discovered that.) How often are your overshopping impulses triggered by the urge to escape from— or express—some negative emotion? It might be sadness, fear, loneliness, shame, anger, or any of a host of other shades of negative emotional experience. Or maybe you've learned that, for you, overshopping is a way of trying to create, maintain, or enhance some positive feeling. You also know by now that, whether your feelings are negative or positive, regulating them by overshopping is ultimately unsuccessful, no matter how attractive in the moment. Let's look at a couple of examples.

Ted, a forty-seven-year-old pharmaceutical rep, compulsively bought CDs and DVDs—to the tune of *twenty-two thousand* discs! (His wife said it was like being married to Crazy Eddie.) Working with his Shopping Journal, he began to realize that the urge to buy was associated with a feeling of fear: his hands would sweat and his heart would speed up when he came across a disc that he didn't already own. Shortly after this physiological recognition, he realized it was the "limited-time-only" sales pitch that particularly triggered him, especially on the Internet. If he didn't buy immediately, he feared, the item would disappear forever—even though he knew that "limited-time-only" offers actually appeared over and over again. Eventually, a startling hypothesis occurred to him: he had lost his father suddenly and unexpectedly when he was eight years old, and he wondered whether his fear of "losing" an item forever was related to the trauma of that early loss. Talking openly about his father's death and gradually "metabolizing" his insight led to a significant decrease in his overshopping. Ted redirected his impulse into saving money; he had recently become a father himself and did not want to abandon *his* child by being unable to provide for his young son's needs.

Recently downsized from her corporate job with a large severance package, Cindy was at a crossroads. Would she rejoin the corporate world or do something more creative, even if it meant less money? Compulsive buying complicated her decision. Even when she'd worked, she could ill afford this habit. Now it threatened to devour her severance money and force her prematurely back to the corporate world. Working with this book, Cindy pinpointed the color and shade of the feeling that accompanied her shopping urge: excited, buoyant. More slowly, she came to realize that her need to feel excited and buoyant was connected with wanting applause, with wanting to impress: she longed to be seen, admired, and accepted as part of the group. Her desire to be creative—a need for self-actualization—became evident, too. And shopping somewhat answered all these needs: Cindy would visit her favorite store, hang out with the salespeople and the other customers, and put together very creative outfits, to her own delight and the delight of the others. She belonged! But then, of course, she felt she had to take the outfits home, even though she often knew she wouldn't wear them. Looking to meet her needs in a healthier way, Cindy hit upon the idea of joining a writers' workshop. She was exhilarated at seeing that she could paint and sculpt, not with a paintbrush or clay, but by pressing her fingers on a keyboard and watching form reveal itself as she worked and reworked her creations. Her excitement about writing was contagious, and she began to feel seen, admired, and accepted by her fellow students.

What these examples underscore is the importance of examining and articulating the trigger emotions connected with your impulse to overshop. Doing so will help you understand that impulse and redirect it. Your trigger emotions correspond with underlying needs that aren't being met; once these authentic needs are acknowledged and identified, you can choose life-enhancing ways to meet them, alternatives far healthier than overshopping.

Emotional Shades

To develop fluency in the language of the heart, you need to pay close attention to nuances of feeling. Finding the right word to express a feeling can be difficult, even frustrating. But sifting through the various shades of an emotional spectrum can give you more useful information than an all-purpose *angry* or *sad*. Often, the process of naming an emotion will help you make connections between that feeling and important issues and events in your life, connections that lead you to the discovery of an underlying need. The list below constitutes a small, suggestive thesaurus of feeling shades, broken down into some of the primary emotional colors; it's merely a beginning, intended to stimulate your search for emotional shades within a dominant color. Note that, as with colors, there are no clear boundaries here, and some words might straddle more than one category.

Negative Emotions

Words related to *anger:* affronted, betrayed, cranky, disgusted, incensed, infuriated, livid, resentful, sullen

Words related to *sadness, hurt,* and *boredom:* abandoned, alienated, depressed, despondent, disappointed, distraught, empty, heartbroken, misunderstood, rejected, sulky, tormented, upset, wretched

Words related to *inadequacy* and *unworthiness:* deficient, incompetent, ineffectual, pitiful, unskilled, useless

Words related to *shame:* degraded, disgraced, dishonored, embarrassed, humiliated, mortified, self-conscious

Words related to *disconnection:* aloof, apathetic, detached, indifferent, numb, withdrawn

Words related to *anxiety, doubt,* and *fear:* agitated, ambivalent, awkward, cowardly, distraught, fidgety, frazzled, hesitant, jittery, nervous, rattled, startled, stressed, uneasy, unsettled, vulnerable, worried

Positive Emotions

Words related to *confidence, fearlessness, interest,* and *eagerness:* absorbed, alert, capable, courageous, creative, daring, enchanted, enthusiastic, fascinated, heroic, independent, intrigued, masterful, spirited

Words related to *excitement* and *exhilaration:* amazed, aroused, dazzled, elated, enthralled, exuberant, giddy, invigorated, passionate, radiant, rapturous, vibrant

Words related to *joy, happiness, love, affection,* and *appreciation:* adoring, ardent, attractive, buoyant, caring, ecstatic, elated, infatuated, inspired, jubilant, lusty, seductive, sexy, tender

Words related to *hope* and *inspiration:* awed, encouraged, expectant, optimistic, positive

Words related to *peacefulness* and *freshness:* balanced, calm, centered, comfortable, contented, fulfilled, mellow, relaxed, renewed, restored, serene, tranquil

ON-THE-GO EXERCISE

Identifying Your Emotional Shades

You've already collected a significant amount of information about your emotions in your Shopping Journal. There, you've been recording your emotional state when you first feel the impulse to shop. You've also been answering the question "How do I feel?" while you're in the *process* of shopping. Now focus on your feelings even more closely. The further you refine your emotional vocabulary, the easier it will be to connect these emotions with the underlying needs they reflect—and then to create truly satisfying tailor-made alternatives to shopping. This is, I promise you, not an academic exercise in vocabulary. It's a psychic treasure hunt whose ultimate prize is the self you wish to become. The more precise you can be about what you feel, the easier it will be both to understand what's behind your behavior and to change it.

So, *for your next three overshopping urges,* really try to pinpoint your emotions, to articulate in your journal just what shades you're feeling. For each of the next three urges to overshop, write down the day, date, and time. First, identify the broad emotional category: is it related to one of the *negative* primary colors (anger, fear, or hurt, perhaps) or to a *positive* one (maybe happiness, exhilaration, or hope)? Next, find the word (or two) that most resonates with what you feel. Now try to identify the authentic need that prompted your trigger emotion when you experienced it. Finally, see whether you can come up with a realistic, tailor-made alternative on the spot. If you can, do it instead! If not, return to this page at a calmer moment and see whether you can think of something that might have worked.

Keep in mind that you're trying to connect the dots between a very specific emotional experience and a very specific emotional need. The more closely and honestly you can look at both your experience and your need—always from that vitally important stance of clear-sighted, nonjudgmental self-care—the more likely it is you'll design a successful and wholly satisfying tailor-made alternative. By the way, don't be surprised if the same emotional shade relates to different needs on different days. Feeling lonely, for example, might on Monday relate to a need for belonging and on Tuesday to a need for comfort.

I know: this work's no picnic. Habits die hard, and we often rationalize and justify them quite well. You may find yourself thinking, "I'm hopeless when it comes to pinpointing my feelings," or "I really don't need to do this written work; I can stop overshopping without it." Or maybe, as a particular tailor-made alternative came to mind and you dismissed it, you said to yourself, "I'd never be able to do that." The next chapter will help you develop fluency in recognizing and releasing the hold that these automatic, negative thoughts have on many of us. Before we get there, though, here's one more way to approach your emotions.

The Money Dialogue:
An Alternative Route to the Language of the Heart

The money dialogue—a deceptively simple yet extraordinarily powerful technique developed by Olivia Mellan (*Money Harmony*, 1994)—is an alternative route to the language of the heart. Mellan created it to cut through the armor that many of us wear over our emotions. As its name suggests, the money dialogue was initially designed to help people gain a greater awareness of their relationship with money and to see how the attitudes of other significant people in their lives have affected that relationship. In recent years, Mellan and her students (myself among them) have expanded the concept. We now regularly ask clients to dialogue with their credit cards, their jewelry, their Dizzy Dean baseball card—anything, in short, that they either *use* for overshopping or overshop *for*. The process begins with these instructions: "Let's imagine that your money (jewelry, credit card, or other desired object) is a *person* with whom you have a relationship. Imagine having a conversation with this *person* about how your relationship is going." The resulting dialogue typically moves back and forth a couple of times until it reaches some closure. It might sound something like this:

Money: Why do you treat me so poorly? You *seem* to value me, because you work hard to get me; but then you throw me away on things you don't really need. It makes me feel as if you don't care about me at all. If you really valued me, you'd take better care of me and be really thoughtful about whom you wanted to give me to.

Overshopper: It's true. I do respect you, or I wouldn't work so hard to get you. But when I see something I want, the issue of need simply evaporates, and I'm driven to trade you in for whatever I want. I guess at that moment, I don't much respect having you.

Money: What about respecting my value for the future rather than focusing only on immediate gratification? If you held on to me longer, I could do something much more meaningful for you.

Overshopper: I know that's true. But it's hard to keep the future in mind, especially because I'm not feeling very good about mine.

Once this initial element of the money dialogue concludes, a second element begins. Now, four voices comment on the just-completed dialogue: your mother, your father, a significant other (or some prominent person in your life, past or present), and a higher power (God, inner wisdom, the voice of reason, or some other spiritual presence). To do this, you imagine these voices responding to what they just overheard. Here's the second element of the preceding dialogue:

Mother: You've *always* been spoiled! Here you are again, trying to keep up your spoiled lifestyle.

Father: You work hard. You should spend your money however you want.

Spouse: Your hard work isn't enough to both support your spending and help us plan a future. Without savings, our dreams will go up in a puff of smoke, and we won't be able to provide well for the kids. I know that's not what you want for us.

Higher power: There's an important part of you that wants something more than "things," more than "stuff." Look beyond the quick fix, find out what you *really* need and what you want your life to be about, and then go out and get it. Do that, and you'll have your life back.

With both elements of the dialogue finished, you pause and reflect. If you've been able to let yourself really engage in this process—to be not only yourself but also your money or jewelry, your mother and father, your significant other and your higher power—then what you've written may bring together previously scattered pieces of your overshopping puzzle. You may discover, as Paula does below, something significant about the origin and nature of your relationship with your jewelry (or your money or your baseball card); you may discover what's keeping you stuck.

Paula's Dialogue

Paula's been secretly buying jewelry on the Home Shopping Network—to the tune of $35,000 in credit card debt, which she has no idea how she'll pay. Though she buys an occasional piece every now and then, the majority of her debt came from three major buying binges over the last five years, each precipitated by a significant loss in her life. The first happened when she lost her job; the second followed the death of her mother; and the third came recently, after her husband's heart attack.

Much of the HSN jewelry is unused, unworn, still in boxes in Paula's home. Her head tells her it'd make sense to sell some of it and begin paying back her debt. Her heart's hanging on to the jewelry for dear life. Until Paula created this dialogue between herself and her jewelry, she had no idea why she couldn't let go of it:

Jewelry: What's the matter? You seem upset.

Paula: Well, I'm worried about what I'm going to have to do. I've listed each piece of you and ranked it 1, 2, or 3, according to how attached I am. But the prospect of selling even my less beloved pieces feels awful, as if I'm getting rid of my best friends. Just writing it down makes me nauseated. *What's wrong with me?* You're only pieces of jewelry, not people—certainly not family like my kids, or like Joe, who's been so good to me throughout this jewelry saga. I feel so guilty. You know, when I talk about you, I sometimes refer to you as buttons, like the buttons I lost as a child; and I feel so ashamed. . . .

Jewelry: Even to *think* of getting rid of me! How *could* you? You love me and you know it; you've always loved me; you *need* me. You feel pretty when you wear me. How could you live without me?

Paula: Yes, I've loved you—but now there are *people* to consider. And I don't have to sell all of you. Maybe some of the 1s and 2s and a couple of the 3s. Maybe that wouldn't be so awful. . . . If I sold the pieces that don't mean so much to me, I could pay down some credit card debt and put a little money into a savings account.

Jewelry: Sounds like maybe I'm not number one anymore. You better think this over, sweetie, 'cause once I'm gone, you'll never have me again.

Paula: Yes, and I feel sad about that. I do love you, jewelry, but I love the people in my life more. Some of you will have to go.

The second element of Paula's jewelry dialogue went like this:

Mother: You've always been a wimp. I could never get you to do *any*thing. I even had to shop for you—you, you, you! I gave up my *life* for you. I could've *been* somebody. I was beautiful, and my hair was so blond that people couldn't stop touching it. I could have been a nurse and married somebody rich. But no, I stayed married to your loser father—just so you could have a house! You make me sick, you ingrate!

Father: I always loved you, no matter what your mother did.

Joe: The jewelry saga's been hard on both of us. When I first found out about it, I felt totally betrayed. But I see the work you're putting into this, and I think we can get past it. I'm gonna really try to support you.

Higher power: This is all pretty intimidating for you—which means you're surely onto something. Don't bury any of this; stay with it. Jewelry is only a means to an end. You're going to be all right, Paula. Be brave; stay in the present.

In therapy, Paula and I worked through her dialogue together. When we began, I was intending to read the whole dialogue aloud so that she could really hear it, but by the time I got to jewelry's second comment, I was so struck by the tone, I felt compelled to ask Paula if anyone had spoken to her the way jewelry was speaking to her now. Her response couldn't have been more spontaneous and deeply felt. "Oh my God!" she said; "that's exactly how my mother talked to me. Narcissistic, controlling, and mean—never caring who I was as a person though she said she had my best interests at heart. I've always felt guilty about my mother and what I didn't do for her when she was alive. I've felt guilty, too, about not having the courage to stand up for myself and have a life separate from my mother. I've never ever thought about this before! It feels so *right*. I can feel the connection between my jewelry and my mother. Yes, for my relationships to thrive—for *me* to thrive—I need to give up some of my jewelry. This is such a *wow* to me! I've got to let it sink in."

Then we talked about how supportive, each in a different way, the other commentaries had been. Paula came to see that she had a lot of compassion for herself when she could internalize the voices of her father, Joe, and her higher power.

JOURNAL TIME

Your Money Dialogue

Not every money dialogue will bring results as dramatic as Paula's, but the technique is almost always productive. It nearly always sheds revealing light on an important relationship. Now it's time for *you* to write a money dialogue. In deciding what to talk to—your baseball cards or your jewelry or your credit cards—think of a particular venue, or a particular category of thing, or a particular means for your overshopping. In your Shopping Journal, follow the examples above: write out what *you* say, what your personified object says in response, and so on. After your initial dialogue has concluded, add commentaries on your dialogue from your mother, your father, a significant other, and a higher power. Then step back and see what you've told yourself.

9 | Recruiting the Mind and the Soul

In this part of the book, we're looking at the four central resources of every overshopper: body, heart, mind, and soul. In the last chapter, we looked at body and heart. Now we turn to mind and soul. First, we focus on the mind's subtlety and examine its unhealthy distortions, discovering how early, unexamined messages can powerfully shape our present feelings and behavior. Then, we tackle the soul, the birthplace of transcendence—whether aesthetic, philosophical, or religious—and learn how it can balance and lighten the weight of our desire for material things.

THE LANGUAGE OF THE MIND: THOUGHTS

The mind speaks in the language of thoughts. These can be rational and conscious (such as the thoughts that are occurring to you as you're reading now and the thoughts you have as you use the strategies you're learning), or they can be automatic and habitual (such as the effortless set of steps you glide through when you get on a bicycle). Both kinds of thought are essential to our everyday functioning. We need rational thinking for all kinds of problem solving; for interactions with other people; and for creating, planning, and organizing. We need automatic thinking for efficiency and ease, to manage routine tasks in the background while we concentrate our attention elsewhere.

The primary modality of this book is rational thought. The very decision to purchase it was, I hope, a rational one. You reasoned that your overshopping problem was causing you substantial difficulties and decided that a carefully designed and successfully tested program, one whose concepts and strategies had worked for others, might help you, too. In your work thus far, you've rationally examined the consequences of your shopping behavior, financial and otherwise, and you've used reason as a tool to prepare and develop alternatives to overshopping. You've also relied on reason as you began—and continue—to connect the dots of separate shopping episodes into telltale patterns.

But until now, we haven't spoken about *automatic thoughts*, a powerful and unexamined part of our thinking that affects every corner of our lives. It's not the useful, positive elements of automatic thinking we're after. We're happy to have those. Rather, we now want to focus on, rethink, and modify instances of *negative automatic thought*, commonly referred to as *distorted thinking*. These thoughts, which we may experience as verbal ideas or as images, are unexamined and often fleeting; they seem to rise up spontaneously and negatively affect our behavior or judgments. Though they come to us in the present, they're outgrowths of early programming, of core beliefs we formed in childhood. And we hold those core beliefs to be true—though they may very well *not* be—simply because they've been with us for a long time and were developed during a period when we lacked the power and capacity to test them.

Distorted Thinking

Suppose that someone formed the core belief "I am a failure" from unhappy childhood experiences. Maybe it was a result of overly harsh and perfectionist parenting, maybe it arose because of an unrecognized handicap, or maybe it was a hypersensitive response to the pressure of highly accomplished siblings. Inside the adult, this kernel festers and grows into distorted thinking. If the adult then embarks on the work of this book and at some point slips up, he or she is likely to think, automatically, "I didn't even last a month! Ah, well,

I was bound to fail." Such thinking is, of course, a setup for further feelings of failure and tends to become a self-fulfilling prophecy. A more rational response, and a far more productive one, would be "OK. This is a huge challenge for me; I'm giving myself a pat on the back for even undertaking it. I've made three and a half weeks of solid progress, and now I've slid back a little. What I need to do is look at what happened, ask why, and figure out how to keep it from happening again."

What's particularly difficult about distorted thoughts is that they *feel like truths,* even though they aren't. And we tend, even as adults, not to examine them, because they lie beneath the surface. What we're conscious of isn't the distortion itself but the emotion that's associated with it—the hopelessness or resignation or fear. In other words, our self-talk typically goes on without any conscious recognition of the intricate connective chain that links core beliefs to underlying assumptions and then to distorted thoughts. But if you slow this process down and look individually at the links, the whole process becomes clearer and easier to manage, because, as with any chain—such as the triggers → actions → aftershocks sequence we looked at in chapter 3—you can target the weakest link. It's particularly important to do this with automatic thinking, because the process so often leads to overshopping and other negative behaviors. Below are a few specific examples of how distorted thoughts, underlying assumptions, and core beliefs are linked:

Distorted Thoughts/Images (situation-specific in most cases)	Underlying Assumptions (often understood as rules with always or never, moral imperatives with should, or conditional absolutes with If . . . then)	Core Beliefs (unconditional)
I am so stupid! I can't even balance my checkbook.	Smart people never have difficulties managing their finances.	I'm incompetent.

I'm a bad and selfish mother: today I bought a pair of shoes I didn't need, when I could've spent that money on my children.	Mothers should always think of their children first.	I'm selfish.
I ordered tickets today to a Broadway show I can't afford. I'll never succeed in this program.	I always do worse than other people.	I'm a loser.

To reiterate, your thinking style and therefore your actions, including your overshopping behaviors, are influenced by automatic thoughts, underlying assumptions, and core beliefs. Whether they were derived from family messages, difficult life situations, or cultural conditioning, we've all learned certain basic beliefs that influence what we pay attention to and how we think about ourselves and the external world. These silent assumptions are so much a part of ourselves that we tend not to recognize them; we wear them like an invisible set of blinders. But, with practice, we can identify and challenge these silent and damaging misconceptions. A rational analysis of the categories into which these misconceptions fall will help us identify the several types of logical errors behind distorted thinking. That's what we'll turn our attention to now.

A Typology of Distortions

The thought pattern errors listed below will seem almost painfully obvious. Surely, you may say, I'm smarter than *that*. Remember, however, that these patterns are the wild stallions that your unexamined core beliefs ride in on; they're the means by which you attempt to square your present life with any crooked messages from your childhood. Once you identify these errors and acknowledge the ones that apply to you, you're in a position to examine and challenge any core beliefs that are contributing to your self-destructive behavior. You'll probably find that as you become familiar with the different types of distortions, you'll recognize them almost as soon as you hear them come out of your mouth—or the mouths of other people.

As is often the case with typologies, one category may shade into another; overgeneralization, for example, is much like obsessive focus. Exact pigeonholing isn't the point here; what you're interested in is recognizing your own general areas of distorted thinking. Categories such as these have been a cornerstone of cognitive behavior therapy, a highly effective form of psychological treatment, first developed by Aaron Beck in the 1960s:[1]

- *All-or-nothing thinking:* You see things as all or nothing, black or white, good or bad—there's no middle ground. If your performance falls short of perfect, you see yourself as a total failure. *Example:* "Every season, I have to go out and buy the latest designer clothes. If I don't, people will think I don't know anything about fashion."
- *Overgeneralization:* You come to a general conclusion based on a single incident or piece of evidence. You see a single negative event as a never-ending pattern of defeat. This type of negative thought frequently involves the use of *always* or *never.* *Example:* "I couldn't stay away from the mall this weekend. I'll never be able to recover from my shopping addiction."
- *One rotten apple spoils the barrel:* You pick out a single negative detail and dwell on it exclusively so that your vision of all reality becomes darkened, like the drop of ink that discolors a whole glass of water. *Example:* "For the first time in five weeks, I bought some things on eBay. I'm a hopeless shopaholic, and I'm wasting my time with this book."
- *Discounting the positive:* You reject positive experiences by insisting they "don't count" for some reason or other. In this way, you can maintain a negative belief that is contradicted by your everyday experiences. *Example:* "I've been resisting my urges and writing in my Shopping Journal on a regular basis. But yesterday I didn't. It's getting cold, and without a word in my journal, I bought a pair of

warm gloves. So I don't really think that I'm making much progress, and I doubt that I'll overcome this problem."

- *Jumping to conclusions:* You come to an arbitrary and negative conclusion that isn't justified by the facts or situation. There are two forms of this error:

  1. *Mind reading:* You make an arbitrary assumption about what someone else is thinking and feeling, you don't check it out with them, and you react on the basis of your assumption. (*Example:* "I know my wife thinks I'm an irresponsible spendthrift. She saw me doing Internet research on tramp art, and she's sure I'm going to add something new to my collection.")
  2. *Self-fulfilling prophecy:* You imagine that something bad is going to happen, you believe in your prediction, and you react as if it has already occurred. (*Example:* "I'll be back to shopping tomorrow or the day after, so what's the point of trying to avoid it today?")

- *Catastrophizing:* You blow things way out of proportion in order to fulfill your negative expectations.
  Example: You're going to give a business presentation. You become distraught as you think about how nervous you are. You feel sure that you won't do a good job, and that even if you did, the people you're presenting to wouldn't be swayed toward your position. You're sure you'll end up getting fired.
- *Denial:* You ignore or seriously minimize important information or events.
  Example: You keep getting late notices from your creditors, then begin to get threatening calls from a collection agency; you tell yourself, "There's nothing they can do to me."
- *Emotional reasoning:* You assume that your negative emotions necessarily reflect the way things are: "I feel it; therefore, it's true."
  Example: "I feel out of control and anxious today. I know I won't be able to avoid buying a lot when I go to the computer store."
- *"Should" statements:* You try to motivate yourself with *shoulds* and *shouldn'ts,* as if you had to be whipped into shape in order to

make choices. (*Must* and *ought to* are also offenders.) The emotional consequence is guilt. Or, if you direct *should* statements toward others, you feel anger, frustration, and resentment.

Example: "I should be able to stop overshopping now that I know why I do it."

Another example: "My family should understand that shopping is my only real pleasure in life."

- *Labeling:* This is an extreme form of overgeneralization. Instead of describing behavior, you attach negative labels, describing yourself or actions or events in highly colored and emotionally loaded language.

  Example: "I couldn't resist that plasma HDTV. I'm such a loser."

- *Personalization:* You see yourself as the cause of some negative external event for which, in fact, you are not primarily responsible.

  Example: "That saleslady looked so angry! I know it's because I was asking her too many questions about the store's return policy."

Challenging Your Distorted Thinking

Once you've looked at the different types of distortions that can fuel overshopping behavior, you need to identify, challenge, and refute the ones that are operating in you.

An old joke is illustrative here. A man buys a cheap suit he's very fond of and shows it to a friend. "Look at this!" he exclaims. "Only twenty-five dollars!" "Well," says the friend, "but that right sleeve's a little short." "No problem," comes the reply, and the man hikes up his shoulder to adjust the sleeve length. Coming upon another friend, he points proudly to the suit: "What do you think? I got it for twenty-five dollars!" "Nice," says the friend, "but that left leg's kind of long." "Easy," says the man, cocking his hip to shorten the pants leg. He proceeds to several other friends. Each notes a flaw in the fit, and at each, he further adjusts his posture. Finally, hunched and wrenched, he hobbles into the town square. "Oh," cries a woman, "look at the poor crippled boy." "Yeah," says her friend, "but don't his suit fit great?"

Distorted thoughts are the mind's postural adjustments, its crippling adaptations to the ill-fitting suit of destructive core beliefs and related underlying assumptions. To straighten things out, use this six-step technique:

1. Describe the situation. Articulate the circumstances and your feelings.
2. What are the primary distortions here? Identify and then label each one.
3. Choose the most prominent distortion.
4. Evaluate that distortion:
   a. On a 0–10 scale, how much do I really believe this distorted thought?
   b. How does the distortion make me feel?
   c. On a 0–10 scale, how strong is this negative feeling?
5. Examine the distortion:
   a. *Evidence for:* What concrete evidence do I have to support this thought? What makes me think it's true?
   b. *Evidence against:* What evidence do I have to refute it? Have I had any past experience that contradicts this distorted thought?
   c. *Common sense:* What does my common sense tell me about this thought? Am I basing it on emotion only, either forgetting facts or focusing on irrelevant ones?
   d. *Impact on my life:* What is the effect of believing the thought?
   e. *Alternative view:* What's another way for me to look at this?
   f. *Believing the alternative:* What if I believed the alternative view? What might happen if I changed my thinking?
   g. *What a friend would say:* Would a trusted friend or loved one believe the thought? How would he or she correct it?
6. Reevaluate the distortion:
   a. On a 0–10 scale, how much do I now believe this thought?
   b. On a 0–10 scale, how strong is the negative feeling associated with your distorted thought now?

To get a feel for this process before trying it out in your Shopping Journal, follow the example below.

EXAMPLE: DO I OVERWORK OR OVERSHOP?

1. Describe the situation. Articulate the circumstances and your feelings.

   It's late morning. I'm at my desk, but I don't want to do any more work because this report I'm writing is going painfully slow. It's an important report and it's due very soon, but I feel lousy about what I've written so far, and I just want to forget how I feel. Either I sit here and suffer for the rest of the day, or I blow off work and go shopping. I can't just go home, because I wouldn't be doing anything constructive there; I'd feel guilty. But shopping for the rest of the day would be OK: I'm feeling really down, and it would lift my spirits; and, anyway, it's the holidays, and I have presents to buy.

2. What are the primary distortions here? Identify and then label each one.

   First, either I work intently for the rest of the day or I spend the day shopping. There are no alternatives and no in-betweens. (All-or-nothing.) Second, during work hours, I should always be constructive. (Should statement.) Third, though the report is due soon, shopping is OK, because it'll make me feel better, and I have presents to buy. (Denial.)

3. Choose what, in your estimation, is the most prominent distortion.
   Though the report is due soon, shopping is OK, because it'll make me feel better, and I have presents to buy.

4. Evaluate the distortion:
   a. On a 0–10 scale, how much do I really believe this distorted thought? *Maybe 7.*
   b. How does the distortion make me feel? *I feel ashamed about it.*
   c. On a 0–10 scale, how strong is this negative feeling? *About 8.*

5. Examine the distortion and answer the questions below.
   a. *Evidence for:* What concrete evidence do I have to support this thought? What makes me think it's true?
      The same thing happened last month with another report I was writing. I left the office and went shopping. The report was late, but I really didn't get into that much trouble.
   b. *Evidence against:* What evidence do I have to refute it? Have I had any past experience that contradicts this distorted thought?

My supervisor bailed me out when last month's report was late, but he told me to look up the word deadline in the dictionary. And we know that our little department is going to lose a position this summer, when the company downsizes.

c. *Common sense:* What does my common sense tell me about this thought? Am I basing it on emotion only, either forgetting facts or focusing on irrelevant ones?

I'm feeling very low in energy and want to take the path of least resistance. But that path's incompatible with my job responsibilities. Besides, one of our five associates will be let go this summer, and I don't want it to be me, so this is a time to shine, not shirk. On top of that, I'm drowning in debt, which will only get worse if I shop.

d. *Impact on my life:* What is the effect of believing the thought?

Who am I kidding? Believing it's OK to shop this afternoon is reinforcing a delusion I have: that if I do it just this once, I'll have had my shopping fix and won't need to shop again for quite a while. I also know that going shopping will only make my addiction stronger, and I'm setting myself up for trouble at work.

e. *Alternative view:* What's another way for me to look at this? Shopping right now is not OK, and it won't make me feel better. What would really make me feel better is finishing the report—and finishing it well. I could get a quick lunch at the mall, energize myself with a ten-minute chair massage, then come back and finish it up.

f. *Believing the alternative:* What if I believed the alternative view? What might happen if I changed my thinking?

No question—if I begin to be more realistic and positive about my choices, I'll definitely feel better about myself. I think it'll expand my life in ways I can't even anticipate yet. Whatever they are, they're definitely going to be better than the way I'm living now.

g. *What a friend would say:* Would a trusted friend or loved one believe the thought? How would he or she correct it?

Angie would smile at the notion that it was OK to shop this afternoon—and gently shake her head. She knows me very well, and I trust her. She's also someone who takes wonderful care of herself. She'd probably recommend a short, comforting chair massage, or maybe she'd suggest skipping lunch at the mall, eating an apple with organic peanut butter on it, and taking a quick sauna and swim at the fitness center instead. She'd tell me to stay out of the stores, buy the presents online, and buy only what's absolutely necessary.

6. Reevaluate the distortion:
   a. On a 0–10 scale, how much do I now believe this thought? *Only 2.*
   b. On a 0–10 scale, how strong is the negative feeling associated with my distorted thought now? *4—more silly than ashamed now.*

JOURNAL TIME

Challenging Your Distorted Thinking

Now it's your turn. In your Shopping Journal, identify a situation as it's occurring and follow the six-step technique outlined above for challenging your distorting thinking.

If you've gone through this section carefully once, and then, as you took pains to do a thorough job with the restructuring exercise, reread this material, you've probably learned that rational thinking can trump the weaker suits of negative automatic thought. You can talk yourself down from the emotional ledges your distortions sometimes bring you to. Hold on to this recognition. Keep your mind's ear tuned for distortions, look 'em straight in the eye, and pounce on them the moment you hear them. Gaining control over these negative thoughts is an important piece of ammunition in the war against overshopping; this skill will generalize to other areas of your life, too.

THE LANGUAGE OF THE SOUL: SPIRITUALITY

In what language does the soul speak? Is spirituality something you think about? Do you have strong and coherent beliefs about a higher purpose or a meaning to the universe? Do you think you fit into a larger scheme? Do your beliefs shape your actions? Are your beliefs a source of comfort to you? What feeds your soul?

Accessing the language of the soul isn't easy. We're so bombarded with external stimulation that we don't often think about, much less attend to, our spiritual needs and hungers. While all of us probably have a consciousness (or an inkling) about something larger than ourselves, our consumer culture continually stimulates and reinforces material desires and wants, leaving little space for the exploration of spiritual ones. Remember the signature strengths work you did in chapter 5? Five of those character strengths or virtues—spirituality, the appreciation of beauty and excellence, gratitude, hope, and humor—are what Christopher Peterson and Martin Seligman call "strengths of transcendence." What these strengths have in common is that "each allows individuals to forge connections to the larger universe and thereby provide meaning to their lives."[2]

- Spirituality is the quintessential transcendent value, "a belief in and commitment to the nonmaterial aspects of life—whether they be called universal, ideal, sacred, or divine."[3]

- The appreciation of beauty and excellence can be seen as transcendent, because people who have it often feel awe and wonder at something larger than themselves. Many things could give rise to this feeling: a brilliantly executed design, an evocative piece of music, a captivating work of art, an individual of profound moral stature, even an athletic performance that goes beyond what seems humanly possible.

- Gratitude is thankfulness for a gift, whether it be tangible and expected, as in a birthday present, or intangible and random, as in accidentally overhearing an opera singer practicing through an open window. Gratitude is a transcendent virtue because it's accompanied by "the emotion of grace—the sense that we have benefited from the actions of another."[4]

- Hope is an emotional color that contains the shade of optimism and represents a positive stance toward the future. What helps us to access hope is often a belief in something larger than ourselves.

- While there are many types of humor—not all of them spiritual nor even well-meaning—some forms of humor do moral good: "They make the human condition more bearable by drawing attention to its contradictions, by sustaining good cheer in the face of despair, by building social bonds, and by lubricating social interaction."[5]

How can we access the various components of transcendence, connect with our higher purpose, commune with some force beyond ourselves? Often what motivates us and shows us the way is pain—either emotional or physical (or both). The pain that overshopping has caused in your life is what's driven you to read this book; that same pain may be the inspiration you need to discover—or rediscover—your spiritual hungers; to find self-actualizing, life-affirming ways to feed those hungers; to balance your material desires with spiritual nourishment.

"Just how," the skeptic inside you may be asking, "can any of this vague spiritual stuff help with the very concrete problem of my overshopping?" Rita Gross, in "Form and Elegance with Just Enough," offers the very useful beginning of an answer. (It's only the beginning, because the complete answer has to come from *you*, has to address *your* personal needs and empty places, has to incorporate *your* particular strengths and capabilities.) Gross suggests that our temptation to overdo—to buy too much, eat too much, drink too much—is the result of "being buried in a mountain of material goods with little sense of how to enjoy what we consume," and she argues that "one of the ways of discouraging consumerism may well be to encourage the love of beauty, elegance, and dignity, so that we know how to enjoy the right amount."[6]

Easy enough, of course, for Goldilocks to know which porridge was just right; our sensitivity to hot and cold is acute and automatic, and is not under constant assault by our culture. But we can also learn to see and value the abstract qualities that Gross speaks of, whether in art or artichokes, living or loving, buying or being. The same sense of proportion that leaves many speechless before Michelangelo's *David* informs Rudyard Kipling's advice that we "meet with Triumph and Disaster and treat those two imposters just the same."[7] The same elegance that informs the harmonious relationship of elements in the Japanese tea ceremony is at work in a few beautifully chosen garments that can be combined half a dozen ways to half a dozen different effects. Proportion and elegance: these underlie everything in the universe, from the face of the sunflower to the paths of celestial bodies. And here we are, smack dab in the middle of it all. When we learn to filter out the assaults of commercial interests and to creatively address our authentic needs, we're well on the way to enjoying the right amount.

The work of this section will help you to begin thinking about these issues. First, you'll be exploring your spirituality by responding to questions and identifying your spiritual needs and hungers. Then you'll be thinking about ways to meet those needs and satisfy those hungers. After that, you'll be counting your blessings and building a gratitude list. And finally, you'll do some further work on mindfulness, the umbrella under which this entire book finds the cool shade of balance and clarity.

We began to look at mindfulness in chapter 4 and saw how it involves *observing or watching our thoughts, feelings, and physical sensations without trying to change or judge them*. Mindfulness lets us tune in to our experience *on a moment-by-moment basis*, giving us increased options for the life we want to live and allowing us, over time, to come to wisdom. Probably the best way to develop this ability to quietly watch what you're doing as you're doing it is to practice sitting meditation. Through mindfulness and meditation, you can overcome the spiritual poverty that rides the coattails of overconsumption.

Spiritual Needs and Hungers Questionnaire

Below is a list of spiritual needs and hungers. Read through it, think about each need or hunger, and decide which of them resonate with you. After you've done that, it will be time to think about how you might fulfill any of your unmet spiritual needs, time to tease out which of your trigger emotions actually relate to underlying spiritual hungers. Doing this can greatly expand your capacity to create tailor-made alternatives.

How important is it to you to . . . ?	Not at all	Some-what	Moder-ately	Very	Extremely
1. Be accepted as a person	❏	❏	❏	❏	❏
2. Have a quiet space to meditate or reflect	❏	❏	❏	❏	❏
3. Be forgiven or forgive others	❏	❏	❏	❏	❏
4. Feel positive or hopeful	❏	❏	❏	❏	❏
5. Protect and foster human life	❏	❏	❏	❏	❏
6. Protect and foster plants and animals	❏	❏	❏	❏	❏
7. Feel a sense of connection with the world	❏	❏	❏	❏	❏
8. Feel a "calling"	❏	❏	❏	❏	❏
9. Experience fresh-ness, see the famil-iar world with new eyes	❏	❏	❏	❏	❏
10. Believe in miracles	❏	❏	❏	❏	❏
11. See the universe as ordered and inter-connected rather than chaotic	❏	❏	❏	❏	❏
12. Feel a sense of wonder and awe	❏	❏	❏	❏	❏
13. Believe in the unbelievable	❏	❏	❏	❏	❏
14. Feel hope	❏	❏	❏	❏	❏
15. Feel love, compas-sion, or kindness for others	❏	❏	❏	❏	❏

How important is it to you to . . . ?	Not at all	Some-what	Moder-ately	Very	Extremely
16. Feel love, compassion, or kindness from others	❏	❏	❏	❏	❏
17. Give to others	❏	❏	❏	❏	❏
18. Feel connected to a boundless universe	❏	❏	❏	❏	❏
19. Access and use your "sixth sense"	❏	❏	❏	❏	❏
20. Feel peace and contentment	❏	❏	❏	❏	❏
21. Experience nature or beauty	❏	❏	❏	❏	❏
22. Experience and appreciate music	❏	❏	❏	❏	❏
23. Laugh, see the light side of things, and make other people laugh	❏	❏	❏	❏	❏
24. Ask for and receive guidance from a higher power	❏	❏	❏	❏	❏
25. Read religious or spiritual materials	❏	❏	❏	❏	❏
26. Participate in religious or spiritual services or rituals	❏	❏	❏	❏	❏
27. Find meaning and purpose in life	❏	❏	❏	❏	❏
28. Address issues about death and dying	❏	❏	❏	❏	❏
29. Have a personal mission	❏	❏	❏	❏	❏

Your Spiritual Action Plan

Even in an area as seemingly abstract as spirituality, you can discover and name specific spiritual needs and hungers and think about the role they play in your life. You've already done some of this in the "Needs: Love and Affection, Belonging, Esteem, and Self-Actualization" section of chapter 5. Developing a concrete action plan will enable you to use what you discover to better access your spiritual side. Devote some space in your journal to such a plan, using anything you may have learned from the questionnaire above and whatever other resources you can bring. Here's the place to gaze into your spiritual mirror and decide how you feel about what you see. Then create a goal and follow through on it. You might even want to share your goal with a loved one who can help shepherd you toward it. Ask yourself:

1. What does spirituality mean to me?
2. What kind of a role does spirituality play in my life? How does it manifest itself?
3. What did I discover about my spiritual needs by completing the questionnaire?

Then work toward creating a goal. Ask yourself:

1. What is my spiritual goal?
2. What active steps can I take to meet this goal?
3. Who will help me to achieve it, and what do I want him or her to do?
4. What are three positive outcomes I can imagine?
5. When and how will I assess my progress toward this goal?

COUNTING YOUR BLESSINGS

Irving Berlin wrote the beautiful song "Count Your Blessings" for the 1954 film *White Christmas*. In the song, memorably sung by Bing Crosby, Berlin invokes the healing perspective to be gained from recognizing the good things in our lives. More than half a century later, his practice remains timely: now as then, a shield of positive perspective deflects the arrows of worry or a diminished bankroll.

Indeed, modern research confirms Berlin's notion. It tells us that gratitude and optimism—in essence, seeing the glass as half full—have significant benefits for our health and well-being. It's important, then, to focus on and appreciate the blessings we each have, whether we consider them dispensations from above or simply good fortune.

To reiterate an important idea, modern research supports Berlin's notion. It tells us that gratitude and optimism—in essence, seeing the glass as half full—have significant benefits for our health and well-being. It's important, then, to focus on and appreciate the blessings we each have, whether we consider them dispensations from above or simply good fortune.

What are you most grateful for? What do you consider a blessing in your life? Aesthetic joys, such as the beautiful paperweight on your desk that you stumbled upon last year in a flea market? Those photos of your great-grandparents, just off the boat after the arduous trip from the old country? That pair of worn-out slippers into which you still love to slide your feet? Maybe it's intangibles, such as the excellent health you enjoy, or a well-functioning blended family, or a warm and supportive network of friends you can count on. Maybe it's a talent—your skill with a needle and thread, or your way with words. The possibilities for blessings are endless. Perhaps you scale peaks like a mountain goat or whip up a memorable meal without cracking a cookbook. Maybe you have deep and abiding integrity or the capacity to inspire people to grow.

Maybe an important blessing for you is knowing that your best friend will drop everything and run when you need her, or that you can rely on the guy you carpool with to calm you down before you overreact to that irresponsible employee with whom you've got a 9:00 A.M. meeting. Perhaps you're grateful for the life lessons you learned when you had cancer. Maybe you feel blessed by the fact that your son feels close enough to you to call and talk over a relationship issue he's having—and then thank you for listening. Maybe you recognize it's a blessing that you have the courage to confront your overshopping problem.

Counting Your Blessings

Where is the nonmaterial wealth and abundance in your life? What are your blessings? Pick a bunch of your most beautiful blessings and make a page for this bouquet in your Shopping Journal. Here's another place where adding something visual would be nice: a photo, a drawing, a memento—anything that will remind you of all that you have, all that you are.

MINDFULNESS AND MEDITATION

As we discovered in the section on demagnetizing in chapter 6, much of our consumer behavior stems from unconscious choices rather than mindfulness of what we're buying and what it's really costing, in either monetary or quality-of-life terms. "Mindfulness is the part of our mind that knows exactly what is happening when it is happening. It is present, aware, and connected to the moment. It contributes to wisdom and helps us distinguish what is skillful, helpful action from what is unskillful, hurtful action. Without mindfulness, we don't know what our minds are doing or what the effects of our actions will be."[8]

An important component of mindfulness is a "willingness to feel all of your feelings more completely, even—or especially—the bad feelings, so that you can live your life more completely. In essence, instead of trying to feel *better,* willingness involves learning how to *feel* better. . . . To be willing and accepting means noticing that you are the sky, not the clouds; the ocean, not the waves[; . . .] that you're large enough to contain all your experiences."[9]

Developing the practice or habit of mindfulness can help us make decisions based on conscious choices as opposed to impulses. Through the power of mindfulness, we can short-circuit the triggers → actions → aftershocks sequence and prevent the automatic response. With enhanced awareness, we're less likely to be manipulated into buying products we don't really need or want.

We can notice, *Wow, I want a pair of boots.* We can feel the desire in our bodies (aching in the chest or gut area, pounding heart) and notice the accompanying thoughts (*They're perfect. I can't live without them*). Then we can apply mindfulness to these sensations or thoughts. When we see them clearly for what they are—merely thoughts and sensations, not truths about ourselves—we can relax some, softening the blow, and notice, *Hey, it's just a thought.* When it sees clearly, according to author Diana Winston, "the mind can let go and stop the forward thrust into attachment, purchase, and the boot-addicted self."[10]

Cultivating Mindfulness

Again, the practice of mindfulness involves observing or watching our thoughts, feelings, and physical sensations, tuning in to them on a moment-by-moment basis—without trying to change them and without judging them. When we learn to see ourselves as we are and genuinely notice, clearly and compassionately, what we're thinking or feeling, we become more intuitive and change is more possible.

It's quite a challenge, though: we're not accustomed to paying close attention to these things, particularly without judging them. So many things distract us. Who hasn't walked down the hall into another room and then been unable to remember what you'd gone there for? As you walked, you thought about what to cook for dinner or what you need to pick up for your daughter, or something else. Walking down the hall is an everyday example of how we are not present to what we're doing in the moment. The first step toward becoming mindful is to quietly watch what you are doing as you're doing it.

The skill we practice to become mindful is coming back to the present moment. This is something that can be learned through meditation. Meditation is helpful not only when you feel the urge to shop but whenever daily activities challenge your tranquility in any way. Learning the discipline of meditation—and then practicing it regularly—takes dedication and commitment. It's like developing a muscle: every time you come back to the present moment and observe what you're doing and thinking, you strengthen the muscle of awareness. Even people who are experienced at being mindful must continue to practice in order to maintain that muscle. Think about the study of a musical instrument—the piano, for example. When you begin to study the piano, scales are the first thing you learn—and you never give up that discipline. Even the world's great pianists still play scales; it's a basic skill that can't be allowed to rust.

Through sitting quietly with yourself, you tune and sharpen the basic mental skills needed to be mindful. As you become more skillful at it, you will also grasp more clearly what you're feeling in a whole host of situations, including being involved in a heated discussion or having a powerful impulse to buy something.

When you first start to sit quietly and simply notice what's going on in your head and body, you may be uncomfortable. Perhaps you'll feel self-conscious, sleepy, or bored; perhaps you'll want to give up. Maybe you'll feel anxious, irritable, or any of a hundred other unpleasant emotional shades. We're so accustomed to input—to television or music, to being active, to cleaning or planning—that when we sit quietly, not moving our bodies, we start to notice what we're doing with our minds, and the loudness of our inner voice discomforts us. Whenever that happens, direct yourself gently back to your breath.

When they sit quietly, different things come up for different people. Some replay past scenarios or fantasize about the future. Others become aware of restlessness, anxiety, or sadness. Still others notice more their physical sensations—rapid heartbeat, say, or pain in the foot. Without outside distractions, the inner workings of the mind can seem very intense. *But what you experience while you are meditating may be what you're experiencing all the time below the threshold of consciousness.* Irritation, restlessness, or fatigue, for example, may be the dominant emotional experience for someone beginning to meditate. The same person may be unaware of the extent to which irritation and restlessness are present in his everyday life. When you meditate, it's as if you're listening to the background tape that's always playing in your mind, but now it's front and center.

During meditation, you can focus on a number of different things. If you're a beginner, I recommend that you start with your breath—it's more constant than anything else, and you can call on it anytime, anywhere, for the rest of your life. In the guided meditation that follows, which I want you to practice, you'll focus on using your breath as an anchor.

In our ordinary lives, we tend to ignore unpleasant things, to put them out of our minds. Practicing mindfulness, however, means being completely honest with ourselves, paying attention to *whatever* is going on inside of us, pleasant, unpleasant, or neutral. As we mindfully watch ourselves during meditation, unpleasant sensations may come up: a pain in a particular body part, perhaps, or a sense of shame regarding something we don't like about ourselves, or anxiety about growing older and getting sick. Don't reject these. Merely notice them and gently let them go while you bring your attention back to your breath.

Looking at thoughts, feelings, and body sensations from without, rather than being caught inside of them, you can have them without letting them warp what you see. But this is easier said than done. One way to create that distance is to *label and depersonalize* the thoughts, feelings, and body sensations that arise. You can do this while you're meditating, and you can do it in your everyday life. It's a basic, yet very powerful technique: something as simple as "I'm feeling restless" becomes "There's restlessness"; "I have more work to do today than I can possibly finish" becomes "I notice the thought that I have more work to do today than I can possibly finish"; instead of acting on the impulse to cough, say "There's an urgent tickling sensation in my throat."

When you start to meditate, your mind will likely be full of thoughts, feelings, and sensations, and it will be difficult to stay focused on your breath. Notice when your attention wanders, and keep bringing it back to your breath. The mind is like a cup of muddy water: the longer you keep the cup still, the more the mud settles and the water clarifies. Stay quiet without moving your body and focus your undivided attention on your breath; your mind, too, will settle and grow clearer. There will always, however, be thoughts, feelings, and body sensations that vie for your attention. Noticing, allowing, and labeling them—and then bringing your focus back to your breath—is the path to stillness.

REGULAR PRACTICE

Sitting Meditation

Let me guide you now in a short sitting meditation. Read the instructions yourself, have someone else guide you through them, or download my voice at www.stoppingovershopping.com/audiofiles. Set aside twenty minutes of quiet, uninterrupted time for this.

I invite you to sit gently erect, with dignity, shoulders relaxed, chest open, head supported by the entire spine. You may want to tip your head slightly back and forth to find a good balance point for you. Make sure you are seated on your sitting bones, supported by the chair and the floor, feet flat on the floor, allowing your eyes to close gently if that's OK with you; otherwise, keep your eyes open with a soft, slightly downward gaze.

You might want to begin by brightening your mind. Bringing to mind some of your good qualities or visualizing your loved ones can brighten your mind. When you've been able to brighten your mind some, become aware of the breath as it enters and leaves the body. Don't manipulate the breath in any way; simply become aware of it. It may be shallow or deep, quick or slow—it doesn't matter, simply watch it the way it is.

Sit for one minute with your eyes open or closed as you get used to just being there. When the mind wanders, as it will, gently escort it back to the breath, without judgment. Often, becoming aware of *not* being present is the first step of mindfulness. We can then choose to be *here*.

Notice that you are breathing, and open your senses to your breath. You might want to say to yourself, "I am breathing in" while you inhale and "I am breathing out" while you exhale. This will help to quiet your mind. Or you might want to say to yourself, "I'm breathing in and making my breath and body light and peaceful. I'm breathing out and making my breath and body light and peaceful." Then, becoming aware of your body as a whole, soften any muscle tightness with the in-breath, and let tension exit with the out-breath to the extent it will.

Find some aspect of breathing that is pleasant to you right now—perhaps the touch of air in your nostrils, down your throat, and into your chest and belly; the rhythmic in-and-out of the breath, the massage of it, the quiet sounds. Focus on the sensation you like most and keep returning to this pleasure.

If you find yourself focused on a body sensation, an emotion, a thought, or a sound, just greet it with friendliness and come back to your breath, to the sensation you like the most. Some people like to think of thoughts as clouds that you can watch pass by and then return to your breath. Your mind will always wander; the key is to be gentle in returning to the breath.

In an easy and casual manner, keep bringing your attention back to the sensual experience of breathing.

When thoughts come, you'll often become totally lost in them and forget that you're breathing. But when you return from the thoughts, you'll have a choice of what to pay attention to, and again, you can enjoy the breath.

And after you've sat for a bit in this way, you can ask, before closing, "Where and how is my mind now? Where and how is my body now? Where and how is my breath?"

Now, if your eyes are closed, allow them to open gently. You might want to wiggle your fingers or your toes, as you return to a more active way of being, taking this experience of simply being with you into every fiber of your body, able to call upon it at any time.

You can practice this exercise, first with verbal guidance and later, when you know the instructions, without it, for one, three, five, even twenty minutes. After your meditation, take a look at the questions below. You might want to jot down some notes in your Shopping Journal. Read and answer these questions every time you meditate until you've internalized them and you answer them automatically after you've meditated.

1. How did you brighten your mind when you first started sitting? Did you bring to mind your good qualities, your loved ones, the gift of this practice, the gift of life, or some combination of these?
2. What was your mind like? Was it calm, quiet, racing, scattered, or some combination of those?
3. How did your body feel? Was it relaxed, alert, tense, jittery, drowsy, achy, something else, perhaps? Were you physically comfortable or uncomfortable during the sitting?
4. What drew your mind away from your breath most frequently? A feeling, a thought, a memory, maybe a physical sensation? Some of the most common states that draw our minds away from the breath are doubts, dullness or sleepiness, sensual desire, aversion or ill will, and restlessness.
5. When you noticed you had lost touch with your breath, what was your response? Was it hard to bring yourself back to your breath? Did you judge yourself? Were you accepting?

6. Overall, what was the sitting like for you? Did you find it to be a pleasant or an unpleasant event? Why?

Meditation takes commitment. Having a group to practice with will make it easier to meditate on your own. Try to find a local class, or explore the abundant resources online. Particularly helpful is "A Moment of Calm," a ten-minute guided meditation by Tara Brach, a much-beloved Buddhist teacher and the author of a deeply moving book, *Radical Acceptance*, upon which our stance of care is based. (You can hear this meditation at www .beliefnet.com/story/3/story_385_1.html.) There are countless Internet sites, books, and tapes about meditation, and classes are available in most areas of the country and online. What's most important is not where or how you study it, but that you do so faithfully.

FOUR TONGUES, ONE LANGUAGE

Body, heart, mind, and soul—each of us speaks these deeply inter-related tongues, and the more fluent you become with the whole, flexible vocabulary of being, the more fully you can live. You can think of them as what linguists call "dictions," forms of a language that are appropriate for certain purposes or audiences or moments. There's one English for the boardroom—it's formal and polite and cautious—and another for the bedroom, where we're a lot freer. We don't speak the same language with taxi drivers that we speak with university professors, and we use quite different dictions with children than we use with drivers who cut us off. The really good speaker has command of many dictions—formal, intimate, and everywhere in be-tween. He or she can coo with a baby, curse like a sailor, charm a lover, persuade a mechanic to stay late, cool down a heated debate, or talk his or her way out of a jam—can, in short, choose and use the language that's best for getting what's wanted or needed. Develop-ing fluency in the four tongues of this part of the book will do the same for you: it will give you different and complementary sets of muscles that, used together, enable you to accomplish the work of stopping overshopping. (By the way, and not inconsequentially, developing this fluency will also enhance your self-esteem, improve your relationships, and enrich your life!)

10 | What If I Start Again?

Perhaps you've made several months of good, steady progress. Perhaps it's been only a few weeks. You might even have finished this book a year ago and then picked it up again because you're beginning to backslide. However long it's been, you *have* had the experience of shopping less and enjoying life more. Little by little, however, you may find yourself reverting to your old ways, edging toward that slippery slope to relapse. Or maybe you've had an unexpected and uncontrolled buying binge. What happens next will make the difference between careening uncontrollably down the relapse run or digging in your poles and steadying yourself. At this point, it's crucial to maintain your careful, clear-sighted, compassionate stance; to abandon it now is to set yourself up for failure. In this chapter, we look at lapses and relapses: how to prevent them, how to prepare for the possibility that they can and will occur, and how to position yourself to learn from any lapse or relapse.

THE FIRST SIP: STARTING DOWN THE SLIPPERY SLOPE

Maybe it begins with the equivalent of a sip to an overdrinker—a small, seemingly harmless act that starts to lead you back to your habit. While some people can take stock of what's happening and stop after just a few sips, others drink themselves right back into oblivion. This is the stuff of lapse and relapse. A *lapse* can be as few as one and as many as a handful of overshopping episodes following on the heels of a period of much greater control. One lapse can easily lead to another, and, before you know it, lapses can escalate into *relapse,* a serious and prolonged return to the full-blown pattern of compulsive buying. In this chapter, we look at two things: how to resist that first sip—and the next two, three, or four—and, if you *have* slipped, how to steady yourself again.

How does the lapse-relapse progression happen? For some people, it starts small: you allow yourself a loophole in your mindful shopping policy. You might find yourself starting to plan a trip to the outlet stores on your way home from work or drifting toward time on eBay. You use some sort of justifier and get a taste of the old high of the buy. Perhaps a favorite salesperson has gone totally above and beyond, offering you not only an extra 40 percent off the already discounted price but also throwing in free alterations and hand delivery. "How can I not take her up on this incredible offer?" you think; "I'd be a fool not to. It's going to cost me so little." (This is not much different from the overdrinker who claims he can't insult people by refusing a sip of champagne for the toast.) Or it may start with a binge, an uncontrollable urge that leads either to one huge purchase or a series of them. Such a binge is often precipitated by some unexpected or highly charged event.

Especially because shopping can't be totally eliminated from your life, it's vital to be aware of any clue, however small, that suggests the imminent triggering of *over*shopping. So it's important to ask yourself such questions as: "Am I thinking too much about shopping?" "Am I shopping too much?" "What's going on? I've started using my credit card again." "Am I going to be able to limit this to one or two purchases, or am I slipping back into my old patterns?"

I've isolated six types of triggering situations commonly associated with lapse and relapse:

1. Negative emotional states (for example, frustration and anger)
2. Interpersonal conflict (perhaps an altercation with a friend, a child, a parent, a spouse, or a supervisor)
3. Social pressure (A friend tells you about a huge sale, invites you, and you say, "I'd love to!"—or your clever child picks just the right moment to ask, and you respond, "Oh, all right . . . whatever.")

4. An excited emotional state (a great success, perhaps, or a windfall or a new relationship)
5. An event that changes your brain or body chemistry, lowers your inhibitions, or lowers your mood (You begin or return to using or abusing alcohol or drugs, or your psychotropic medication seems to have stopped working, or you develop a medical condition.)
6. Any big change in habit or life circumstance (You go on a very strict diet, for example, or stop smoking; perhaps you've been taking care of an elderly parent and that parent dies; or you begin working part-time, or your young adult child comes back to live with you after graduating from college.)

You can't completely avoid these situations—nor would you want to avoid some of them. But recognizing them when they occur will help you ward off the overshopping they can trigger. Compulsive habits run deep, as your work with this book has shown you, and their impulse is never wholly eradicated. Reformed drinkers call themselves "recovering" alcoholics, and the grammatical force of that *ing* stresses the ongoing process of the recovery. So it is with stopping overshopping. When there's a break in the new routine, an upsetting of the new applecart, old habits tend to resurface. Watch out for this. Guard against it.

And if it happens? There's an important tipping point the first time you lapse; what follows will be strongly influenced by your perceptions and reactions. Either of two extremes, denial or despondence, are apt to steepen the slope, making your slide into relapse more likely. So don't ignore or rationalize your lapse—and don't throw up your hands and pull the covers over your head. This is the moment for clear-sighted compassion. Look carefully at what's happened—what does the detective in you detect?—and form a plan for resteadying yourself.

If you find yourself in danger of more overshopping after that first nonmindful purchase, realize that you need to get yourself away from the shopping venue, whatever it is, *immediately.* Change the scene; different scenery will lead to different thoughts. Then, think about what's just happened and recommit yourself to stopping overshopping. If you've stopped Weighing In, start again. If you've quit working with your negative, distorted thoughts, resensitize yourself to hearing them—and begin asking yourself the questions that help you restructure them. If you've started using your credit card again, stop! If you've stopped planning your purchases, start! If you've ceased to align your purchases with your values and goals, recommit to doing so. If you've lost touch with the blessings in your life, review your list and write some new ones. Meditate. Talk to your Shopping Support Buddy about what's happening. Even if you've stopped carrying your Shopping Journal, you can still answer the Reminder Card questions; at this point, you know them by heart. But it's a good idea to rekindle your intimacy with your Shopping Journal by rereading it, keeping it with you, and working with your urges in a systematic way.

It's important at this point that you work to strengthen your self-efficacy, your positive expectations about your ability to cope. As you avoid overshopping, as you maintain the changes gained through healthier shopping patterns, you'll experience a sense of control. This reinforces the healthier patterns, which continue to strengthen the longer you abstain from overshopping. In contrast, temptations threaten your perceived control. The longer you're exposed to them, the weaker your self-control—and the greater the probability of a relapse. So remind yourself of your earlier successes, rearm yourself with the tools and strategies you've learned to use, close your ears to the siren song of "stuff," and reclaim your self-efficacy.

Below, we'll look at a couple of techniques—the mental rehearsal and the dress rehearsal—to help you avoid lapses and relapse. Before doing so, however, a few words about outside help. If doing the work of stopping overshopping has begun to feel like pulling a truck across sand, consider consulting an expert. There may be a psychological issue—depression, substance abuse, some form of trauma, or bipolar disorder, for example—that's making it hard to stay on track. These problems can be diagnosed and treated quite successfully. There might be a medication issue that's interfering with your capacity to commit to the work of the book. This is particularly possible if you adjust dosages yourself or have taken a medication holiday. (It's also possible that your medication is no longer working for you; some people become habituated to drugs, and a change can make all the difference.) This is *your* life. Don't be afraid to get whatever help you need to live it richly and rewardingly, free of the burdens of overshopping.

JOURNAL TIME

Potential Lapse or Relapse Triggers

The very first sign of backsliding is the time to troubleshoot. Scan your environment for potential temptations, invitations, or excuses to overshop. Look for changes in brain or body chemistry, changes in habit or life circumstances. Are there sources of negative emotion, interpersonal conflict, social pressure, or excitement in your life for which shopping might be an all-purpose response? What potential lapse or relapse triggers do you see? Jot them down in your Shopping Journal, and then choose one for the mental and dress rehearsals that follow.

THE MENTAL REHEARSAL AND THE DRESS REHEARSAL

The mental and dress rehearsals are two experiments that fortify you against lapses by preparing you for and familiarizing you with a high-risk situation from which you emerge triumphant: *without having bought anything!* In the first, the mental rehearsal, you create in your imagination a movie; you play the starring role. In this film, you're drawn to shop by a triggering situation that you've chosen from the list above, and you see and experience every frame. It's an important first step in developing a plan to handle this temptation when it actually and naturally occurs. The dress rehearsal is the second part of the experiment. There, you put yourself in a *real* shopping situation—one as close as possible to your movie—and, again, you commit to buying nothing. Highly empowering, an effective dress rehearsal will give you the confidence to star in a live performance—to succeed when this situation arises in real life.

To give you a feel for the process and its level of detail, we look at the written reports of Joanne, a legal secretary, as she does both exercises. First, the mental rehearsal (the movie):

I picture myself getting out of the office, getting into my car, and driving to the mall. I've had a really crappy day: my boss raged around the office and blamed me for something I had nothing to do with. Even though I know she was being crazy, her unreasonableness still pushed my buttons. And guess what I tend to do when my buttons are pushed? So I'm off and running to the mall. I park very close to the entrance of Macy's and go straight to the jewelry floor—just to look, of course, because I'm not buying anything. I don't *need* anything. Then I see a Bulova watch: it has a woven leather strap and a delicate face—and it's really beautiful. In the case right opposite it, there's a friendship ring in three different colors of gold, all twisted together. I feel my heart beating. My palms and brow actually start to sweat. I'm really stirred up.

The salesman asks me if I'd like him to take the watch out of the case. Is he kidding? On my wrist, the watch is perfect; I can hardly contain myself. But then that small, quiet voice in my head gently reminds me of my credit card debt. Longingly, I give the watch back to the salesman, who seems a little annoyed that he's not going to get his commission.

This doesn't stop me from trying on the ring. It's gorgeous! Besides, my old friendship ring disappeared last summer, and I've missed it every day since. The salesman says he can give me 20 percent off if I use my Macy's credit card. I *really* want to buy it. The urge is visceral; I can almost point to the spot in my belly where it starts. I *deserve* the ring, I tell myself: I've been so good lately about overshopping, and it's such a good deal. I feel my resolve melting away. But then I remember why I'm here. I *know* I'd have to give the watch a big fat 0 as a Necessity Score, so I try to make a case for buying the ring—how much I've missed the one I lost, the good deal. But I can't kid myself. It, too, would have to get a 0: I clearly don't need it. I thank the salesman and tell him I'll think about it.

I leave the store and find a place to sit down in the center of the mall. I take some deep breaths, and then I open my Shopping Journal and think about my urge and answer the urge questions. I write about what's going on in my body; how I'm feeling; what I'm thinking; and, now that I've decided not to buy, what's happening to my urge. I think about and write down what my heart's saying (what would be good about buying it) and what my head's saying (what would be not so good about buying it).

I'm feeling calmer now, and I think I can handle it, so I go back for a second look at both of them. It feels a little weird to be bothering the same salesman, but I remind myself that I'm not here to take care of *him;* I'm here to take care of *me.* What I'm doing will help me confront stores like this—jewelry like this—without fear. I look at the watch again, and I tell the salesman that I'm still not sure—and I say this as if that's OK. I look at the ring, too, but I don't ask him to take it out again.

Then I go back to the same place to sit down. I take out my Shopping Journal again and try to tease out what I'm *really* needing and what else I might do, and I write about this. Quite a mental rehearsal! Then I leave the mall, congratulating myself for not buying anything.

All hats off to Joanne! Her imaginative engagement with every aspect of this experiment makes it particularly strong. Now she reflects on what she's just done by answering a short set of post–mental rehearsal questions.[1]

1. How did it feel to imagine letting go of the item(s) that you rehearsed with?
   I can't say that I'm 100 percent happy; in fact, I'm aware of some disappointment. But I'm also aware of feeling a low-key confidence that I think will grow as I see what I've been able to do.
2. On a scale of 1 to 10, with 1 being the worst and 10 being the best, how bad are those feelings?
   Since I had a mixture of both good and bad feelings, I kind of took a mental average and said that the bad feelings were only at a level of 3–4.
3. How long do you think it would take you to get over those feelings?
   As long as I get involved in something else and don't keep second-guessing myself, I think I'd get over the disappointment pretty quickly: within twenty minutes, I'd say.

4. What bad outcome might there be if you didn't purchase the item(s)?

    I can think of two potentially bad outcomes. One is the possibility that when I do have the money to buy the ring, either the store won't have it or the price will be a lot higher. The second possibility is that when I leave the store without having bought these things and try to find something to take my mind off my disappointment, I won't be able to.

5. What would it take for you to recover if that bad thing happened?

    Truthfully, I don't think it would take that much. As far as the first bad thing, the store not having the items or selling them for a higher price, it wouldn't be a big deal. There are always other stores and the Internet. I'd be able to find it somewhere for sure. As far as the second fear, that I won't be able to find something to take my mind off my disappointment, I think that's unlikely because I have several Shopping Support Buddies, and someone is bound to be reachable. And it wouldn't be so terrible either if I didn't take my mind off my feelings but noticed them and allowed them to be there, hopefully with the help of one of my friends or some tapes I've been listening to about feeling my feelings. It would be a good experiment to remind myself that these kinds of feelings eventually go away.

6. What conclusions have you drawn from this experiment?

    One conclusion I've drawn is that even a mental rehearsal takes a lot of effort to pull off. There are so many little details to think about, and I didn't even get into any contingencies, like what would happen if the salesperson had offered me a much bigger discount. I think, though, that it's going to be great preparation for my dress rehearsal, which up until now I'd felt shaky about even attempting.

Poised and ready for her dress rehearsal, Joanne went to Macy's the following day. Here's what happened:

I did it! I went to Macy's. It was rather odd: though I felt fine when I got there, I began to be genuinely upset when I remembered my boss's behavior in the movie. I've done a lot of shopping when I felt hounded, and it was very easy to recapture that feeling. At the jewelry counter, I saw a gorgeous watch—it was a Movado rather than a Bulova—and the urge came flooding back. It didn't matter that this was a dress rehearsal or that this new watch was much more expensive; *I wanted that watch.* I felt simultaneously "up" and upset. I tried on the watch and a couple of cheaper ones, and then I thanked the saleslady and told her I might come back.

I had trouble finding a good place to sit down. I was embarrassed at how upset I felt, since I'd rehearsed this already. I wanted to calm down. Finally, I got in the car and drove to a nearby park. It was a beautiful day, and I just wanted to get away and think. As I started to write in my journal, I began to see that I was *mad,* mad as hell: mad at my "imaginary" boss (who's a lot like my real one) for her unjustness and her indirect shaming, madder at myself for not standing up to her, for not even *considering* doing so. So I didn't calm down very much.

Instead, I drove back to the mall, marched up to the jewelry counter, and practically demanded to see the Movado watch again. But I almost couldn't focus on it; I was thinking about my boss. I made an excuse about having forgotten something and told the saleslady I'd be back. I found a bench at the mall and again got out my journal. I recognized that maybe I wasn't ready to confront my boss—and that confronting her might make matters worse—but I needed to do *something.* Then I had an idea: why not call Brenda, a coworker and one of my Shopping Support Buddies? She knows the quality of my work. She'll reassure me—and remind me that in our frenetic office, everything blows over by the following day. I realized that when my boss gives me a hard time, what I *really* need is affirmation and validation, which I can get in a lot of places in my life. One important source for these is my group of Shopping Support Buddies. I can also remind myself about Carla, the little girl I've been Big Sistering for several years now: how well she's done since I've started spending time with her. *That's* validation. And now I did feel myself calming down.

Once more, I returned to the jewelry counter. It was almost a joke now, but the saleslady wasn't busy, so she humored me. I grew less and less anxious, and although I still wanted that watch, the urge was not nearly as strong as before. I experienced in my gut what my head had been telling me—that I don't have to buy, certainly not now. Watches like this one aren't going anywhere. And if they do, there'll be another one, just as lovely, right behind it. I even allowed myself a little fun, asking what kind of movement the watch had, how long a warranty, how many diamonds, and the carat weight. By the way, for whatever reason, the rings weren't calling my name the way they were in the mental rehearsal.

At that moment, I realized that I could see, touch, try on—*and not have to buy anything!* If I use the tools and strategies I've learned—and take my time—I can really and truly get unhooked. I felt great the rest of the afternoon: I'm in control of my life! The dress rehearsal pushed a lot more buttons than I'd expected, and it was extremely valuable to do anyway—probably, it occurs to me, *because* of those buttons. I now feel ready to take on the real urge, whenever it comes.

Once again, Joanne has put herself fully into the experiment and written an admirably detailed report of it. Now let's listen as she answers a similar set of questions, this time post–dress rehearsal:

1. How did it feel to actually let go of this item?
   At first, it felt pretty bad. I really wanted it, started to justify to myself how I could afford it and why I should have it. But because I'd committed to doing this dress rehearsal, I was able to stand back and let it go. Not easily, mind you. But I called Brenda, and she was so positive and congratulatory, some of the affirmation and validation I wanted from having a gorgeous new watch were coming my way for not *buying. Now there's a switch!*
2. On a 1–10 scale, with 1 being the worst and 10 being the best, how bad were those feelings?
   When I first left the store, I'd say 5 or 6, but after I talked to Brenda,

they were almost entirely gone, replaced by feelings of pride in myself.

3. How long did it take you to get over them?
   Only until I'd talked with Brenda.
4. Was there a bad outcome?
   No. Truthfully, only good came of this.
5. If so, what did it take for you to recover, and how long did it take?
6. What conclusions did you draw from this experiment?
   I'd resisted finding Shopping Support Buddies until recently, but that extra help is invaluable. Opening up to a close friend who understands and really wants to help, knowing that I have someone to call—this makes a huge difference.

The detailed practice of these rehearsals breaks down the over-shopping sequence into manageable pieces, allowing you to step back and examine each piece—and then step away from the temptation to lapse. While the intensive nature of these exercises precludes doing both of them regularly, the more manageable of the two, the mental rehearsal, is a great preparation for any high-risk encounter. Whenever you feel the temptation to lapse, it offers you an imaginative way to walk past your demons and ward them off.

JOURNAL TIME

Your *Mental Rehearsal*

Now write out your own mental rehearsal of a highly tempting shopping encounter, using the lapse or relapse trigger you selected above. (Because you'll follow this with a dress rehearsal, don't pick the highest-risk scenario on your list; choose a situation you think you can manage.) Give your movie plenty of detail; let it follow you from the moment you enter the situation until you exit—*without buying anything*. If, for example, the situation involves Internet or catalog shopping, describe all the elements: you at the computer or in your favorite chair, the Sundance catalog on your lap and the phone nearby. If your scenario takes place in a store, bring it to life with your description.

Write about what you know: yourself, the feel of the event, the triggers and aftershocks that make the situation risky, and the coping techniques and strategies you've learned. Are you likely to experience physical symptoms? Write about your underlying needs, the tailor-made alternatives you might choose, the Necessity Scores of prospective purchases, what else you might do with your time and money, what blessings you might remind yourself of. Give yourself at least a half hour to do this; forty-five minutes is even better. Once you've written out your mental rehearsal, take a deep breath, step back a little from the experience, and then answer the same six post–mental rehearsal questions that Joanne did:

1. How did it feel to imagine letting go of the item(s) that you rehearsed with?
2. On a scale of 1 to 10, with 1 being the worst and 10 being the best, how bad are those feelings?
3. How long do you think it would take you to get over those feelings?
4. What bad outcome might there be if you didn't purchase the item(s)?
5. What would it take for you to recover if that bad thing happened?
6. What conclusions have you drawn from this experiment?

EXERCISE

Your *Dress Rehearsal*

This actual walk-through of a risky situation is a lot riskier than the mental rehearsal that precedes it. Will you need to talk it through with someone and get support before, during, or after? Will you need to take somebody with you or, conversely, *avoid* going with a particular person? What will it take for you to succeed in this venture?

Use the same situation you imagined above, and this time actually go to the store or log on to the shopping site. The dress rehearsal is unlikely to be entirely comfortable, so be sure to maintain your caring stance. *Arrange* the structure and the support you need to ensure success. If, for example, a supportive friend is part of your mental rehearsal, see that he or she is available for the walk-through and informed about its purpose and goal. If your Shopping Journal is a part of the mental rehearsal—and I certainly hope it is—don't fail to bring it with you. Follow your mental rehearsal as closely as you can. There'll be differences, of course, because imagination and reality never entirely dovetail, but closely approximating your movie will give extra authority to your walk-though. Finally, consider planning or scheduling a pleasurable activity for afterward; this will help to combat anxiety and give you a reward to look forward to.

After you've done your dress rehearsal, it could be useful to write about it in your journal. At the very least, think about it in detail. What were your thoughts and feelings and behavior before, during, and after the walk-through? (You may afterward want to acknowledge these further by talking to a supportive friend, a family member, or a therapist.) In your write-up, include answers to any of the following questions that apply: How close to the movie was the walk-through? Did you come out of this high-risk situation without buying anything? Did anything happen that you hadn't anticipated? Did you get stage fright and chicken out? Did you forget your lines? If you weren't fully successful, what would you have to do next time to ensure success?

Congratulations! Completing your initial walk-through is another big step forward—and the journey continues. Later, allow yourself to confront other triggers, to enter other tempting situations and practice not buying, until you can comfortably handle them. If at any point you don't succeed, look at what went wrong, determine where in the process you had problems, and make notes in your Shopping Journal. If you slip up, be sure to arrange the support you need before trying again. And be prudent: don't take on more than one item at a time.

THE BINGE: PLANNING FOR UPCOMING HIGH-RISK SITUATIONS

OK. Say you've worked with this book for a while, and it's going well. You take to the new strategies and techniques like a duck to water, and you're already holding your shopping demons at bay. You're feeling good—self-confident and optimistic. OK!

But not so fast. It's one thing to stop overshopping for a focused and somewhat intensive period. It's quite another when you're zapped by something big, something you haven't prepared for, something that blindsides you.

Sometimes it comes out of the blue. You fall madly in love and suddenly realize you've been spending money hand over fist on getaway weekends and gifts for your new sweetheart. Sometimes you can see it coming from miles away. You started the work of this book in January, after badly overshopping last December, and now it's October and the good vibes of your nine months' success are giving way to dread: the approaching demands of your family's annual extravaganza—the gifts, the decorations, the parties, more gifts— these reach for you like the ghostly fingers of Christmas Past Due.

Sometimes you're just unprepared. Suddenly it's your tenth anniversary, and you want something very special to mark your first decade of togetherness. More typically, it's not one major purchase but a string of them: setting up a basement office for your new, part-time, work-at-home business, for example.

Forewarned is forearmed. You need an effective *plan* for your next big overshopping challenge. You also need to keep a keen eye out for any demons lurking round the corner, ready to pounce and drag you back into their lair. Maybe there'll be special events—birthdays, celebrations at work, business meetings, a vacation, a visit, a presentation at the office. Maybe there'll be some change in routine: your child's going to camp, your boss will be out of the office for a month, you've lost your job, or your closest friend is being relocated to China. Maybe you'll simply get some spare time, enough to relax with a catalog or go surfing on the auction sites . . .

Something will come up. Something always does. Soon you'll learn how to prepare for a high-risk situation by creating a Lapse and Relapse Prevention Plan. (It's great to get into the habit of making these early, and as often as needed.) First, though, take a look at these general principles and specific tips for lapse and relapse prevention.

Tips for Lapse and Relapse Prevention

- *Acknowledge and anticipate.* Admit that you could easily lapse or relapse if you fail to look ahead toward prospective high-risk situations. Note how different this is from *predicting* that you'll overshop (which creates an expectation of failure). Predict that you *won't* overshop, because you're going to create a good prevention plan and follow it through. Simply *naming* an upcoming high-risk situation on a Lapse and Relapse Prevention Plan (see the end of this section) gives you a leg up; writing it down in black and white is far more powerful than only worrying about it (or trying not to think about it at all).

- *Identify and avoid triggers.* As soon as an urge starts to stir in you—or you even worry that one *might* stir in a future high-risk situation—pay attention to your radar. Back in chapter 2, you identified your situational, cognitive, interpersonal, emotional, and physical triggers for previous overshopping urges; by now you're probably a pro at this. (If you need a refresher, review chapter 2 and the list of triggers you wrote in your Shopping Journal.) Just what is it that this upcoming situation is stirring in you? Note any bodily sensations; any negative or positive feelings; any thoughts, images, or memories that bubble up as you anticipate. What do these tell you?

- *Evaluate and troubleshoot possible aftershocks.* Don't be so afraid to think about the possible consequences of a lapse that you put the whole thing out of your mind. Nothing's happened yet! Better to think ahead, anticipate, and grapple now with your feelings than to overshop later. Consider the worst possible consequences of a lapse; then consider damage control. Is there a realistic way to altogether avoid aftershocks? What might you do, even if you slip, to minimize the consequences? Could you return an overshopped item or sell it on eBay? Cancel a reservation, even if you're charged a fee to do so? Let go of the $100 layaway deposit you put down on a $900 leather sofa, now that you're seeing clearly and realize you can't buy it?

- *Listen to your heart and head, and identify and restructure automatic thoughts.* First, simply listen to what your heart and head are saying about the prospective high-risk situation—just as you've done for earlier urges. Then, see if you can restructure any thoughts that aren't serving you well. (Refer back to the "Language of the Mind: Thoughts" section of chapter 9 if you get stuck.) Create a Metta Tag that affirms your control as the high-risk situation approaches.

- *Ferret out what you'll really need in this upcoming situation.* What exactly is it in the upcoming situation that's especially challenging for you? What old buttons get pushed when you think about it? What do you *really* need, and how can you get it without overshopping? Is there something you can do before, during, or after the event that will meet your needs without overspending? Beware of overloading high-risk situations with unrealistic expectations; give up on the fantasy that they can or should be perfect. Refer to chapter 5 and to your tailor-made alternatives list for ideas on how to get what you really need. Be creative!

- *Don't give yourself an excuse for failure. Create self-control strategies well in advance.* High-risk situations often feel unavoidable: you *have to go* to your sister's wedding, and so you *have to get* an amazing new outfit—or so it seems. Think this through. Yes, of course you want to go, and of course you want to look your best. But with all the tools at your disposal, you can avoid the worst and cope with the rest. If you decide to shop, do so mindfully. Plan your purchase, determining the maximum amount you can afford to spend. Don't shop with that wealthy bridesmaid who'll look only at designer gowns; plan and practice what to say to her, so social pressure doesn't end up driving your purchase. When you go for your outfit, bring your Shopping Journal with you, your debit card tucked into the back pocket; leave your credit card at home.

- *Evaluate any expenditures against your values and goals.* Keeping your values and goals uppermost in your mind will help to sharpen and refine them—and will help you to embrace them and yourself.

THE LAPSE AND RELAPSE PREVENTION PLAN

A useful maxim for prevention plans is "Strike while the iron is cold": prepare your plan when you're not feeling stressed by urges to buy. This will help bolster your resolve. A Lapse and Relapse Prevention Plan is a series of prompts you respond to in your journal as a high-risk situation approaches. The process activates the tools you've learned to use, fortifying you against the heat of the upcoming moments. First, let's look at an example, as a woman named Tammy creates a plan and puts it to work. Then you'll start to think about creating one of your own.

Tammy's Well-Deserved Vacation

After Tammy spent many years in an unsatisfying and sometimes destructive marriage, her divorce has become final, and though she's got a lot of complicated, mixed feelings, the dominant one is relief. Even though she's had to move out of an apartment she loved and will be relocating to a smaller one, this one has some outdoor space—and several of her friends live nearby. She wants to take a trip to celebrate the beginning of this new chapter in her life. In the old days, she'd put everything on her credit card and worry about paying for it later. As you can see below, she's now trying for balance, hoping to go on the trip, not break the bank, not feel deprived, and still have a great time. See what you think about her Lapse and Relapse Prevention Plan.

1. What's the upcoming high-risk situation that could trigger overshopping?
   My vacation, and the many feelings I have about my marriage ending.
2. What about this situation might trigger you to overshop?
   I've been holding it together so tightly! Now that my divorce is final, I just want to relax and let go! I'm worried I'll just take off, selecting a destination without regard for the expense. Already I was doing this on the Internet last night. I can see myself overspending on personal items and services while I'm gone: beach garb, piña coladas, spa treatments, a new tote bag—acting as though it's the last vacation I'll go on for a long time.

3. If you did overshop, what might the consequences be?
   I could easily get back into overspending to "make up for" how difficult this period in my life has been. Then I'd have to move into my new place already stressed about additional debt.
4. What automatic or dysfunctional thoughts are you having about this situation?
   First, I've just come through a traumatic divorce. If I don't take a really first-class vacation, I'll feel deprived. Second, I need to get far away to really relax and recharge. I couldn't do it here.
5. How can you restructure those irrational thoughts?
   First, my divorce doesn't entitle me to splurge—certainly not with all my credit card debt. But sun and beach are luxurious enough, and last time I checked, they were both free! Second, there's no real reason I can't relax and recharge closer to home. In fact, spending less will help me relax. In short, spend less on "fixes," Tammy; go for real self-care: reduce stress by not overspending.
6. What are you *really* shopping for—what is the authentic underlying need that's fueling your impulse to overshop?
   First, a "carefree" feeling; second, experiencing the beauty of nature, especially sun and sea; third, returning refreshed and more peaceful, energized, and excited to move into my new apartment and start this next chapter of my life.
7. Instead of overshopping, how could you successfully meet that need?
   First, I could find a reasonably priced hotel with beautiful gardens, meals, and a hammock included. Second, I could walk on the beach and soak up the sun. And, third, I could commit to eating lunch in the park when I get back instead of shopping on my lunch hour.
8. Write a special Metta Tag to help you specifically with this upcoming high-risk situation.
   I spend only what I can afford. I truly relax, enjoy my vacation, and return refreshed.
9. What danger zones do you have to avoid?
   High-end "luxury" travel packages on the Internet and tourist-gear shops on the vacation.
10. What sources of social pressure do you have to avoid or deflect, and how will you do that?

I'm my own source of pressure, telling myself I "deserve" a luxury vacation. What I deserve is the freedom that comes from being able to manage my money wisely and pay back my debt.

11. If you've made the decision to shop, how will you plan your shopping to minimize the risk of overshopping? Make notes in advance of when, where, with whom, for whom, and for how long you'll shop; also, how you'll pay. Think about how much you can comfortably afford for each item and how necessary each one is. Finally, think about the risk of overshopping with this plan.

   I'll shop tonight and some on the trip. Tonight I'll shop for the air/hotel package on the Internet for a maximum of two to three hours. I can afford $1,500 for that. I'm going to shop with my most responsible self and for my tired, lovable self! I'm going to get a much-needed spa treatment on vacation, and I can afford $150 for that. If I get a tote bag, which I really don't need, I'm only going to spend $50 more, and I won't spend a lot of my vacation time look-ing for it either. I'll use my debit card for all of this. I feel confident that I'll be able to follow this plan and not overspend.

12. After the situation is over, make some notes about how you managed it and any ideas you have for future high-risk situations.

   I actually found a beautiful, affordable, small hotel on one of the nicest strips of beach and spent a wonderful five days there. I read, relaxed, snorkeled, and soaked up sun and sea. I got a great spa treatment, found a tote bag for even less than I'd allocated, and returned home completely refreshed. I'm eager to move and put my marriage behind me, and I'm doubly committed to planning and living more thoughtfully.

JOURNAL TIME

Your Lapse and Relapse Prevention Plan

Now it's your turn. What potentially high-risk situations do you foresee in the next six to twelve months? Maybe you're in line for an important promotion, or you're about to graduate from some course of study, or you're about to retire. Perhaps a friend or relative is moving away—or moving in, for that matter. Maybe it's *you* who'll be doing the moving. Any of these is likely to give rise to intense feelings, either positive or negative, feelings that might trigger an overshopping lapse or even a full-blown relapse. As the first of these situations approaches, begin working on a Lapse and Relapse Prevention Plan; continue to do this as you see potentially high-risk situations on the horizon. (You might want to mark this page with a Post-it so it's easy to find when you need it.) Remember, it's important to begin to create your plan *well in advance* and keep refining it as the high-risk situation approaches. Use the same twelve prompts that Tammy responded to:

1. What's the upcoming high-risk situation that could trigger overshopping?
2. What about this situation might trigger you to overshop?
3. If you did overshop, what might the consequences be?
4. What automatic or dysfunctional thoughts are you having about this situation?
5. How can you restructure those irrational thoughts?
6. What are you *really* shopping for—what is the authentic underlying need that's fueling your impulse to overshop?
7. Instead of overshopping, how could you successfully meet that need?
8. Write a special Metta Tag to help you specifically with this upcoming high-risk situation.
9. What danger zones do you have to avoid?
10. What sources of social pressure do you have to avoid or deflect, and how will you do that?
11. If you've made the decision to shop, how will you plan your shopping to minimize the risk of overshopping? Make notes in advance of when, where, with whom, for whom, and for how long you'll shop, and also how you'll pay. Think about how much you can comfortably afford for each item and how necessary each one is. Finally, think about the risk of overshopping with this plan.
12. After the situation is over, make some notes about how you managed it and any ideas you have for future high-risk situations.

You now know what you need to do if you've lapsed or relapsed, or if a really high-risk situation is coming straight at you. If you return to overshopping after a long period of abstinence, see it as a bump in the road, a detour on the journey—and rededicate yourself to the strategies and techniques that have worked best for you in the past. Like Dorothy and her friends in the land of Oz, you already have everything you need to get where you want to go. And you don't have to buy ruby-red slippers to get there! Follow the yellow brick road of this book, and it'll lead you straight to stopping overshopping.

THE HANGOVER: AFTER THAT FIRST SIP (OR THE WHOLE GLASS)

Deeply ingrained habits die hard, and compulsive shopping is certainly no exception; so it's essential to recognize that your progression away from it probably won't be linear. Far more typical is the "three steps forward, one step back" model. Don't let this throw you. Simple arithmetic tells us that this model will get you where you need to go—with a net gain of two steps at a time. What's critical for maintaining your overall progress in the face of occasional regressions is preparation and attitude.

In spite of all of your planning and intentions, lapses and relapses can happen—do happen. When you've done all you can to avoid or handle the urge to shop and you still find yourself heading home with packages you don't really need, it's vital that you not compound the slip with either of two very typical responses. *Don't minimize* and *don't catastrophize*. Instead, reassert your central stance of seeing clearly and with nonjudgmental compassion. Then brush yourself off and move forward.

Tips for Lapse and Relapse Recovery

Reframe a lapse or relapse. All-or-nothing thinking can turn a slip into a slide, with hopelessness and despair precipitating ever-worsening overshopping. Avoid this by abandoning perfectionist thinking about a lapse or relapse. Instead, *reframe* it. Step back and see it at a different scale—as an event that's not unimportant but is still only a ripple in the pond of your life.

Watch your self-talk, and be forgiving. Avoid self-punishing talk. It's natural to feel bad about falling off the wagon, but a lapse isn't the end of the world. Don't denigrate yourself as "out of control," "unable to do this recovery thing," "a loser." Whatever may have happened, the reins of control are always before you; it's you who dropped them, and it's you who can pick them up. Credit yourself for the progress you've made, which began with your decision to read this book and work the exercises in it and has continued through a host of positive steps. Stick to the reality of what's happened; being too tough on yourself will harm rather than help you. Renew your commitment to stopping and you can climb right back on the wagon.

Limit the damage. During a lapse, implement damage-control procedures; for example, leave the store after your first purchase, and, if you've brought a credit card, mail it home. (Keep a stamped, self-addressed envelope handy for this purpose.) After a lapse, return what you can, and, when you do, *don't buy anything else.* If you can't get a refund, get a store credit, which you can use when there's a genuine need. You can refuse delivery of impulsive catalog orders or, if you've opened them, pay the return postage and send them back. Reread your Shopping Journal and parts of the book you found particularly helpful—this will minimize the chances for a lapse to become a relapse.

Get back to your techniques. Start practicing alternative behaviors. Go to a peaceful place, either literally or in your mind's eye, when you're in trouble. Meditate. Connect with your support network. If you skipped over any parts of this book originally, do them now. Return to a plan of shopping without *over*shopping.

See and use your slips as learning opportunities. A lapse is several things, but one of them is a message, a letter to you about yourself; work hard to read what it tells you. Ask yourself the central questions: What are my real needs here? What triggers are operating? What thoughts and feelings came with the urge? When could I still have walked away? If you have experience with prior slips, look back and try to see what *they* were telling you. The more you can learn from a slip, the more control you'll gain for the next temptation. (Sometimes writing a dialogue will give you a deeper understanding of what a slip is about and how it happened.)

Seek treatment or a self-help group if a relapse is prolonged. If you're in therapy, talk about any relapse with your therapist. If you're not, a prolonged relapse might well point you in that direction—ideally, to a therapist who has worked with overshopping issues. If overshopping has created serious problems in your primary relationship, it might be helpful to seek couples counseling with a therapist familiar with money disorders. Debtors Anonymous is another resource, as are online self-help groups. If you're on medication, a lengthy relapse would suggest a consultation with your prescriber. If you're not, a psychopharmacologist is yet another possible resource. Don't let a relapse go on and on. Get help.

Make lifestyle changes that will support your recovery. Learn how to create a more balanced lifestyle. If you're overworking, for example, and that tends to trigger your overshopping, allow yourself—force yourself, if need be—to play, to have fun. If your lapses occur with particular friends, even if you'd thought them safe to shop with, explore a new way to be together, even if only temporarily. Stretch a little; try something entirely new.

Again, attitude is everything. After a lapse or relapse, you're particularly vulnerable. All the barriers you've erected against overshopping have been breached; all the focus and energy you've poured into the program has, for the moment, come to naught. Your habit, which wants to maintain itself, seizes the opportunity of this leak to try to open the floodgates. If you kid yourself with minimizing—"It's just this once, and I deserved it, even though it wasn't on my list"—you're ignoring the crack in the dam. If you wring your hands and feel sorry for yourself—"I'm hopeless! This proves it"—you're accepting the flood as inevitable. Instead, this is the moment for a clear-sighted, compassionate perspective. Reassert it and you won't feed into the negativity of the lapse. Instead, you'll have the perspective to recognize it as a detour, not a washout, as part of the continuing journey rather than a premature and abrupt end to the trip.

Conclusion

Wrapping It Up and Bringing It Home

Congratulations on having arrived at this final leg of our long and arduous journey! I know there were things you didn't want to read, didn't want to write, didn't want to learn; yet you read, you wrote, and you learned. Getting here means you've really stretched yourself. You've developed and practiced new skills, begun to master the use of new tools, and created and tested important strategies. I hope you'll continue to use all that you've learned to stop overshopping. I hope, too, that these changes are an integral part of something larger: that you'll come away from this book equipped to live a richer, freer, happier life. Toward that end, I want to leave you with a few ideas for expanding your everyday living options and one final exercise where you distill your experience of the program to its essence.

SHOP IS NOT A FOUR-LETTER WORD

The first idea I'd like to leave you with is this: *shop is not a four-letter word*. Though you've got to turn away from compulsive, mindless overshopping, let me reiterate my belief that shopping can be both positive and productive. To shop is to taste, touch, sift, consider, and talk our way through an endless landscape of possibilities as we try to determine what we want and need. A vital and challenging process of search, shopping offers opportunities for self-definition, self-expression, creativity, sometimes even healing. Shopping—whether for a mutual fund, a pair of pumps, a movie, a political candidate, or a lifestyle—is a way we search for ourselves and our place in the world.

But shop with a wide-angle lens! Focus more of your attention on ideas and experiences than on goods and services. Remember, an extensive body of research shows unequivocally that *we get far more lasting satisfaction from experiences than we do from material goods.* That research confirms what we all know in our hearts: the good life comes from *doing* things, not from *having* them. When we invest our discretionary resources in life experiences rather than material possessions, we see it as money better spent—and we're happier.

There are several reasons for this. First, experiences (unlike most material goods) grow *more* valuable over time, giving us pleasure in the memories we have—and the stories we tell—about them. Also, experiences aren't nearly as likely as material goods are to disappoint us or lead to regrets. Because they're unique to us, experiences aren't usually subject to negative comparisons, while this can easily happen with material goods when somebody else gets a bigger, nicer, newer, or more expensive thing than yours. Finally, experiences tend to be shared, whereas acquiring things is more often a solo act.[1] We'll go on at length, if our listener is interested, about a movie we've seen or a trip we've taken. How often do we have as much to say (or as willing an ear) when we talk about our sunglasses or iPods?

Even when it's for things rather than experiences, conscious, thoughtful shopping is a way we align outer and inner, squaring our material existence with who we are, what we need, and what we want out of life. By developing a thoughtful approach to the search process, you're slowly untying the knot that binds shopping and buying so tightly together. Conscious shopping—which is a conversation with your heart, your head, your mind, and your soul—opens you to important opportunities for growth. Stepping off the consumption escalator, you put both feet solidly on the ground; and balanced there, in control, you can *select* rather than *seize*.

HOW MUCH IS ENOUGH?

While the most obvious prerequisite for selecting rather than seizing is to break free of the *compulsion* behind compulsive shopping—that desperate need, that enslavement to desire—it's also crucial that you make a sensible determination of just *how much* is *enough*. Clearly, if you live without essential goods and services, uncertain of a roof over your head or your next meal, you don't have enough. There comes a point, however—and we reach it much sooner than most overshoppers recognize—of sufficiency, a point where you can provide for your needs and some of your wants. Beyond this lies the land of diminishing returns, where the benefits of having more stuff are outweighed by the costs of getting and maintaining it. Here, instead of liberating us, things bind us—to useless tasks, to negatively impacted relationships, to decreased productivity, and to impaired overall health.

Many of us who live beyond this point of diminishing returns live in material abundance—but in abject poverty when it comes to joy. As life flashes by us on our feverish work-spend bullet train, we ignore the stress this constant state of overdrive puts on our engines. It's a fundamental law of systems that as they get more complex, they get *much* more difficult to maintain. For those of us with a lot of money (or aspirations to get a lot), a significant portion of our time and energy is spent in its acquisition—and another large dollop goes to finding and maintaining the possessions that our money has made possible. The more we have, the more administration and management we must do—and the further removed we are from the hands-on activities that bring the joy of total engagement, of being at one with our experience. Rather than apportioning our time to such activities as woodworking, making music, painting, mowing the lawn, tending a garden, cooking, writing, arranging flowers, helping our kids with their homework or teaching them to play ball or fly kites, we overwork so we can pay other people to do these for us, robbing ourselves of those pleasures.

Enough makes life rich; *too much* leans toward misery. But in our culture, we're led to wolf down more than we can digest. We supersize work and ambition just as unhealthily as we supersize fast food. In the process, our intuitive balance, our instinct for knowing how much is enough, is thrown off. Regaining it involves clear seeing, compassion toward yourself, restraint, and the capacity to be still in the present moment, with nothing added. This can be a struggle; in today's brave, fast world, we are not encouraged to sit quietly and be with what is, and we're actively *dis*couraged from seeing that less is more.

LESS *IS* MORE

As I've said earlier, and want to reiterate here, hyperabundance is far from a blessing. "More is better" is a bill of goods we've been sold, but research and experience agree on its falsehood. The American Dream has a dark underbelly. Money and possessions will *not* make us happy; when acquisition is the standard, happiness is always the next purchase away, or the one after that—an infinitely receding horizon that keeps sliding farther into the distance. Always bear in mind, to say it one last time, *you can never get enough of what you don't really need.*

After all, we can do only so much. Ultimately, an intense focus on materialistic pursuits takes us away from spiritual and psychological growth. It also signals an alienation from ourselves, our families, and our communities. Constant acquisition demands so much of us that it leaves little quality time and energy for the central people in our lives; instead, we wind up having relationships with the things we purchase, which are neither deep nor very satisfying. We treat one another in less and less humane ways; grammar notwithstanding, objects take precedence over subjects! Even the earth itself, our communal home, suffers; in the grip of "aspendicitis" or luxury fever, we ransack the planet. It's no accident that Americans, who represent maybe 5 percent of the earth's population, consume nearly *one-third* of its resources.[2]

It would be a formidable leap, but maybe we need to start thinking like the government of Bhutan, which in 1972 threw out the usual economic progress indicators and replaced them with a "Gross National Happiness" index. This revolutionary concept, embracing everything from the protection of natural resources to the promotion of a strong culture and the ensuring of democratic governance, puts the overall well-being of citizens at the forefront of national policy. No dark underbelly there!

TRUE WEALTH, VOLUNTARY SIMPLICITY, AND *WABI SABI*

Throughout this book, you've been fortifying yourself with an arsenal of tools, skills, and strategies to fight off affluenza, our national (and, increasingly, global) epidemic of overconsumption. Before we conclude our work together, I want to introduce you to three powerful and intimately related ideas: the cultivation of "true wealth," the consideration of voluntary simplicity, and the contemplation of wabi sabi. All three are designed to optimize present and future happiness.

True Wealth, a 1990 book by Paul Hwoschinsky, offers a persuasive antidote to rampant materialism. Hwoschinsky suggests that true wealth is attained by leveraging those nonfinancial assets, different for each person, that invigorate and vitalize: talents, hobbies, close connections with other people and animals, communion with nature—food for our neglected spiritual and emotional appetites. Materialism, he notes, focuses on status, power, and control; it cannot fulfill us. True wealth can and does, by embracing self-acceptance, personal growth, intimacy, creativity, curiosity, courage, integrity, compassion, forgiveness, and community feeling. Hwoschinsky's arguments, strong when the book first appeared, seem more and more powerful with each passing year.

A second lifestyle idea, voluntary simplicity, whose origins go back to the nineteenth century, is more popular today than ever before. It's a movement that encourages people to redefine the good life, to seek lives outwardly simple and inwardly rich. Calling into question the values of material wealth and status, it focuses instead on frugal consumption, ecological awareness, moral responsibility, and the development of the wisdom to think through—and act upon—what really matters. Lao-tzu poured the foundation for this movement twenty-four centuries ago, saying "He who knows he has enough is rich." (The converse is true as well: he who has enough but *doesn't* know it is poor.) Voluntary simplicity turns away from activities that have repeatedly failed to deliver satisfaction and contentment—mindless shopping, for example, or competitively scrambling up the career ladder—and embraces instead the joys of creativity and community. It celebrates everyday life.[3]

A third stance toward life, wabi sabi, is an integral part of traditional Japanese culture. It "appreciates and accepts complexity" even as it values simplicity, tranquility, and naturalness.[4] *Wabi* suggests rustic simplicity: freshness, quietness, and understated elegance. *Sabi* is "the gloom of time," the natural progression of tarnish and rust, the extinguished gloss of that which once sparkled.[5] It accepts and embraces the patina that comes with age. In contemporary American culture, objects are discarded well before they reach this point; instead, something new is acquired.[6] We're so busy trying to stay new, young, and unworn, constantly updating, upgrading, renovating, and attempting to reinvent ourselves, that we miss precious opportunities to form deep and abiding attachments to objects we already have—to say nothing of the people we love. Wabi sabi acknowledges that nothing lasts, nothing is finished, and nothing is perfect. "To accept these realities is to accept contentment as the maturation of happiness, and to acknowledge that clarity and grace can be found in genuine unvarnished existence."[7]

Each of these stances I've just lightly sketched—true wealth, voluntary simplicity, and wabi sabi—is a way of looking at and living your life beyond the incessant gravity of consumerism, out of the centrifugal whirl of overshopping. Each can anchor the work you've done in this book.

JOURNAL TIME

Distilling Your Experience of the Program to Its Essence

In this final inventory, it's time to step back, to look clearly at your journey through these months and many chapters, and to embrace yourself. Then write in your Shopping Journal about the essence of *your* particular experience: what you've discovered, what it's felt like to get to this point, what the biggest obstacles and triumphs have been, and what it feels like to be here now. Don't shortchange yourself; make sure you create the time and space to do this final piece of writing fully and openheartedly. Then give yourself the credit you so richly deserve for having gotten here.

ONWARD

This is the end of one journey and the start of another. You've looked hard at what goes into your overshopping behavior and comes out of it. You've worked hard to blunt the sharpness of your urges with newly learned strategies and techniques. And you've thought hard

Acknowledgments

Writing the acknowledgments for a project like this is a consummate pleasure. Not only does getting to this point mean that the book is finally finished but it also means that I get a chance to look back, count my blessings, and express my gratitude to a team of generous friends and colleagues, each of whom supplied something vital. As I pause to recognize them at the close of this fierce year of labor, I offer my heartfelt thanks. Quite simply, the book would not exist without them.

From the time I first decided to morph and update the Stopping Overshopping Program into a format that would make it available to countless overshoppers, my long-time editor (and even longer-time brother), Gary Lane, has done what he's always done for me: provided the sage counsel of a loyal and loving older sibling, shaped and immeasurably extended my thinking, and worked his particular alchemist's magic with the copy I supplied him.

Over the course of this writing project, and especially over the last three months, Eden Steinberg, my editor at Shambhala, enthusiastically championed *To Buy or Not to Buy* and helped me to reign in a lifelong tendency toward overconsumption—this time, of words. Her editorial suggestions in no small measure account for what I hope is a book that's manageable and motivating.

Five colleagues who contributed chapters to my earlier book, *I Shop, Therefore I Am: Compulsive Buying and the Search for Self,* also helped me with this one. Helga Dittmar, senior lecturer in psychology at the University of Sussex, in England, was always eager to share the latest research in the field with me. Donald Black, professor of psychiatry at the University of Iowa, gave me valuable feedback on the Shopping Patterns Checklist and on the issue of psychopharmacology for compulsive buying. James Mitchell, president of the Neuropsychiatric Research Institute in Fargo, North Dakota, who began running groups for compulsive buyers well before I did, was extremely generous, sharing his group treatment manual with me and patiently answering my many questions about his experience using it. Karen McCall, as a teacher and a writer, demystified for me the process of "keeping your numbers." Olivia Mellan, who introduced me to the money dialogue, leads a monthly money psychology teleclass that's a fertile place for brainstorming about projects like this one.

Nancy Ridgway, of the Robbins School of Business at the University of Richmond, shared the results of her compulsive buying research, and Lorrin Koran, of the Stanford University School of Medicine, provided useful suggestions about the introduction and about the section on medication. Irene Tobis helped shape the section on social pressure and conceived the dialogue about self-kindness. Laura Longville helped me with the needs section of the book, and Nick Lessa taught me about Motivational Interviewing.

My meditation teacher, Peter Doobinin, and my meditation sisters, Carol Coburn, Cynthia Del Mastro, Harriet Dorosin, Karen Heller, Andrea Raskin, Amy Selzer, Gail Spindell, and Elaine Vipler, have all helped me to experience, from the inside out, the joy and importance of stillness, the impermanence of thoughts and feelings, and the wisdom of the dharma. Sandra Shapiro, Nancy Bravman, and Judy Rabinor helped me to think through and write the visualizations and the body scan. Celia Berliner introduced me to the book *Hooked!;* Judi Hollis to *wabi sabi.* Lynn Lawrence, ever watchful for news relevant to her friends, came across and referred me to three books related to materialism and overconsumption before I had any idea the books existed; in a former life she must have been a librarian. For additional assistance, I thank Marcela Torres and Kathleen Galek, my associates at Stopping Overshopping, Julie Saidenberg and Ben Gleason of Shambhala Publications, and Elisa Michel.

The Institute for Contemporary Psychotherapy, my professional home for more than three decades, has provided me with an extremely fertile learning environment. And the overshoppers I've had the privilege of working with, both those I see in person and those I work with over the telephone, also deserve mention here. They've taught me more about the problem of overshopping and its solution than any book or course ever could. Your reminder card exists because of Sue from Houston's thoughtful suggestion.

And finally, deepest thanks to my husband Jim and my sons Eric and Corey. Each stuck by me when I was short on time, energy, sleep, or patience. Typical of my hero of a husband's contributions was his willingness to painstakingly proofread every word of the manuscript, to say nothing of the countless times he tamed my wild computer. For blessings conferred, for uncountable help, I thank all of these. For any shortcomings that remain, I take full responsibility.

Appendix A |
Shopping Support Buddies

A Shopping Support Buddy is a person who agrees to become your advocate, to work with you and help you stop overshopping. The exact form and nature of your relationship will be determined by the two of you; no two of these relationships are alike. Choose someone you know and respect, someone you consider trustworthy and non-judgmental, someone you can be yourself with—typically, a friend or relative, or perhaps a coach, counselor, or therapist. You might want to have more than one Shopping Support Buddy, to make it more likely you'll get the help you need when you need it.

How can your buddy support you? He or she can be on the other end of the phone when the going gets tough. Your buddy can share some of the work you've done in your Shopping Journal and bring a second pair of eyes to the search for patterns. Your buddy can be a confidant, revisiting with you what you've discovered about why you overshop and how it all began, or what you've observed about your personal shopping triggers and aftershocks, or what you consider the costs and benefits of either stopping or continuing. An understanding and encouraging voice, your buddy can celebrate your triumphs with you, buck you up when you slip a little, or give a gentle push and remind you to get back to the work of the book if you've stopped.

Don't underestimate the importance of a Shopping Support Buddy. Not being alone in this struggle makes a big difference. Knowing there's somebody else who understands what you're going through, who's on your side and cheering for you, can keep you motivated.

In addition, sharing your problem will help you feel your feelings and communicate about them rather than expressing them in self-defeating behaviors such as overshopping. It will also help you move beyond any denial you have, reduce your feeling of shame, and lead to greater self-acceptance.

Choose a buddy as soon as you prudently can, as soon as you've verified to yourself that your prospect is nurturing and wise. And if, for countless possible individual reasons, a prospect refuses, don't take it personally. Instead, find someone else. If you think positively and really want a buddy, you'll find one. People like to be of service to others, and this is a very unusual opportunity to be helpful.

Activate your search for a buddy by using the little table below. To give a prospect some idea of what you're asking, provide a copy of the Guidelines for Shopping Support Buddies following the table.

Candidate's Name	Have I approached the prospect?	Have I given the prospect Guidelines for Shopping Buddies?	Has the prospect agreed to be my Shopping Support Buddy?
	❑ Yes ❑ No	❑ Yes ❑ No	❑ Yes ❑ No
	❑ Yes ❑ No	❑ Yes ❑ No	❑ Yes ❑ No
	❑ Yes ❑ No	❑ Yes ❑ No	❑ Yes ❑ No
	❑ Yes ❑ No	❑ Yes ❑ No	❑ Yes ❑ No
	❑ Yes ❑ No	❑ Yes ❑ No	❑ Yes ❑ No

GUIDELINES FOR SHOPPING SUPPORT BUDDIES

Somebody who respects and trusts you wants your help in learning to control his or her overshopping behavior. This person is asking you to serve as a Shopping Support Buddy. He or she wants to be able to share difficulties, doubts, and successes with you, as well as to be reminded and helped to use the skills he or she is in the process of acquiring. Your role as a Shopping Support Buddy isn't to treat or cure; it's simply to be there with understanding and empathy when the opportunity arises. You're a listener and a cheerleader and a positive, creative coach. If, after a setback or two, your buddy loses confidence in his or her ability to change, you can be of tremendous help by remaining hopeful. If, on the other hand, your buddy accomplishes a program goal, celebrate with him or her. If your buddy calls you in the grip of an overshopping urge, calmly remind him or her that there are skills and techniques to control it.

Change can't be forced or rushed, not even by the most well-intentioned Shopping Support Buddy; it will happen only when the overshopper is ready. So be prepared for ambivalence; one part of your buddy very much wants to stop; and there's often just as big a part that wants to continue. Overshopping, despite its many costs, has powerful short-term rewards, and it's entirely normal for someone to have mixed feelings about stopping. Your job is to stay empathic. If your buddy weakens, don't express disapproval but rather solidarity, empathy, and comprehension: "I can see how hard it is for you to give this up. Let's you and I figure out together what you can do instead of shopping today."

Here are a few specific tips for the relationship:

Tips for Shopping Support Buddies

1. You and your buddy are a team. Two people on the same page are a recipe for success, whereas two people working at cross-purposes are seldom productive.
2. Help your buddy to stay focused on the stopping overshopping task. If he or she begins to avoid the work or to make excuses, remind your buddy of the ultimate objective.
3. If your buddy gets upset with you, stay calm. And if he or

she is unmotivated to do the work on a given day, allow your buddy to save face and temporarily opt out of your help.

4. Always provide emotional support. Don't scold or argue with your buddy. Acting like a taskmaster or a drill sergeant makes people nervous or angry and interferes with their ability to learn new approaches; they feel even more isolated and misunderstood, and retreat into bad habits.

5. Help with decision making, but don't try to make decisions for your buddy. It's probably better for you to ask good questions, questions that will help your buddy zero in on the right answer for him or her.

6. Be a steady cheerleader. Support even the slightest progress. Stay in touch with your buddy in whatever way the two of you have discussed and agreed on.

7. Accompany your buddy on a dress rehearsal or an actual shopping trip, one for which he or she has planned the purchase(s) in advance. Remind your buddy of his or her commitment and tools for stopping overshopping.

8. Don't go beyond your own comfort level. In order to be a useful Shopping Support Buddy, you need to know and set limits on what and how much you can do at any given time. If you think your buddy needs more than you can offer, help him or her to research additional options.

9. Acknowledge yourself for your generosity and willingness to tackle what can be a difficult role. And allow yourself to lovingly say "no" if, after reading these guidelines, you don't feel fully prepared to take on this role.

Appendix B |
Psychotherapy, Medication,
and the Work of This Book

PSYCHOTHERAPY

You don't need to be in any kind of formal psychotherapy to undertake the work of this book. But if you *are* in treatment, discuss your plans to work the program with your therapist; you might even want to bring some of the work to sessions. If you're in a self-help group or traditional group therapy, you might want to let the group know about this work. Sharing your experience in a safe, supportive setting can keep you motivated when the going gets tough and can help you put what you've learned to use.

If you're not in therapy and find yourself unable to stay with the work, several things could be happening. Sometimes a change in circumstances—such as divorce, serious illness, job loss, or a death in the family—can understandably cause you to lose focus and motivation. Sometimes, a co-occurring disorder will have flared up. Talk the situation over honestly and fully with a trusted friend or family member who's willing to serve as a Shopping Support Buddy. (Guidelines for Shopping Support Buddy relationships are in appendix A.) If you continue to have difficulty after that, consider a consultation with a therapist and/or psychiatrist. This additional support may very well get you back on track.

A FEW WORDS ABOUT MEDICATION

The use of psychotropic medication for the treatment of compulsive buying has been reported in the psychiatric literature since 1991. Antidepressants—typically, selective serotonin reuptake inhibitors (SSRIs)—have been used most frequently, although the use of mood stabilizers and naltrexone, an opioid antagonist, has also been reported, either alone or in combination with an antidepressant. A 1996 review of studies reporting treatment of compulsive buying with antidepressants suggested that antidepressant treatment was markedly successful when uncontrolled buying was associated with depression.[1] Other studies have suggested that the value of the medication involves its ability to control buying thoughts and impulses rather than mood elevation.[2] In any case, this early research had looked promising.

In 2000, however, the results of two other studies called the optimism sharply into question.[3] In these studies, all of whose subjects were randomly assigned to drug or placebo groups, the drug and placebo were equally effective at controlling overshopping. But all the subjects met on a regular basis with the study psychiatrist and a research nurse to talk about details of their shopping behavior, and all constructed shopping diaries that included daily records of their buying. The researchers hypothesize that this support and attention outweighed any effect the drug might have had.

To further cloud the issue, two recently published, identically designed studies treating compulsive buying with antidepressants showed contradictory results. In the first, the majority of patients using the medication reported a loss of interest in shopping and rated themselves "improved" or "very much improved."[4] Some of the responders were then switched to a placebo. More than half of those resumed overbuying, while none who continued on the medication relapsed. But when researchers repeated the study two years later with new subjects, relapse rates for initial positive responders were now the same whether they'd been continued on the medication or switched to a placebo.[5]

What to do? At this point, there's some evidence that in some people, medication can reduce the intensity of buying urges and the preoccupation with buying and therefore make it easier to work with this program. Referral for medication requires consultation with a psychiatrist, preferably one familiar with the latest research on drug treatment for compulsive buying. The psychiatrist will take into account whether or not a compulsive buyer has co-occurring conditions and/or other addictions. If you're already on psychotropic medication, it's important to discuss your plans to work this program with your prescriber.

Appendix C |
Resources

Organizations and Websites Related to Overshopping

Debtors Anonymous (www.debtorsanonymous.org)

Debtors Anonymous is a fellowship of men and women who share their experience, strength, and hope with one another in order to solve their common problem and help others recover from compulsive debting. The only requirement for membership is a desire to stop incurring unsecured debt. There are no dues or fees for DA membership. There are DA meetings in every state, as well as telephone and online meetings.

Shopping Addicts Only (http://health.groups.yahoo.com/group/ Shoppingaddictsonly)

This Yahoo online support group is a forum in which overshoppers exchange support, guidance, and companionship with other overshoppers. It's free. Members can post messages, contact other members, and gain access to helpful links.

MySelfHelp.com

This website provides an online, interactive self-help program for illuminating compulsive shopping. It's staffed by health-care professionals. There's a discussion board for both members and visitors, a free newsletter, and a free online program about how to help loved ones cope with issues.

Addicted.com

This website provides a variety of recovery resources for people struggling with addiction and for their families and friends. Highlights include a panel of experts in specific areas of addiction who answer readers' questions; a directory of addiction treatment centers, including virtual tours; and a directory of addiction counselors. The site offers addiction self-tests, links to twelve-step programs, and current articles on many types of addiction.

HypnosisDownloads.com

This eighteen-minute downloadable audio file details the steps of the compulsive buying cycle and uses guided imagery and visualization to help overshoppers gain control. For more information visit www.hyp nosisdownloads.com/downloads/hypnotherapy/shopping-addiction .html.

Talking Bookstore (www.talking-book-store.com)

Healing Addictions: Compulsive Shopping is a 1-hour and 8-minute downloadable audio file that includes instructions for deep relaxation, stress management, mental biofeedback, and healthy goal setting as they pertain to gaining control over compulsive shopping.

Help for People Who Hoard and for Their Families Buried in Treasures

Buried in Treasures: Help for Compulsive Acquiring, Saving, and Hoarding, by David F. Tolin, Randy O. Frost, and Gail Steketee (New York: Oxford University Press, 2007), outlines an effective, scientifically based program for helping compulsive hoarders dig their way out of the clutter and chaos of their homes. Includes self-assessments to determine the severity of the problem, tips and tools for organizing possessions and filing paperwork, strategies for changing unhelpful beliefs about possessions, and behavioral experiments to reduce the anxiety of discarding.

The Compulsive Hoarding Website (www.ocfoundation.org/hoarding)

This website provides information and assistance to people who hoard and to their families. Included on the site is a useful definition of hoarding, professional articles on multiple aspects of hoarding, a research digest for hoarding-related scientific papers, information about self-help and support groups, and a hoarding / compulsive buying screening test.

You can contact the foundation by telephone at (617) 973-5801. It recommends that clients and families with hoarding issues seek the help of a licensed professional with specialized training in treating this compulsion. For a list of specializing clinicians as well as other important information about hoarding behavior, e-mail Dr. David Tolin at dtolin@harthosp.org.

Consumer Education, Media Literacy, and Voluntary Simplicity

The Center for a New American Dream (www.newdream.org)

This website provides consumer education materials, including the video *More Fun, Less Stuff: The Challenges and Rewards of a New American Dream*. The center works with individuals, institutions, communities, and businesses to protect the environment, enhance quality of life, counter the commercialization of American culture, and promote social justice.

The New Road Map Foundation (www.newroadmap.org)

This is a nonprofit educational and charitable foundation that aims to cultivate a cooperative human community by creating and distributing practical tools and innovative approaches to personal and cultural change. Since 1980, a big focus of the foundation has been on teaching the program in *Your Money or Your Life*, by Joe Dominguez and Vicki Robin (New York: Penguin, 1992). In 2001, the New Road Map Foundation, in partnership with Seeds of Simplicity, launched the Simplicity Forum, a leadership alliance dedicated to honoring and achieving simple, just, and sustainable ways of life for all.

New Mexico Media Literacy Project (www.nmmlp.org)

Founded in 1993, the New Mexico Media Literacy Project is an outreach project of Albuquerque Academy and is one of the most successful media literacy organizations in the United States. Centered on building healthy communities, the New Mexico Media Literacy

Project supports critical thinking concerning today's media culture. The site offers educational media literacy presentations for youth and adults, training opportunities, media literacy curricula on CD and DVD, and a free newsletter.

Action Coalition for Media Education (www.acmecoalition.org/home)

Founded in 2002 in Albuquerque, New Mexico, the Action Coalition for Media Education (ACME) is an emerging global coalition run by and for media educators. It is dedicated to teaching about media literacy; developing and distributing media education curricula and tools; advocating independent media production; and supporting local, state, national, and global media reform, and media justice efforts. Using a wide variety of multimedia curricula and resources, ACME helps individuals and organizations gain the skills and knowledge to access, analyze, evaluate, and produce media in a wide variety of forms.

Don't Buy It: Get Media Smart! (www.pbskids.org/dontbuyit)

This media literacy site for young people encourages users to think critically about media and become smart consumers. Activities are designed to provide users with some of the skills and knowledge needed to question, analyze, interpret, and evaluate media messages.

The Media Education Foundation (www.mediaed.org)

Founded in 1991 by University of Massachusetts communication professor and media scholar Sut Jhally, the Media Education Foundation is the nation's leading producer and distributor of educational videos. The foundation encourages students to critically consider the structure of the media industry and the content it produces. It aims to stimulate reflection on the social, political, and cultural impact of American mass media.

The Simple Living Network (www.simpleliving.net/main)

Since 1996, the Simple Living Network has been providing resources, tools, examples, and contacts for conscious living that's simple, healthy, and restorative. This site offers a free online newsletter; discussion forums; in-person and online study groups and simplicity circles; and a wide variety of materials—including CDs, DVDs, e-books, and brochures—on topics related to voluntary simplicity.

The Simplicity Resource Guide
(www.gallagherpress.com/pierce/index.htm)

This site offers "a wide spectrum of resources related to voluntary simplicity, a way of life that addresses the widespread yearning in North America and other western countries for a slower pace of life with more time for joyful relationships, fulfilling work, and living one's dreams." Included are book reviews, articles and essays, and information about organizations and activities related to simplicity.

Reverend Billy and the Church of Stop Shopping (www.revbilly.com)

Reverend Billy (Bill Talen) and the Church of Stop Shopping are an advocacy group that believes consumerism is overwhelming our lives. They warn of the coming "shopocalypse." They perform throughout the country in a variety of venues to proffer their message that our neighborhoods are "disappearing into the corporatized world of big boxes and chain stores" and expose companies without "fair-trade" policies.

Financial Literacy, Debt, and Credit

SmartAboutMoney.org (http://smartaboutmoney.org)

A division of the National Endowment for Financial Education (NEFE), this site offers Web visitors the opportunity to take a financial assessment and then, on the basis of their answers, be directed to appropriate resources. There's also a life events and financial decisions section that helps consumers think about the financial issues that are relevant to a variety of life events and stages. In addition, you'll find here the NEFE Financial Literacy Resource Center[SM], a collection of free materials contributed by many organizations and reviewed by NEFE to provide credible and unbiased money management information and materials.

National Endowment for Financial Education (NEFE) (www.nefe.org)

The mission of NEFE is to help Americans acquire the knowledge and skill necessary to take control of their financial destiny. The endowment sees itself as having "nothing to sell and a lot to tell." NEFE provides informative and user-friendly articles, tools, and other resources. There's a financial-planning program that's been offered to more than 5 million high school students.

InCharge Debt Solutions (www.incharge.org)

InCharge Debt Solutions is a nonprofit organization that provides confidential and professional credit counseling, debt management, and financial education programs to people behind the financial eight ball. Its website, available in English and Spanish, offers educational and personal financial management tools, helping debtors learn to use credit responsibly and set a course for a financially stable and successful future.

InCharge Education Foundation (www.inchargefoundation.org)

The InCharge Education Foundation provides award-winning products and materials, including a variety of innovative personal finance tools ranging from content-rich magazines and websites to print, CD, and Web-based educational programs. All support the personal financial literacy needs of consumers worldwide, including children in grades kindergarten through twelve, eighteen- to twenty-four-year-olds, military families, new home buyers, the Hispanic population, and those going through bankruptcy.

MyMoney.gov (http://mymoney.gov)

This U.S. government website is dedicated to teaching all Americans the basics about financial education. Whether your questions relate to budgeting and taxes, credit, financial planning, home ownership, paying for education, retirement planning, or saving and investing, MyMoney.gov has useful and detailed information.

AnnualCreditReport.com

This central site allows you to request a free credit report once every twelve months from each of the nationwide consumer credit reporting companies: Equifax, Experian, and TransUnion.

Association of Independent Consumer Credit Counseling Agencies (www.aiccca.org)

The AICCCA is a member-supported national association representing nonprofit credit-counseling companies that provide consumer credit counseling, debt management, and financial education services. Consumers can find a directory of accredited consumer credit-counseling agencies on the site, and there are monthly press releases on a variety of topics relevant to consumers.

National Foundation for Credit Counseling (www.nfcc.org)

The NFCC is another site where consumers can find a directory of the credit-counseling services that belong to the organization. Housing counseling, to address the deepening foreclosure crisis, is available at almost all NFCC member agencies, and there's comprehensive information on credit counseling and how NFCC member agencies can make a difference to the consumer.

SaveKaryn.com

On this site is the story of Karen Bosnak, who found a creative way to get out of debt and, in the process, became an inspiration for others in debt. The site offers helpful, down-home suggestions for getting out of debt by a former debtor.

Recommended Videos

The Secret History of the Credit Card (1 hour)

"In 'Secret History of the Credit Card,' FRONTLINE® and *The New York Times* join forces to investigate an industry few Americans fully understand. . . . Correspondent Lowell Bergman uncovers the techniques used by the industry to earn record profits and get consumers to take on more debt." You can watch the whole video online at www.pbs.org/wgbh/pages/frontline/shows/credit/view.

Affluenza (56 minutes; Bullfrog Films, Oley, Pa.)

This videotape takes a simultaneously lighthearted and serious look at "affluenza," our modern-day plague of overconsumption and materialism, and explores its personal, familial, societal, and environmental impact. Visit www.bullfrogfilms.com/catalog/affl.html for more information.

Escape from Affluenza (56 minutes; Bullfrog Films, Oley, Pa.)

This sequel to *Affluenza* presents humorous and thought-provoking vignettes to show how people from many walks of life are reducing their consumption, simplifying their lives, and feeling more satisfaction. Visit www.bullfrogfilms.com/catalog/efa.html for more information.

The Story of Stuff *(20 minutes)*

This fast-paced, fact-filled, and often funny look at the underbelly of our production and consumption patterns raises critical social and environmental issues. It calls us to work together to create a more sustainable and just world. To watch, download, or order a DVD, visit www.thestoryofstuff.com.

What Would Jesus Buy? *(90 minutes)*

Produced by Morgan Spurlock (*Super Size Me*) and directed by Rob VanAlkemade, *What Would Jesus Buy?* follows Reverend Billy and the Church of Stop Shopping Gospel Choir singing their way across the country in December 2005, preaching their anticonsumerist message at the Mall of America, Wal-Mart headquarters, and on Main Street in Disneyland on Christmas Day. Entertaining and eye-opening, it's a sharp poke at holiday consumerism. Visit www.wwjbmovie.com for more information.

Additional Readings for Overshoppers, Friends, and Family

The following items are not in the bibliography of works cited.

Boss, Shira. *Green with Envy: Why Keeping Up with the Joneses Is Keeping Us in Debt.* New York: Warner Business Books, 2006.

Boundy, D. *When Money Is the Drug: Understanding and Changing Self-Defeating Money Patterns.* Woodstock, N.Y.: Maverick Media Resources, 1993.

Carlomagno, Mary. *Give It Up! My Year of Learning to Live Better with Less.* New York: William Morrow, 2006.

Catalano, E., and N. Sonenberg. *Consuming Passions: Help for Compulsive Shoppers.* Oakland, Calif.: New Harbinger Publications, 1993.

Damon, J. *Shopaholics: An 8-Week Program to Control Compulsive Spending.* New York: Avon Books, 1988.

Debtors Anonymous. *A Currency of Hope.* Brainerd, Minn.: Bang Printing, 1999.

Dittmar, Helga. *Consumer Culture, Identity, and Well-Being: The Search for the "Good Life" and the "Body Beautiful."* New York: Psychology Press, 2008.

Easterbrook, G. *The Progress Paradox.* New York: Random House, 2003.

Eliot, E. *Attention Shoppers! The Woman's Guide to Enlightenment through Shopping.* Deerfield Beach, Fla.: Health Communications, 2003.

Ford, Amanda. *Retail Therapy: Life Lessons Learned While Shopping.* York Beach, Maine: Conari Press, 2002.

Houlder, Kulananda, and Dominic Houlder. *Mindfulness and Money: The Buddhist Path of Abundance.* New York: Broadway Books, 2002.

Johnson, J. *Appearance Obsession: Learning to Love the Way You Look.* Deerfield Beach, Fla.: Health Communications, 1994.

Kasser, Tim. *The High Price of Materialism.* Boston: MIT Press, 2002.

Kilbourne, J. *Can't Buy My Love: How Advertising Changes the Way We Think and Feel.* New York: Touchstone, 1999. (Originally published as *Deadly Persuasion: Why Women and Girls Must Fight the Addictive Power of Advertising.*)

Klontz, T., R. Kahler, and B. Klontz. *The Financial Wisdom of Ebenezer Scrooge: 5 Principles to Transform Your Relationship with Money.* Deerfield Beach, Fla.: Health Communications, 2006.

Kottler, J. *Exploring and Treating Acquisitive Desire: Living in the Material World.* Thousand Oaks, Calif.: Sage Publications, 1999.

Lee, M. *Fashion Victim: Our Love-Hate Relationship with Dressing, Shopping, and the Cost of Style.* New York: Broadway Books, 2003.

Levine, J. *Not Buying It: My Year without Shopping.* New York: Free Press, 2006.

Mellan, Olivia. *Overcoming Overspending: A Winning Plan for Spenders and Their Partners.* With S. Christie. New York: Walker & Company, 1995.

O'Connor, Karen. *Addicted to Shopping . . . and Other Issues Women Have with Money.* Eugene, Ore.: Harvest House, 2005.

Sander, P., and J. Sander. *The Pocket Idiot's Guide to Living on a Budget*. 2nd ed. New York: Alpha, 2005.

Shulman, T. *Bought Out and $pent*. West Conshohocken, Pa.: Infinity Publishing, 2008.

Twist, Lynne. *The Soul of Money: Transforming Your Relationship with Money and Life*. New York: Norton, 2003.

Underhill, P. *Call of the Mall: The Geography of Shopping by the Author of "Why We Buy."* New York: Simon & Schuster, 2004.

Wesson, C. *Women Who Shop Too Much*. New York: St. Martin's Press, 1990.

Notes

Introduction

1. Some people who think of themselves as compulsive buy-
   ers really have a *hoarding* problem. In *Buried in Treasures*,
   Tolin, Frost, and Steketee offer three criteria, all of which
   they deem necessary for the diagnosis of hoarding:
   A. "You accumulate, and then have great difficulty discard-
      ing, objects that most other people would consider use-
      less or of limited value," 12.
   B. "The clutter is so severe that it prevents or seriously
      limits the use of living spaces in the manner for which
      those spaces were intended," 13.
   C. "The clutter, acquiring, or difficulty discarding causes
      significant impairment or distress," 14.
   There are resources for people who hoard and their loved
   ones in appendix C.
2. Koran et al., "Estimated Prevalence of Compulsive Buying
   Behavior in the United States," 1806.
3. Schor, *The Overspent American*, 3.
4. Underhill, *Why We Buy*, 31.
5. Ridgway, N. M., Kukar-Kinney, M., and Monroe, K., "An
   Expanded Conceptualization and a New Measure of Compulsive Buying," *Journal of Consumer Research* (2008): 35.
6. www.money-zine.com/financial-planning/debt-consolida
   tion/credit-card-debt-statistics.
7. www.washingtonpost.com/wp-dyn/content/article/2007/
   02/01/AR2007020101276.html.

8. Kaza, *Hooked!* 9.
9. Durning, *How Much Is Enough?* 23.

Chapter 1

1. Faber, "Self-Control and Compulsive Buying."
2. Dittmar, "The Role of Self-Image in Excessive Buying," 125.
3. Elliott, Eccles, and Gournay, "Man Management?" 658.
4. Dittmar, "Understanding and Diagnosing Compulsive Buying," 441.
5. Eccles, "Lived Experiences of Women as Addictive Consumers," 20.
6. Horne, "Incandescent Shopper," 104.
7. Goldstein, "Desire, Delusion, and DVDs," 18.
8. Lawrence, "Psychodynamics of the Compulsive Female Shopper," 68.
9. Williams, *Cat on a Hot Tin Roof,* 73.
10. McCall, *Financial Recovery Workbook,* 1.

Chapter 2

1. Hayes, *Get Out of Your Mind and Into Your Life,* chapter 11.
2. Miller and Rollnick, *Motivational Interviewing,* 19.
3. Ibid., 53.
4. Graef, "Penetrating the Tangle," 123.
5. Goldstein, "Desire, Delusion, and DVDs," 23–24.
6. Chödrön, "How We Get Hooked, How We Get Unhooked," 32.
7. Here and in the previous paragraph, I'm indebted to Stephen Hayes's discussion of the consequences of attempting to ignore pain in *Get Out of Your Mind and Into Your Life.* See chapters 1, 3, and 4 of this book for a series of deceptively simple exercises for increasing your capacity to witness and tolerate your feelings as they are.
8. Mellan, *Money Harmony,* 80.

Chapter 3

1. The Shopping Patterns Checklist and the You and Your Stuff Questionnaire are copyright © 2006 April Lane Benson and Irene Tobis.

Chapter 4

1. McCall, "Financial Recovery Counseling," 466–67.
2. Bach, *Finish Rich Workbook,* 42.
3. An eye-opening discussion of this is "Secret History of the Credit Card," which you can view free at www.pbs.org/wgbh/pages/frontline/shows/credit/view.
4. Bach, *Finish Rich Workbook,* 85.

Chapter 5

1. Kinnell, "Saint Francis and the Sow," 98.
2. Maslow at MrDowling.com, www.mrdowling.com/602-maslow.html.

Chapter 6

1. Mulpuru, "U.S. eCommerce Forecast: 2008–2112"; Pew Internet Project, "September 2007 Survey," quoted at www.infoplease.com/ipa/a0931236.html.
2. We now have hard evidence to demonstrate this, in two recent British studies that focused on compulsive buying tendencies online. See Dittmar, Long, and Bond, "When a Better Self Is Only a Button Click Away."
3. Garner and Kearney-Cooke, "Body Image," 55.
4. Ridgway and Kukar-Kinney, "Hi, I'm a Compulsive Buyer."
5. Linn, *Consuming Kids,* 26.
6. Schor, *Born to Buy,* 62.
7. Bee-Gates, *I Want It Now.*
8. Schwartz, *Paradox of Choice,* 18.
9. Schor, *Born to Buy,* 31.
10. Gallo and Gallo, *Financially Intelligent Parent,* 135–50.
11. Schor, *Born to Buy,* 25.

Chapter 9

1. See Beck, *Cognitive Therapy.*
2. Peterson and Seligman, *Character Strengths and Virtues,* 519.
3. Ibid.
4. Ibid.
5. Ibid., 530.
6. Gross, "Form and Elegance with Just Enough," 165.

7. Kipling, "If," 170.

8. Hayes, *Get Out of Your Mind and Into Your Life*, 178.

9. Goldstein, "Desire, Delusion, and DVDs," 26.

10. Hayes, *Get Out of Your Mind and Into Your Life*, 45.

11. Winston, "You Are What You Download," 81.

Chapter 10

1. The post–mental rehearsal and post–dress rehearsal questions later in this section are adapted from Tolin, Frost, and Steketee, *Buried in Treasures*, 118.

Conclusion

1. Van Boven, "Experientialism, Materialism, and the Pursuit of Happiness."

2. http://earthtrends.wri.org/updates/node/236.

3. Several fairly extreme anticonsumerist lifestyles, growing in popularity though still far from mainstream, may be considered radical forms of voluntary simplicity. One is the Compact, which advocates buying no new products of any kind, only (with a very few exceptions) borrowing and buying *used*. Another is freeganism, which advocates salvaging discarded, unspoiled food.

4. Powell, *Wabi Sabi Simple*.

5. R. G. Lawrence, *The Wabi-Sabi Home*, 20.

6. Powell, *Wabi Sabi Simple*, 7–8.

7. Ibid., ix.

Appendix B

1. Lejoyeux, et al., "Phenomenology and Psychopathology of Uncontrolled Buying," 1524–29.

2. Black, Monahan, and Gabel, "Fluvoxamine in the Treatment of Compulsive Buying."

3. Black et al., "Double-Blind Comparison of Fluvoxamine versus Placebo"; Ninan et al., "Placebo-Controlled Study of Fluvoxamine."

4. Koran et al., "Citalopram for Compulsive Shopping Disorder."

5. Koran et al., "Escitalopram for Compulsive Buying Disorder."

Bibliography

Bach, D. *The Finish Rich Workbook.* New York: Broadway Books, 2003.

Beck, J. *Cognitive Therapy: Basics and Beyond.* New York: Guilford Press, 1995.

Bee-Gates, D. *I Want It Now: Navigating Childhood in a Materialistic World.* New York: Palgrave Macmillan, 2006.

Benson, A., ed. *I Shop, Therefore I Am: Compulsive Buying and the Search for Self.* Lanham, Md.: Aronson Press, an imprint of Rowman & Littlefield Publishers, 2000.

Black, D. W., J. Gabel, J. Hansen, and S. Schlosser. "A Double-Blind Comparison of Fluvoxamine versus Placebo in the Treatment of Compulsive Buying Disorder." *Annals of Clinical Psychiatry* 12, no. 4 (Dec. 2000): 205–11.

Black, D. W., P. Monahan, and J. Gabel. "Fluvoxamine in the Treatment of Compulsive Buying." *Journal of Clinical Psychiatry* 58, no. 4 (1997): 159–63.

Brach, T. *Radical Acceptance: Embracing Your Life with the Heart of a Buddha.* New York: Bantam, 2003.

Bynner, W. *The Way of Life, According to Lao Tzu.* New York: Penguin Putnam, 1986.

Chatzky, J. *Pay It Down! From Debt to Wealth on $10 a Day.* New York: Portfolio, 2004.

Chödrön, P. "How We Get Hooked, How We Get Unhooked." In S. Kaza, ed., *Hooked!*

Dittmar, H. "The Role of Self-Image in Excessive Buying." In A. Benson, ed., *I Shop, Therefore I Am.*

_____. "Understanding and Diagnosing Compulsive Buying." In R. Coombs, ed., *Handbook of Addictive Disorders: A Practical Guide to Diagnosis and Treatment.* Hoboken, N.J.: John Wiley & Sons, 2004.

Dittmar, H., K. Long, and R. Bond. "When a Better Self Is Only a Button Click Away: Associations between Materialistic Values, Emotional and Identity-Related Buying Motives, and Compulsive Buying Tendency Online." *Journal of Social and Clinical Psychology* 26, no. 3 (2007): 334–61.

Durning, A. T. *How Much Is Enough? The Consumer Society and the Future of the Earth.* New York: Norton, 1992.

Eccles, S. "The Lived Experiences of Women as Addictive Consumers." *Journal of Research for Consumers* (a Web-based interdisciplinary journal) 4 (2002). www.jrconsumers.com/academic_articles/issue_4/Eccles.pdf.

Elliott, R., S. Eccles, and K. Gournay. "Man Management? Women and the Use of Debt to Control Personal Relationships." *Journal of Marketing Management* 12, no. 7 (1996): 657–69.

Faber, R. "Self-Control and Compulsive Buying." In Kasser, T. and A. Kenner, eds., *Psychology and Consumer Culture.* Washington, D.C.: American Psychological Association, 2004.

Gallo, E., and J. Gallo. *The Financially Intelligent Parent.* New York: New American Library, 2005.

Garner, D., and A. Kearney-Cooke. "Body Image." *Psychology Today* 29, no. 2 (1996): 55–56.

Goldstein, J. "Desire, Delusion, and DVDs." In S. Kaza, ed., *Hooked!*

Graef, S. "Penetrating the Tangle." In S. Kaza, ed., *Hooked!*

Gross, R. "Form and Elegance with Just Enough." In S. Kaza, ed., *Hooked!*

Hayes, S. *Get Out of Your Mind and Into Your Life: The New Acceptance and Commitment Therapy.* With S. Smith. Oakland, Calif.: New Harbinger, 2005.

Horne, D. "The Incandescent Shopper: An Existential-Phenomenological Perspective." In *Serious Shopping: Essays in Psychotherapy and Consumerism,* edited by A. Baker. London: Free Association Books, 2000.

Hwoschinsky, P. *True Wealth.* Berkeley: Ten Speed Press, 1990.

Kaza, S., ed. *Hooked! Buddhist Writings on Greed, Desire, and the Urge to Consume.* Boston: Shambhala Publications, 2005.

Kinnell, G. "Saint Francis and the Sow." In *A New Selected Poems.* New York: Mariner Books, 2001.

Kipling, R. *Kipling Poems.* New York: Everyman's Library, 2007.

Koran, L., E. Aboujaoude, B. Solvason, N. Gamel, and E. Smith. "Escitalopram for Compulsive Buying Disorder: A Double-Blind Discontinuation Study." *Journal of Clinical Psychopharmacology* 27, no. 2 (2007): 225–27.

Koran, L., H. Chuoung, K. Bullock, and S. Smith. "Citalopram for Compulsive Shopping Disorder: An Open-Label Study Followed by Double-Blind Discontinuation." *Journal of Clinical Psychiatry* 64, no. 7 (2003): 793–98.

Koran, L., R. Faber, E. Aboujaoude, M. Large, and R. Serpe. "Estimated Prevalence of Compulsive Buying Behavior in the United States." *American Journal of Psychiatry* 163, no. 10 (2006): 1806–12.

Lawrence, L. "The Psychodynamics of the Compulsive Female Shopper." *American Journal of Psychoanalysis* 50, no. 1 (1990): 67–70.

Lawrence, R. G. *The Wabi-Sabi Home: The Japanese Art of Imperfect Beauty.* New York: Clarkson Potter, 2004.

Lejoyeux, A., Tassain, and Solomon. "Phenomenology and Psychopathology of Uncontrolled Buying." *American Journal of Psychiatry* 155 (1996), 1524–29.

Linn, S. *Consuming Kids: Protecting Our Kids from the Onslaught of Marketing and Advertising.* New York: Anchor Books, 2004.

Maslow, A., at mrdowling.com. www.mrdowling.com/602-maslow.html.

McCall, K. "Financial Recovery Counseling." In Benson, ed., *I Shop, Therefore I Am.*

————. *Financial Recovery Workbook.* San Anselmo, Calif.: Financial Recovery Press, 1995.

————. *MoneyMinder Financial Recovery Workbook.* San Anselmo, Calif.: Financial Recovery Press, 2002.

Mellan, O. *Money Harmony: Resolving Money Conflicts in Your Life and Relationships.* New York: Walker & Company, 1994.

Miller, W., and S. Rollnick. *Motivational Interviewing: Preparing People for Change.* 2nd ed. New York: Guilford Press, 2002.

Mulpuru, S. "U.S. eCommerce Forecast: 2008–2112." www.interactivedevelopment.net/facts.php.

Mundis, J. *How to Get Out of Debt, Stay Out of Debt, and Live Prosperously.* Rev. ed. New York: Bantam Books, 2003.

Ninan, P., S. McElroy, C. Kane, B. Knight, L. Casuto, S. Rose, F. Marsteller, and C. Nemeroff. "Placebo-Controlled Study of Fluvoxamine in the Treatment of Patients with Compulsive Buying." *Journal of Clinical Psychopharmacology* 20, no. 3 (2000): 362–66.

Orman, S. *The 9 Steps to Financial Freedom.* New York: Crown Publishers, 1997.

Peterson, C., and M. Seligman. *Character Strengths and Virtues.* Washington, D.C.: American Psychological Association, 2004.

Pew Internet Project. "September 2007 Survey," quoted at http://infoplease.com/ipa/A0931236.html.

Powell, R. *Wabi Sabi Simple.* Avon, Mass.: Adams Media, 2005.

Ramsey, D. *The Total Money Makeover: A Proven Plan for Financial Fitness.* 2nd ed. Nashville: Thomas Nelson, 2007.

Ridgway, N., and M. Kukar-Kinney. "Hi, I'm a Compulsive Buyer: A Content Analysis of Themes from Testimonial Telephone Calls at QVC." *Advances in Consumer Research* 32 (2005): 431–36.

Schor, J. *Born to Buy: The Commercialized Child and the New Consumer Culture.* New York: Scribner, 2004.

_____. *The Overspent American: Why We Want What We Don't Need.* New York: Basic Books, 1998.

Schwartz, B. *The Paradox of Choice: Why More Is Less.* New York: HarperCollins, 2004.

Tolin, D., R. Frost, and G. Steketee. *Buried in Treasures: Help for Compulsive Acquiring, Saving, and Hoarding.* New York: Oxford University Press, 2007.

Underhill, P. *Why We Buy: The Science of Shopping.* New York: Simon & Schuster, 1999.

Van Boven, L. "Experientialism, Materialism, and the Pursuit of Happiness." *Review of General Psychology* 9, no. 2 (2005): 132–42.

Wachtel, P. *The Poverty of Affluence: A Psychological Portrait of the American Way of Life.* New York: Free Press, 1983.

Weston, L. *Deal with Your Debt: The Right Way to Manage Your Bill$ and Pay Off What You Owe.* Upper Saddle River, N.J.: Pearson Education, 2006.

Whitman, W. *Leaves of Grass.* New York: Oxford University Press, 2005.

Williams, T. *Cat on a Hot Tin Roof.* New York: New Directions, 1955.

Winston, D. "You Are What You Download." In S. Kaza, ed., *Hooked!*

Visit Us Online

www.stoppingovershopping.com

Whether you're an overshopper, a concerned family member, or a mental health professional, at this site you'll find useful information and resources, including:

- a quiz to aid in determining whether you or someone you love has a shopping problem that's serious enough to warrant professional help
- a ready-made shopping journal that can be used in conjunction with this book
- a quarterly newsletter with further insights, tips, and strategies
- the introduction to the book *I Shop, Therefore I Am: Compulsive Buying and the Search for Self*
- a detailed description of the *Stopping Overshopping Guided Self-Help Program*
- information about individual and group coaching, teleclasses, and therapist training
- help in finding a therapist trained in the Stopping Overshopping method
- a schedule of upcoming workshops and events.
- links to information on financial literacy, credit, debt, and voluntary simplicity
- links to addiction recovery resources, self-help and online groups, and residential treatment centers
- an annotated list of relevant books, videos, and articles.

About the Author

APRIL LANE BENSON, PHD, is a nationally known psychologist who specializes in the treatment of compulsive buying disorder. The editor of *I Shop, Therefore I Am: Compulsive Buying and the Search for Self,* she has appeared on numerous national television programs, including the *Today* show, *Good Morning America,* and the *CBS Evening News.* Her work has also been quoted in the *New York Times* and the *Wall Street Journal.* She lives in New York City.

For more information on Dr. Benson and for further resources, visit her website, http://stoppingovershopping.com.